The Living Earth Book of
NORTH AMERICAN
TREES

THE LIVING EARTH BOOK OF

NORTH AMERICAN
TREES

GERALD JONAS

Foreword by Ed Zahniser

THE READER'S DIGEST ASSOCIATION, INC.
Pleasantville, New York/Montreal

The Living Earth Book of North American Trees

A Reader's Digest Living Earth Book

Produced for The Reader's Digest Association, Inc.,
by Redefinition, Inc.

The credits and acknowledgments that appear on pages 214–216 are
hereby made a part of this copyright page.

Library of Congress Cataloging in Publication Data
Jonas, Gerald, 1945–
      The living earth book of North American trees / Gerald Jonas.
            p.   cm.—(Reader's Digest living earth)
      Includes index.
      ISBN 0-89577-488-7
      1. Trees—North America.   2. Trees—North America—Identification.
  I. Title. II. Series.
  QK110.J665   1993
  582. 16'097—dc20   93-2633

Printed on recycled paper

Printed in the United States of America

FOREWORD

WHEN I SERVED in Korea with the U.S. Army in the late 1960's, the drive to our rifle range took us through a village that possessed one lone, mature hardwood tree. It was like a shrine, so remarkable because so rare in that time and place. Former occupying powers had thoroughly denuded Korea of its prime trees, shipping back home those they did not consume on the spot. Years later my older sister told me she had adopted a tree growing in a city park near where she lived. To her it was a personal shrine and place of healing.

Those trees recalled for me another sacred grove of sorts. My father, Howard Zahniser, once took our family to visit a small stand of ancient trees some distance from his childhood home in the mountains of western Pennsylvania. An isolated plot was all that remained from hundreds of acres of the virgin forest through which his father could have walked as a child. From the depth of my own father's feeling beneath those grand trees, I could sense that we were somehow on a pilgrimage.

A few years later I hiked with my father and brother in Washington State through ancient forests of towering Douglas fir. Earlier that summer my father had finished drafting

the bill that 8 years later evolved as the federal Wilderness Act of 1964. That landmark piece of legislation now protects those magnificent trees in the Glacier Peak Wilderness and in many other areas of the nation.

At age 15 I saw primeval western coastal forests for the first time while I was flying over Washington state, British Columbia, and the Yukon into Fairbanks, Alaska, and then further into central Alaska, with biological explorers Olaus and Mardy Murie. I was used to forests in the eastern United States and southern Ontario, Canada, where trails are like green tunnels through dense wilderness. I vividly recall climbing the hill behind our camp on Lobo Lake in the Brooks Range. Before me stretched a vast expanse of tundra, dotted with isolated clumps of scrub trees, that stretched to the horizon. Low-growing wild rhododendrons were in full bloom, their bright pink flowers standing out against the drab surroundings. Looking out on that scene 150 miles north of the Arctic Circle, I thought: "How can this be wilderness? You can see forever."

That Alaskan summer we were near Wiseman, the arctic village from which, in the 1930's, forester Robert Marshall had studied trees at their limit of growth on the North American continent. Soon afterward—with like-minded professional foresters Aldo Leopold, Benton MacKaye, Bernard Frank, and others—Marshall founded the Wilderness Society, for which my father went to work the year I was born.

Harking back to Henry David Thoreau and John Muir, Marshall and others like him sought to save large samples of pristine American landscape. Robert Marshall's philosopher-guide was fellow forester Aldo Leopold, a fitting choice, since conservation in North America was born in concern for trees and forest practices. Leopold's land ethic, set forth in his classic little book *Sand County Almanac*, launched a new consciousness. "We abuse land because we regard it as a commodity belonging to us," Leopold wrote. "When we see land as a community to which we belong, we may begin to use it with love and respect."

Long ago, the Buddha recognized the "unlimited kindness and benevolence" of trees. They make no demands for sustenance and are generous with the products of their living, he said, even offering shade to the axmen who would cut them down.

As this book makes clear, for all our delight in trees and our awe of them, they do sustain our material lives. European inventories of North America's resources in the early 1700's inspired early probes inland, intent on forest exploitation. The goal of the Voyageurs' Highway that spanned the continent in the 1700's was the beaver, whose pelts were fashioned into hats that adorned the heads of European gentry. Beavers are direct consumers of trees for food, shelter, and dam building. The great seafaring nations particularly sought large white pines for ship masts. That the King of England later reserved the best white pines for the Crown incubated the disquiet that led some colonists to revolt in the name of freedom.

Today we derive foods, fuel, shelter, paper, and plastics from tree products. Between the era of the voyageurs and the work of Robert Marshall and Aldo Leopold, our attitude toward trees and forests has turned from unbridled consumption to thoughtful management and even to preservation.

Appreciation for trees is all around us. While writing this brief essay, I listened to a professor of religion mourn the accidental cutting of a mature hardwood on his campus. That same day I received two offers of tree seedlings to plant, one by mail and one in our county newspaper. Those offers recalled John Muir's advice, that in planting a tree we plant ourselves: "Every root is an anchor" on which we rest and become "sufficiently calm to feel the joy of living."

As the mutual dependency of humans and trees finds increasing appreciation worldwide, new hope builds for an ethic to balance sustainable use and the preservation of the Earth's sensational experiment in evolution. From the Garden of Eden to the Buddha, from Sir Isaac Newton to my own father, trees have revealed knowledge, the powers of mind, and natural law. We must now turn our evolved intimacy with trees, the lungs of our planet, to saving their niche in the immortal genius that is the Earth's biosphere.

The case of the Pacific yew, so recently considered a trash tree in logging operations, is instructive. When random research isolated within the tree's properties a chemical adversary to ovarian cancer, the Pacific yew joined the chincona and willow—sources of quinine and aspirin— as wonder-drug trees. This book embodies the great hope that an awareness of our mutual dependency with trees will move us to respect them—where we live, across the continent, and around the globe.

ED ZAHNISER

CHAPTER ONE

The Presence of Trees

THE BIGGEST AND OLDEST LIVING THINGS on Earth are trees. The record holders are all found on the North American continent, where—since the glaciers of the last ice age receded some 10,000 years ago—conditions have favored the exuberant growth of trees and of those extensive arboreal communities we call forests.

Before European colonists began settling in earnest in the 17th century, close to half the landmass of what is now the United States and Canada was covered with forests. Later observers noted, with only some exaggeration, that a branch-hopping squirrel could journey from the Atlantic seaboard to the Mississippi River without once touching ground. Beyond the Great Plains, the Rocky Mountain system north to the Yukon and the Pacific Coast were also thickly wooded. Even the apparently treeless grasslands and deserts between forested areas were host to tree varieties representing ingenious adaptions to adverse climatic challenges.

Since 1600 the human population of North America has increased 5,000-fold, and immense numbers of trees have been cut down to make room for farms and to satisfy an ever-growing appetite for wood and wood products. Yet nearly a third of North America is still covered with forests—more than 770 million acres, home to an estimated 245 billion trees. Vast regions of Canada, between the populated border areas and the treeless tundra of the Far North, are heavily forested. Although most of these trees are second growth—meaning that they are growing on lands where the old growth forests have already been burned or harvested—a few outposts of the Forest Primeval still remain. In the timeless hush of such virgin groves, the beauty and grandeur of trees older than the cathedrals of Europe continue to inspire awe.

Its roots anchored deep in a rock outcropping, a bristlecone pine endures one more winter in the California Sierras. Some individual bristlecone pines have survived as many as 5,000 winters, making them Earth's oldest living species.

Cutting a broad swath through eastern Florida (opposite), the St. Johns River meanders northward through thick deciduous forests. William Bartram, an American botanist, navigated the St. Johns in 1775; his journal describes the fragrant orange, magnolia, bay, oak, and palmetto trees that once covered these banks.

Along the fog-drenched coast of northern California grow the coast redwoods—nature's skyscrapers. The tallest of these, known as the Tall Tree, towers nearly 370 feet from base to crown; a bird perched on its very top could look down on a 37-story building. According to annual growth rings counted in similar giants that were felled for their lumber, coast redwoods have a life expectancy of up to 2,000 years.

Even longer-lived are their close cousins, the giant sequoias that rise from the western slopes of California's Sierra Nevada range. While few sequoias today stand taller than 300 feet, the biggest of them support up to 600 tons of wood on trunks that measure as much as 100 feet around. These are without question the most massive organisms that ever lived. By way of comparison, the largest animal alive today, the blue whale, tips the scale at 150 tons; the bulkiest dinosaur, the brachiosaurus, probably weighed in at a mere 75 tons.

Starting from a seed the length of an eyelash, a giant sequoia takes some 3,000 years to reach its full growth. Yet such a tree is a mere youngster compared to the most venerable of the bristlecone pines that grow in the high country of Utah, Nevada, and California. Some bristlecones were already clinging to their precarious mountain perches when Moses led his people out of Egypt and Odysseus lost his bearings on the way home from Troy. The oldest bristlecone found so far is a wind-stunted, fearsomely gnarled patriarch that has survived as many as 5,000 winters and summers. By tracing the life histories of these trees through the science of dendrochronology— comparing the growth rings of dead trees with those on pencil-thin cores extracted from living specimens—scientists have been able to construct an accurate calendar of climatic conditions in North America dating back some 9,000 years. Of course, when it comes to the history of trees on Earth, this is just scratching the surface.

This towering coast redwood on the Irvine Trail in California's Prairie Creek Redwoods State Park measures 58 feet around and tops out at about 250 feet. Coast redwoods are taller than any other trees on Earth.

A single seed of the giant sequoia, shown actual size below, stores the genetic material that can become the planet's most massive living thing. Fully mature after 3,000 years, a sequoia outweighs a hundred elephants.

All life is shaped by a struggle for survival. Competition for nutrients and reproductive success is unceasing. In contrast to animals, which must move around in search of food and mates, the plant kingdom places a premium on patience. At first glance trees appear to embody this vegetative strategy to perfection: they seem to achieve all their goals by standing still. What could be more emblematic of patience than a tree that has been rooted in the same spot for hundreds or even thousands of years, taking all it needs from the air, the sun, and the soil?

As for competition with other forms of life, a tree seems to operate on the principle that a good defense is the best offense. Tannins in the outer bark of many trees repel potentially harmful insect pests. Desert trees like the paloverde, the mesquite, and the giant saguaro cactus

Its symmetry preserved in stone, a fossil *Asterotheca arborescens* dates from the late Carboniferous era, 300 million years ago. This giant fern lived and died in what is now the state of Illinois.

guard their internal hoard of moisture with nasty spikes. Even fire, the great scourge of mature trees, is usually turned back by the asbestoslike protection that its thick bark affords the coast redwood.

But first glances can be deceiving. From an evolutionary perspective, trees are among the most dynamic, even aggressive players of the survival game that the planet has known. In the Carboniferous Era—which began some 345 million years ago—giant treelike ferns, some of which were the ancestors of today's common woodland ferns, thrived in the rainy subtropical climate that prevailed over much of the Earth. Where the overarching tops of these giant ferns came together to form a continuous canopy similar to that found in today's rain forests, animals and other plants had no choice but to evolve in their endless green shadow. So abundant were the ferny forests of the Carboniferous Era that the vast compost heap of their remains, driven underground over hundreds of millions of years, forms most of the planet's extensive coal deposits.

Few experiences compare with the awesome tranquility of an ancient forest. Here on Cummins Creek in Oregon's Siuslaw National Forest (*left*), spruce trees and hemlock snags stand in a carpet of fern and moss.

It may take decades for these two immature cones of giant sequoia (*right*) to release their seeds. Often germination occurs only after fire melts resins that seal the cone scales.

THE PRESENCE OF TREES 15

Ferns reproduce themselves through a relatively primitive process: minute spores are unceremoniously released from a mature plant to make their own way into the world. Once separated from the parent plant, a single-celled spore cannot develop into a new individual unless it chances upon a favorable brew of soil and climatic conditions.

When the world's climate became colder and drier some 280 million years ago, the giant ferns fell behind in the struggle for survival. In their place evolved the giant seed-bearing plants we know as trees. Compared to ferns, seed plants are more versatile, better equipped to keep pace with new and changing habitats; one reason perhaps is that they are more solicitous parents.

Each fertilized tree seed is a complete plant in miniature, sealed in a protective coat and packed with enough food to sustain the seedling until its own roots and leaves are ready to supply the plant's needs. To ensure the production of viable seeds from the union of "male" and "female" genetic material, trees have developed elaborate mechanisms for sexual propagation. Conifers, or needle-bearing evergreens, bear their seeds in scaly, spiral-shaped structures known as cones. Male cones supply the peripatetic pollen, and female cones the receptive ovule. Flowering trees tender their offspring even greater protection, clustering their pollen and ovules in partially enclosed receptacles called flowers, and their fertilized seeds in the compact travel containers that we call fruit.

The advent of seed-bearing trees, both cone-bearing and flower-bearing, ushered in a new epoch of forestation. The spread of conifer and hardwood forests across the temperate zones of the planet in the last 200 million years belies the misconception that trees are essentially sedentary. A grain of pollen flicked aloft by a puff of wind or borne on a bee's knee to a nearby flower; a cherry pit dropped from the bill of a contentious blackbird; an undigested apple seed hitching a ride in the belly of a satiated doe—in each instance, a tree is on the move as surely as a rider on a horse or a passenger on an airplane.

To succeed in the quest for survival of their species, trees have developed competitive techniques for regeneration. The male staminate cones of a Monterey pine (*left*) release pollen that will drift on the wind in search of receptive female cones. A honeybee transports pussy willow pollen (*center*) in the sacs on its legs. Seeds that pass through the digestive tract of the golden-mantled ground squirrel (*right*) may be deposited far from the tree that bore them.

Even a rooted tree keeps moving in ways not immediately obvious to the casual observer. The eastern cottonwood, one of the fastest-growing North American trees, increases its height by as much as 4 or 5 feet a year. The endlessly expanding root system of a bur oak competes so voraciously for water that nothing else, not even the toughest prairie grass, is able to thrive in soil that the tree's roots have colonized.

Wherever forests flourish, other forms of life must come to terms with the demands of trees. The first Europeans to reach North America left behind a continent where big trees had been a scarce resource for centuries. The forests these colonists encountered in their New World led them to conclude they had stumbled on an "untouched" wilderness. In long stretches of forest without natural clearings, the rays of the sun barely reached the ground. Just as they had in the Carboniferous Era, animals and plants lived in and under the all-enveloping domain of trees.

The earliest human inhabitants of North America, people that anthropologists refer to as Paleo-Indians, were no exception. Although they grew crops in natural clearings and opened new clearings with controlled fires, trees were their principal resource for shelter, sustenance, and survival. Tools, weapons, fuel, medicine, food, houses, transportation, artistic and spiritual inspiration—these were among the boundless rewards to be gained from learning to live with trees. But with the arrival of more territorially conditioned European cultures, the long-standing equilibrium between people and trees on the North American continent was about to be challenged by the new ideas and advanced technologies of the newcomers.

Europeans had been thinking about trees in two very different ways—the scientific and the mythological—for a long, long time. The person generally credited with founding the science of botany was Theophrastus, a Greek philosopher and naturalist who wrote a series of treatises on plants in the fourth century B.C. A disciple of Aristotle, the great systematizer, Theophrastus divided plants into three categories—trees, shrubs, and herbs—based on their appearance. The most important marker that identified a plant as a tree was whether or not it appeared "woody."

Every child is entranced by the maple tree's winged seed pod. Its graceful aerobatics have a vital purpose, however, spinning the seed far from the parent tree in search of the sunlight and rich soil essential for its survival.

Down through the centuries other investigators, notably the Swedish botanist Carolus Linnaeus (1707-78) and the English naturalist Charles Darwin (1809-82), devised more complex systems of plant classification. They made categories of species based on both genetic and physiological distinctions, some of which could be seen only with the aid of the microscope. None of these botanical systems, however, is without shortcomings.

The generally accepted way for the amateur botanist to distinguish trees from other types of plants relies on a time-tested rule that Theophrastus would understand: single-stemmed woody plants that survive from year to year and grow to a minimum height of about 15 feet are considered to be trees. Their supporting stems, called trunks, hold aloft crowns of limbs and branches that produce some form of foliage. *Shrubs*, which are also woody plants, are typically shorter than trees; their branches diverge from the central stem closer to the ground. As for *herbaceous plants,* they have fleshy central stems that die after flowering. The only time in the life of a tree that it might be mistaken for an herb is in the sapling stage, when the slender stem has not yet grown its rind of protective bark. From then on, most trees are easily distinguishable for what they are.

Even so, there are exceptions to the most general guidelines, and deciding whether a plant is a tree from appearances alone can sometimes be tricky. Mature willows and birch trees often appear quite shrublike, with several stems rather than a single trunk emerging from the roots. The low-lying desert tree called paloverde conserves water by putting out little foliage, concentrating its chlorophyll in its naked green branches instead. There are also plants that only mimic the character of true trees. For example, the "trunk" of the so-called banana tree, which may reach a height of 30 feet, is actually not wood but a structure consisting of tightly rolled leaf stalks. Botanically speaking, the treelike banana is actually a perennial herb.

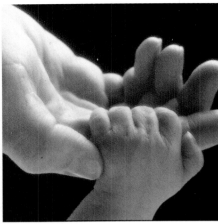

Prominent finger pads give the East Indian tarsier (*left*) superb tree-climbing prowess. The instinctive grasping reflex of a human baby recalls the same inherent survival mechanism.

The intimate relationship between trees and human beings goes back some 60 million years. Our ancestors were prosimians, small primates that climbed and jumped and swung through subtropical forests in Africa, Eurasia, and the Americas. The direct descendants of these four-footed arboreal animals—tree shrews, tarsiers, and lemurs—live today in the tropics. Our own ancestors—the hominids—came down from the trees some three million years ago to walk on the grasslands of Africa, and later spread to more temperate climes. But deep within our bodies and our brains we still carry mementos of our long sojourn in the trees.

The structure of the human hand with its opposable thumb, as well as the near-universal joint in the human shoulder, suggest an early adaptation for swinging on branches—a form of arboreal travel technically known as brachiation. Newborn humans still exhibit a brachiating reflex: their tiny hands will automatically close around any branchlike object, such as an extended parental finger, and hold on tight. It is easy to see that this reflex action is a potentially lifesaving response for young animals raised high above the ground. And along with other airborne creatures who have to maneuver in three dimensions, we have binocular vision: our eyes, like those of some birds, are close together in front of the face. Unlike animals with eyes on opposite sides of their heads, our brains can extract reliable depth information from these overlapping images.

Of course, long after our ancestors stopped swinging from branches, they continued to rely on trees for a substantial portion of their diet. When writers describe early human beings as hunters and gatherers, attention is usually focused on the manly activity of the hunt, with its inherent demands for cooperation, communication, and efficient tools or weapons. But the pedestrian business of gathering fruits and nuts, along with edible roots and leaves, from nearby trees may have provided most of the daily fuel of survival.

Certainly when our ancestors took the first steps toward modern civilization with the development of farming, the tree was there. Olive trees were cultivated on the island of Crete in the Mediterranean more than 5,000 years ago, and it is possible that domesticating wild fruit trees and vines provided humans with the impetus for what has come to be called the Agricultural Revolution. As bands of people migrated over the Earth, they took seeds with them, spreading fruit trees far beyond their original habitats. Apples and pears originated in Afghanistan, apricots and peaches in China; the first plums probably came from Persia. Like olives, such fruits as grapes, dates, and figs are native to the eastern Mediterranean basin.

The importance of trees to the establishment of stable human communities went far beyond their value as a food source. Without tools and fire, early humans could hardly have held their own against their evolu-

Four figures harvest a bountiful olive tree on this 6th-century Athenian black-figured amphora. An important Mediterranean staple, the olive tree has provided edible fruit, valuable oil, and durable wood for thousands of years.

ary competitors, much less gained some measure of control over their destiny. When we think of early toolmaking, we tend to think of stone; entire epochs of human prehistory are named according to the different types of stone tools unearthed by archeologists. This is partly because stone endures to be dug up millions of years later. Except under rare circumstances, wood quickly decays and vanishes into the soil without a trace. Yet it is entirely possible that an important, perhaps even a primary, use of early stone tools was the cutting and shaping of wood. It is certainly reasonable to believe that wood preceded stone as the first material used for human tools.

Chimpanzees, advanced primates whose diet in the wild includes ants and termites, have been observed stripping the foliage from small twigs and inserting them into anthills to lift out a mouthful of protein-rich insects.

The importance of fire—and therefore firewood—to early human communities cannot be underestimated. To make the copper, bronze, and iron tools that mark more advanced stages of human progress, artisans needed fire to smelt usable metal from raw ores. It is only logical that during these same eras the range and utility of wood tools increased enormously. In fact, so widespread has wood been in the story of human civilization that it might be more proper to speak not of the Stone Age, the Bronze Age, and the Iron Age, but of the Wood-and-Stone Age, the Wood-and-Bronze Age, the Wood-and-Iron Age, and so on.

The prehistory of North America offers some intriguing hints of what life might have been like in those distant ages. In a climate that is relatively conducive to the survival of wood artifacts, archeologists have been able to peer back in time with some confidence. The evidence indicates that, until the arrival of European settlers, the way of life of the inhabitants of the North American woodlands had remained essentially unchanged for some 7,000 years. While their culture has been described as Neolithic—that is, New Stone Age—wood was indispensable in nearly every aspect of their lives.

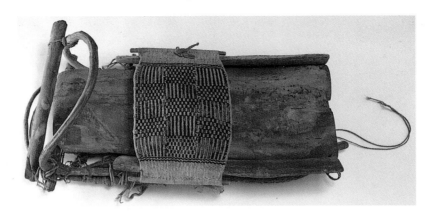

This bent-frame cradle was made almost 9 centuries ago for a child who lived in what is now Canyon de Chelly National Park, Arizona. The craftsman used resilient Spanish oak, a pine board, and reed matting. All remain remarkably preserved in the dry desert air.

Hunters killed large game—everything from deer to walruses—with bows and arrows, sharp-pointed spears launched with throwing sticks, and wood-shafted harpoons. Along with thongs of animal hide, strips of bark and tree roots served all the purposes that rope and string

do; for example, fish were landed with large nets woven from strands of twisted bark. Depending on the region and tribal traditions, families lived in wigwam-type structures framed with flexible saplings covered with bark and hides, in sod houses reinforced with posts and beams, or in log-walled, bark-thatched longhouses. Even on barren shores where no trees grew, the ocean currents often cast up driftwood that was used for fires and dwellings.

Objects fashioned from wood made possible quicker and safer travel. Snowshoes made from supple branches laced with rawhide facilitated walking in deep wintry drifts. A person pulling a travois, two saplings lashed together into a V-shaped platform, could haul a load with

For the Inuit and Tlingit peoples of the north Pacific coast, carved totems of western red cedar are tangible reminders of tribal and family history, as well as a folk art.

Bows of flexible wood and arrows of strong, straight branches are common to many cultures as tools for the hunt and as weapons of war. This Karriaquit Eskimo from the Kodiak Islands bent his sinew-backed bow for the camera a century ago.

far less effort than a person balancing the same weight on head or shoulders. As for water travel, until the advent of iron and steel hulls in the 19th century, there was virtually no alternative to the buoyancy of wood.

The earliest boats were probably drifting logs commandeered by observant—and intrepid—travelers. By lashing several logs together into a crude raft, stability could be improved. Even more navigable were dugouts—large logs hollowed out with stone scrapers or a controlled fire—and the bark canoe—typically, a frame of cedar covered with sheets of birch bark sewn together with slender tamarack roots or threads of twisted bark, and caulked with pine resin. Dugouts were common in the southern and far western parts of the continent, bark canoes in the northeast.

From the trees of North America came an endless bounty of useful wooden products: buttons, knives, slit-eyed snow goggles, even natural medicines brewed in wooden cooking utensils. To fortify permanent villages, palisades of logs were erected. And spiritual and artistic impulses found expression in a broad range of wood carvings, the most spectacular of which were the cedar totem poles of the Northwest coastal region.

Since trees were so important to their survival, it is hardly surprising that the native peoples of North America maintained a reverent attitude toward the forests. Trees figured prominently in many of their creation myths and religious ceremonies. In some parts of the continent a person who damaged a tree, for whatever reason, was expected to offer an apology for causing it pain.

This is not to say that Native American communities put the welfare of trees ahead of their own well-being. Most communities raised food crops, especially maize, that required direct sunlight to ripen. In the heavily wooded parts of the continent, maize could be grown only in large clearings. Where these occurred naturally—as the result of fires, storms, landslides, insect infestations, periodic flooding along riverbanks, or the tree-felling activities of beavers—the Indians took advantage of them. But where natural clearings were insufficient, they did not hesitate to make their own, using the only tools at their disposal.

Cutting down large numbers of mature trees with stone axes is an impossible task. Individual trees can be felled by a method known as girdling; this involves stripping the bark all around the trunk to disrupt the tree's internal

North American Indians knew how to use natural resources without destroying them. In June of 1871, a band of Bannock-Sheepeaters near Medicine Lodge Creek, Idaho, borrowed a few supple saplings for temporary shelter.

circulation. Planting can begin as soon as the foliage begins to wither. But a girdled tree may take months or even years to fall. To clear wooded land more quickly, Indian farmers sometimes resorted to controlled burning. As an added benefit, fire left behind nutrient-rich ashes that enhanced the fertility of the newly exposed soil.

There were limits to the environmental changes that could be brought about by these methods. Living in the shadow of immense trees that literally dwarfed their settlements, the native inhabitants of North America had no choice but to coexist with the forests around them. The Europeans who began settling in North America in the 17th century were mightily impressed by the abundance of trees they saw all around them, but their attitudes toward this new wooded "wilderness" were shaped by a different mind-set and by the superior metal tools, particularly saws and axes, that they brought with them from their former homes.

Trees, of course, loomed large in the central myths of Near Eastern and European religions. According to the Hebrew Scriptures, in the garden that God planted "eastward in Eden" could be found "every tree that is pleasant to the sight, and good for food; the tree of life also in the midst of the garden, and the tree of knowledge of good and evil." The fruit that Adam and Eve were forbidden to eat is not identified by name in the Book of Genesis, but according to Jewish tradition it was a pomegranate. In Norse mythology the entire universe is supported by a giant ash tree known as Yggdrasil. Among the ancient Celts, whose learned priests were called druids—a name that means knowing or finding—it was the oak tree. To ancient Greeks both the laurel and the palm tree were sacred to

The tempting fruit on the Tree of the Knowledge of Good and Evil symbolizes the Judeo-Christian concept of human frailty and imperfection. This version of Adam and Eve in the Garden of Paradise was drawn about 1825 by Durs Rudy, in Lehigh County, Pennsylvania.

Apollo, and the fragrant cedar was widely venerated throughout the Mediterranean world as a symbol of strength and majesty.

Europeans had been chopping down trees with sharp-edged metal axes for some 2,000 years. Since the heyday of the Roman empire—whose far-flung legions fought with maple lances—the wooded slopes of the heavily populated Mediterranean basin had been denuded to supply fuel and building materials for a wood-hungry civilization. As the Romans colonized northern Europe and Britain, forests were still dense enough to shelter all manner of mysterious creatures, from legendary elves and goblins to all-too-real bands of outlaws. By the end of the Renaissance, when cities flourished and commerce grew steadily, the Age of Exploration was about to change the world. At the end of the 17th century the largest trees, sought after as masts and timbers for the ever-expanding navies of the European nation-states, were already in scarce supply.

Unable to find sufficient tall timber in their own backyard, the British had been forced to go as far afield as the shores of the Baltic Sea, where the Russians, Prussians, and Swedes sold "sticks" of light but strong pine that could be stepped together to make masts for the Royal Navy. The danger of being dependent on foreigners for such a vital resource was apparent to the overseers of His Majesty's war machine. So it is not hard to imagine their joy when the first reports reached London that the forests of New England and eastern Canada were filled with great pine trees 200 feet tall and 6 feet in diameter, with straight, thick trunks free of branches for the first 80 feet or more.

Early morning sunshine sweeps over a Wisconsin apple orchard in full bloom (*above*). Such a sight is a sure sign of spring almost anywhere on the continent. The protective petals of the apple blossom (*left*) unfold to reveal elongated stamens yellow with pollen.

Along with fish and furs, timber quickly became the principal export of the North American colonies. The first ships returning to England from Jamestown in the early 1600's carried a load of "clapboards and wainscott." A commercial sawmill was operating near York, Maine, as early as 1623, long before sawmills were introduced into England. By midcentury white pine from New Hampshire was being shipped not just to the home country but to the rival maritime powers of Spain and Portugal, and to markets in Africa and the West Indies as well. In fact, timber formed one corner of the so-called triangle trade that created the first great American fortunes. Oak-hulled and pine-masted merchant ships built in New England ports sailed to the west coast of Africa, where they exchanged cargoes of white pine for cargoes of enslaved Africans destined for the sugar plantations of the West Indies. There the empty holds were filled with barrels of rum and sugar for the return trip to the ports of Massachusetts and New Hampshire.

By the middle of the 18th century the British Crown was issuing proclamations that reserved for the exclusive use of the Royal Navy all pine trees "fit for Masts" in the Crown lands of North America. These attempts to meddle in what the colonists saw as "their" forest enterprise provoked sharp resistance; agents of the Crown were assaulted in the pine woods of Maine, New Hampshire, and New Brunswick by loggers disguised as Indians years before colonial merchants protesting the Stamp Act of 1765 staged their Boston Tea Party. On the eve of the Revolution, the Continental Congress halted all exports, including that of precious mastwood, to Britain. It was no accident that the first Revolutionary flag, which was raised aloft at the battle of Bunker Hill in 1775, bore the picture of a white pine.

Tall masts of native white pine and hoops of supple ash gave American sailing ships mastery of the seas from colonial times into the present century.

Crafted from white oak timbers, the massive keel and symmetrically curved ribs of a traditional wooden boat hull (*opposite*) typify the role that native trees played in the economy of pre-industrial North America.

The young nation that emerged from the American Revolution made full use of its greatest natural resource—the continent's apparently endless expanses of usable trees. Not without reason has this era been called America's Wooden Age. From chestnut cradles to pine coffins, from oak barrels to walnut gunstocks, from hickory firewood to maple rolling pins, from sour-cherry chairs and clocks to beechwood butter churns and table legs, wood was the material of choice—and necessity—for virtually every task of daily life.

The specific properties of each kind of wood were commonly known and cleverly matched to the job at hand. White pine, strong for its weight and resistant to warping, was favored for building bridges, including the famed covered bridges of New England. Because oak is odorless and tasteless, cider, beer, and whiskey were stored in oak barrels, and as the heaviest and sturdiest of American hardwoods, oak gave its strength to ships' hulls, including that of the U.S. Frigate *Constitution*, fondly nicknamed "Old Ironsides" for her ability to shrug off enemy cannonballs.

Since almost any road surface was preferable to bare earth, which turned dusty in summer and muddy in spring and fall, the turnpikes of North America were typically paved with bone-rattling oak logs, until they were replaced, in the early 19th century, by sawn planks

of oak or pine. The same twisted, interlocking grain that made elm logs so hard to split destined that wood for use as shock-resistant wheel hubs, ox yokes, and blocks that held blacksmiths' anvils.

Although log cabins were introduced to North America by Swedish settlers along the Delaware River in the 1630's, they were never, contrary to later misconception, widespread in the original Thirteen Colonies. Only as pioneers moved west in the late 1700's did the rough-and-ready virtues of the hand-hewn cabin, featuring round logs notched at the corners with protruding ends, recommend this basic structure to ax-wielding homesteaders. The earliest settlers imitated, at considerable expense and labor, the construction methods of their home countries: walls of brick, stone, or clapboard siding over elaborate jointed oak frames. What virtually all these houses had in common were roofs made from wood shingles or shakes, typically split with a hand tool called a froe, out of peeled logs of pine or oak.

The importance of trees to the economy of the United States was well understood by Thomas Jefferson, who planted a variety of uncommon species at Monticello and carried on a lively correspondence with other botanists in this country and in Europe. One of his correspondents was John Bartram, a Quaker farmer who established America's first botanical garden, in Philadelphia. In 1803, when President Jefferson selected Meriwether Lewis and William Clark to explore the vast extent of the Louisiana Purchase, he charged them with gather-

North American settlers learned to improve on traditional European-style tools. The double-bit ax is a design recognized as a true American original. The traditional choice for ax handles is springy hickory wood.

ing information on all flora and fauna west of the Mississippi River. Among its other achievements, the expedition is credited with the discovery of 34 species of trees.

Jefferson envisioned the development of the United States as an agrarian democracy, with the typical citizen tending his fields and orchards on his own land. But by the time of Jefferson's death in 1826 the nation was already beginning to turn toward a future that would be dominated by industrial production. Nowhere was that direction more clearly foreshadowed than in the burgeoning timber industry.

Between 1800 and 1850 the continental population increased fivefold to 25 million. To supply these people with homes, fuel, and the necessities of life, the forests of North America were systematically cut down and sent to market as wood products. A pattern was established that continued until the early decades of the 20th century. Logging and sawmill operations would proliferate in one area until all the largest and most profitable trees had been felled; the entire logging operation was then picked up and moved to another part of the country, where fresh stands of virgin timber awaited.

Statistics tell the story. In 1839 New York State succeeded Maine as the nation's leading producer of timber. By the 1870's the states bordering the Great Lakes dominated the industry. With the depletion of the forests in the Lake states over the next 30 years, dominance passed to the southern states; by the 1920's the lead was passing to the western states.

Each region presented different challenges to the loggers. In New England, oxen dragged sleds loaded with white pine down snowy slopes to spring-swollen streams; the buoyant logs were then floated downstream to water-powered mills. Bangor, Maine, on the Penobscot River, was America's first lumber boomtown. The river drained millions of acres of prime timber from the north, providing a natural sluice to flush the felled logs to Bangor's mills. To break up log jams on these "drives," which sometimes covered 200 miles, lumberjacks in caulked boots balanced atop the rolling, rushing mass of wet timber, pushing logs apart with long poles.

When stands of white pine gave out, logging entrepreneurs moved their operations to the Great Lakes region and adapted their methods to new conditions. Where waterways were not sufficiently broad and deep for log drives, the loggers "improved" them with splash dams. Strategically placed dams extended navigability of log drives on Wisconsin's St. Croix river system from 338 miles to 820 miles. The largest rivers, such as the Ohio, were choked with tremendous rafts of logs; one raft that floated past Cincinnati on its way downriver to New Orleans contained an estimated 1.5 million feet of pine and covered 3 acres.

Meanwhile, Yankee ingenuity was also improving the traditional tools of the trade. The first saws for cutting logs into useful lumber had appeared in Europe about 1500 B.C. The Romans invented the frame saw—a long-toothed blade secured to a rectangular frame for easier handling.

Frontier ingenuity and the need for shelter gave birth to the log cabin. Adapted to New World materials from a Scandinavian model, the log house came to typify westward movement throughout the United States and Canada.

To handle large logs, pit saws were devised, with one sawyer standing atop the log being sawed while his partner worked the other end of the saw from a pit beneath. Eventually sawmills in colonial and early 19th-century New England harnessed water wheels to power their huge reciprocating saws. By 1850 the traditional straight-bladed saw was being replaced by enormous belt-driven circular saws, which gave way, some 20 years later, to band saws, toothed loops of steel that ran endlessly over pulleys.

The middle decades of the 19th century also saw the development of practical steam power which, together with the advent of the railroad, set the timber industry free from its long-standing dependence on waterways. With mechanical devices to haul felled trees out of the forest and railroads to transport them to mill and market, loggers were no longer restricted to the lighter, more buoyant species like pine. They could now target the heavier hardwood trees as well. One result was the new practice of clear-cutting; by the 1890's some 50 million acres of timberland were laid bare across the northern Great Lakes region.

The new methods made possible economies of scale that left much of America's timberlands in the control of large corporations. Like other industries, logging monopolies were the order of the day. It was in the Lake states that Ezra Cornell amassed a half million acres of pine lands—and the fortune he later used to found Cornell University. Even more successful was Frederick Weyerhaeuser, the wood baron whose

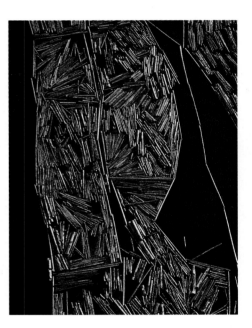

Logging still relies on assistance from nature. Above, logs float down the Fraser River in south-west British Columbia, taking advantage of a natural transportation system.

A century ago, trees provided both a valuable raw material and the means of transporting it. Deep in the Washington wilderness, a wood-burning donkey engine (*left*) hauled fresh-cut logs over a 100-foot-high trestle constructed from logs and timbers cut and assembled on the spot.

George Harvey put a good face on toil in his 1841 painting *Spring: Burning Fallen Trees in a Girdled Clearing (Western Scene)*. While a pioneer father and his sons use fire and oxen to clear their land, a girdled tree dies slowly in the foreground. To Harvey, the scene typified the smiling cheerfulness of the open landscape.

exploits have been compared to those of John D. Rockefeller in oil and Andrew Carnegie in steel. Syndicates controlled by Weyerhaeuser owned forests, logging companies, mills, transportation companies, retail and wholesale marketing concerns.

The onset of the Industrial Revolution brought no slackening in the demand for wood products. Not only were railroads fueled almost entirely by wood until the 1880's, but their construction consumed vast quantities of wood in the form of railroad ties, bridges and trestles, fencing and telegraph poles. In the last decades of the 19th century, up to 25 percent of the nation's annual wood production went to the railroads. But the primary consumer of lumber in the United States was the building industry.

A distinctive American innovation, the balloon-frame house, revolutionized this industry in the 1830's. It was made possible by the availability of cheap machine-cut nails, which American machine shops began turning out in large numbers at the end of the 18th century. With these nails a relatively unskilled carpenter could put together a simple house frame out of wooden studs—typically 2 inches by 4 inches—without the need for positioning heavy beams and securing them with elaborate mortise-and-tenon joints.

Between 1850 and 1900 the population tripled to 76 million; consumption of wood products increased an estimated fivefold—and the first voices began to be raised about the wisdom of such wholesale exploitation of the continent's forest resources.

One early eloquent voice of dissent belonged to Henry David Thoreau. In an 1858 book called *The Maine Woods*, Thoreau challenged the notion that the

forests of North America were valuable only as raw material for human industry. "When the chopper would praise a pine," he wrote, "he will commonly tell you that the one he cut was so big that a yoke of oxen stood on its stump; as if that were what the pine had grown for, to become the footstool of oxen." In that same year, George Perkins Marsh, a Vermont native who represented the United States as a diplomat in Italy, warned that deforestation could turn the Earth's surface from a "sponge" to a "dust heap" that would no longer be capable of supporting human life.

This concern about preserving the forest environment for a larger good was enthusiastically embraced by John Muir, a native of Scotland, who immigrated with his family to a Wisconsin farm in 1849. He pursued a successful career as an industrial inventor until 1867, when he nearly lost his eyesight in a machine-shop accident. At the age of 30, Muir decided to become a naturalist, hiking from the Midwest to the Gulf of Mexico to acquaint himself with the land. His ardent writings ignited a save-the-forest movement that led at the turn of the century to the establishment of a system of national parks and forests.

As founder and first president of the Sierra Club, Muir fought against attempts to allow commercial exploitation of national park land—a stance now known as "protectionist" to distinguish it from more lenient "conservationist" views. The man who became Muir's adversary in the debate between preservation and conservation was Gifford Pinchot, a proponent of rational forest management, whose work led to the establishment of the U.S. Forest Service in 1905.

Today the debate over the proper use of forest resources continues. Fears expressed in the late 19th century that the unrestricted cutting of trees would lead to a

"timber famine" proved unfounded. After diminishing steadily until about 1920, the total acreage designated as forestland in the United States has increased by some 20 percent since then. Although the virgin forests that greeted the European settlers are gone, New England now has more forestland than during Thoreau's time—in some places, like Vermont, nearly twice as much.

Some of this reforestation, especially in the northeastern United States, is due to natural reseeding following the abandonment of economically marginal farmland. Since 1941 lumber companies have planted nearly 100 million acres in so-called tree farms, which are managed to provide profitable crops for the future. All told, about one-third of the total land area of the United States, and a larger percentage of Canada, is now forested, including the 97 million acres in U.S. national parks and forests. Since the early 1940's new growth has consistently exceeded the annual harvest of trees.

But the pressures on our forest resources continue to mount, driven not only by the expanding worldwide market for lumber but also by ever-increasing demands for paper, plywood, and other wood-based products such as synthetic fibers and chemicals. Meanwhile, serious questions have been raised about the net loss to the ecosystem when old-growth forests—which contain trees of many species and many ages—are replaced by tree farms in which a few commercially valuable species are planted in acre after acre of single-age stands; to some observers, a tree farm managed for easy harvesting has more in common with a field of hybrid corn than with a fully diversified old-growth forest that sustains a wealth of plant, animal, and insect life.

The science of forest management is a relatively new discipline. Just a few years ago, when there was little understanding of the role that fire plays in the natural life cycle of forests, the goal was to prevent or contain all

Acres of Douglas firs cover Hurricane Ridge in Olympic National Park, Washington. Heavily timbered mountain ranges like these provide some of the continent's most valuable renewable resources.

John Muir, a native of Scotland, devoted most of his life to protecting American forests. Today, the system of U.S. national parks he inspired is permanent testimony to his remarkable vision—wilderness conservation for the benefit of the nation and its people.

forest fires. Now that fires are seen as one of the natural agents that periodically rejuvenate a forest, firefighting efforts are much more selective. By reducing the amount of sunlight that would otherwise pass through clearings opened by wildfires and by preserving dead wood that harbors insect pests, overzealous fire suppression can actually threaten the lives of healthy trees.

The fearsome blazes that swept through nearly a million acres in Yellowstone National Park during the arid summer of 1988 did extensive damage to trees and wildlife, but the destruction was less severe than a concerned viewer of television news shows might have guessed. Of the 32,000 elk that roamed the park, only 257 were killed; two moose and four deer died, and none of Yellowstone's 200 grizzly bears succumbed. Within a year new seedlings were sprouting from the ash-covered ground, and scientists are now closely monitoring the recovery of the forest to learn more about the complex interactions between the diverse components of a natural ecosystem—which includes the periodic incursion of fire.

At the forefront of recent arguments about the preservation of biodiversity in our forestlands are two apparently unrelated species of wildlife: the Northern spotted owl and the Pacific yew tree. Both live in old-growth forests in the Pacific Northwest, where most of the continent's remaining virgin forests are found. To prevent the destruction of the owl's habitat under provisions of the Endangered Species Act, a federal court restricted lumbering operations in large parts of Oregon and northern California. When lumber companies protested, the Secretary of the Interior appointed a committee of experts who were empowered to override the Endangered Species Act if they found its enforcement caused undue strain on the local economy. The committee, known as the "God squad" because of the life-or-death impact of its decisions, had been assembled only twice before. In May 1992 the "God

Raging through Yellowstone National Park in the summer of 1988, uncontrollable waves of fire incinerated thousands of acres of old-growth wilderness. Whether such fires are disasters or desirable natural events is the subject of continuing dispute.

squad" decided to open up the spotted owl's habitat to logging, apparently dooming the species to extinction.

But the already complex issue has been further complicated by the discovery that taxol, a substance derived from the bark of the Pacific yew tree, has remarkable cancer-fighting properties. In clinical studies, about a third of patients with formerly untreatable ovarian cancers responded positively to treatment with taxol, and there are indications that it is also effective on breast and lung cancers. So far, the drug has not been synthesized in the laboratory, and it takes more than one 100-year-old tree to yield enough taxol to treat one patient. Some 20,000 women contract ovarian cancer every year; according to an estimate submitted by the National Cancer Institute, one year's supply of taxol for treatment and research would require cutting down and stripping 38,000 Pacific yew trees.

Until the discovery of taxol, the Pacific yew was considered a worthless "weed" tree. Some lumber companies burned Pacific yews on slash piles after clear-cutting operations, a practice that environmentalists say is still going on. Meanwhile, other companies have begun to raise yew seedlings, and the search is on for alternative species that might yield significant quantities of taxol.

No one can say for sure what other useful, perhaps lifesaving, products remain hidden in the vast reservoirs of life that make up our forestlands. The task of preserving the biodiversity of the forests while promoting sustainable economic development poses one of the great challenges facing environmentalists in

Just days after the smoldering forest floor in Yellowstone cooled from the 1988 fire, a glacier lily signals the start of natural reclamation. The charred log will itself crumble into nutrients to feed a new generation of trees.

the coming century. But as Henry David Thoreau suggested more than a hundred years ago, there is something about a tree that appeals to us on a level far more profound than that of mere cost-benefit analysis.

When John Muir set out to learn about the landscape of America firsthand, he was determined to get close to trees in a way that his long-vanished ancestors in the long-vanished forests of an earlier geological epoch might have appreciated. Pushing through the California Sierras in a raging storm, Muir decided to climb a tree in order to "obtain a wider outlook and get my ear close to the Aeolian music of its topmost needles." He chose a young 100-foot Douglas fir whose "lithe, brushy tops were rocking and swirling in wild ecstasy.... The tops fairly flapped and swished in the passionate torrent, bending and swirling backward and forward, round and round, tracing indescribable combinations of vertical and horizontal curves, while I clung with muscles firm braced, like a bobolink on a reed." Instead of fear, Muir felt "safe, and free to take the wind into my pulses and enjoy the excited forest from my superb outlook."

Learning to live with trees is nothing less than a test case of our ability to live in harmony with the planet as a whole. ★

Wildlife survives even as forest fires burn out of control. This bull elk will wait for flames to subside and then will forage for fresh vegetation and new tree shoots as the forest begins to reclaim itself.

What Is a Tree?

A NORTH AMERICAN FOREST IN summer, seen from the vantage point of a mountain climber standing above the timberline, strikes the eye with the same beguiling blend of restlessness and repose that characterizes the Earth's oceans.

Agitated by breezes, the interlocking treetops undulate in place. Wave after gentle wave seems to billow up over the hills, then cascade down slopes to flow together into the sunlit valleys and the shadowed ravines. Except here and there, where old landslides and swift-running streams interrupt the verdant tide, it is impossible to tell where one tree ends and another begins.

The superficial movements of the treetops give only the faintest hint of the energies and transformations being generated in the trees below. No human manufacturing enterprise matches the efficiency, the varied capacity, the sheer concentrated power of a mature forest in full leaf. From the outspread leaves that capture the sun's radiant energy to the buried roots that seek out water and nutrients in the soil, from the twin pipelines that carry fluids and foodstuffs up and down the trunk to the internal assembly lines where new cells are made to order, each tree is a living factory that functions in concert—and sometimes in competition—with its woodland neighbors.

Given the right mix of raw materials and climatic conditions, a tree takes care of its own water transport, chemical processing, food production, energy conversion, air

Red maple, sugar maple, and beech leaves reveal the range of their autumn colors as they float on the mirrorlike surface of a pond in the Adirondack Mountains. Color is present in a leaf when it sprouts but is suppressed by green chlorophyll all summer.

The springtime shadow thrown by a sunlit oak's branches (*opposite*) paints the tree's image across young grass. For a deciduous tree like an oak, warm weather signals the start of a new growing season.

A stand of quaking aspen, like this grove in Snowmass Canyon, Colorado, is actually a single living organism, each tree cloned from a centuries-old ancestor and growing from one gigantic root system.

conditioning, reproduction, and nutrient storage. To fire its metabolic furnace, it consumes carbon dioxide, a waste product of animal respiration that would otherwise soon accumulate to life-threatening levels. As a byproduct of its own maintenance systems, every tree produces and releases into the atmosphere great quantities of oxygen, the prerequisite for all animal life on Earth. In addition, the tree puts in overtime as an erosion fighter and soil enricher, as well as a provider of shelter, nourishment, and insulation for other trees and plants, animals, insects, and microscopic organisms.

To add a pound of wood to its own frame, the average tree consumes nearly $1\frac{1}{2}$ pounds of carbon dioxide; at the same time, it releases nearly a pound of oxygen into the air. To keep a person alive for a year takes about 365 pounds of oxygen—the approximate output of $\frac{1}{12}$ of an acre of forestland. But the process works the other way as well. When wood decays or burns, oxygen is consumed and carbon dioxide is released back into the air. Older trees that grow slowly or trees that cannot get sufficient sunlight in an overcrowded, decaying forest may become net consumers of oxygen. What replenishes the world's oxygen supply is a continuously renewed stock of healthy, vigorously growing trees.

Of an estimated 40,000 species of trees in the world, approximately 750 are found in North America. While varying greatly in appearance and in details of structure and function, all share certain growth characteristics that distinguish trees from other members of the plant kingdom. The most distinguishing characteristic of a mature tree is its self-supporting woody spine, or trunk. The trunk's inner core consists of vertically oriented cells closely packed together in parallel rows. The cell walls consist primarily of a material called cellulose. The great majority of these cells, even in a healthy tree, are dead. Seen under a microscope, each cell resembles an empty tube without protoplasm or nucleus. Millions upon millions of such cells, the largest of which measure no more than a centimeter in length, form the heartwood of the trunk—the nonliving central pillar on which the living tree hoists itself skyward.

While the branches of a mature tree put forth new growth each year, its trunk simply thickens and cracks with age. The hollowed trunks of these giant sequoias belie their strength.

The trunk holds aloft a scaffold of branches so that its crown of leaves can receive optimal exposure to sunlight and air. While strong enough to bear the weight of the crown, the trunk and branches must be flexible enough to bend with strong winds instead of breaking. Surrounding the trunk and branches is a layer of bark, which protectively encircles all surfaces of the tree except for the leaves, flowers, fruits, and the thinnest tentacles of the root system.

On new twigs and recently sprouted saplings, the bark may be no more than a single cell thick—a transparent

Sycamore

sheath through which can be seen the cells underneath, green and rich with chlorophyll. Over the years the bark matures into a multilayered security system. The waterproof outer layer, known as the cork, insulates the tree from the elements, fends off hungry animals, and forms a barrier against decay-causing fungi. Just beneath the cork lies the cortex layer, where the tree stores new cork cells that have been manufactured by the cork cambium layer underneath.

As most trees grow older, the outermost cork

Coast madrone

Like skin, hair, and eye color in humans, the color and texture of bark distinguish trees from one another. Clockwise from top are specimens of sycamore, incense cedar, ponderosa pine, and coast madrone.

cells die and harden while new cells produced deeper inside the trunk push outward. This puts enormous pressure on the outer layer, causing the characteristic cracks and fissures seen on the trunks of many mature trees. One notable exception is the beech, whose outer bark cells continue to proliferate and expand as the tree matures, allowing the trunk to remain smooth. Variations in the texture, color, and thickness of bark tend to be characteristic of a given species—so much so that differences in the appearance of the bark provide one of the more reliable methods of identifying mature trees. Birches, for instance, have paper-thin bark that can be easily peeled off in large sheets;

Incense cedar

certain pines have deeply creviced bark that may be more than an inch thick; the more prominently furrowed bark of the giant sequoias of California may be more than a foot thick and so saturated with flame-resistant tannic acid as to be virtually fireproof.

Safe within the embrace of the bark is the tree's circulatory system: two cellular pipelines that transport water,

mineral nutrients, sugars, and other organic substances to all living tissues of the tree. One pipeline, called the phloem—or inner bark—carries the downward flow of foodstuffs from the leaves to the branches, trunk, and roots. The other, called the xylem—or sapwood—

Ponderosa pine

carries water and nutrients up from the roots to the leaves. The phloem lies just beneath the cork cambium; the xylem lies deeper inside the trunk, just outside the heartwood.

Sandwiched between these two pipelines is the vascular cambium—a single-cell layer usually too thin to be seen by the naked eye. Despite its seeming insignificance, this is the tree's major growth organ, responsible for the outward widening of the trunk, branches, twigs, and roots. During each growing season—usually spring and summer in temperate climates—the vascular cambium produces new phloem cells on its outer surface and new xylem cells on its inner surface.

Within the plump, elongated xylem cells of the sapwood, water molecules adhere to each other and are pulled upward through the trunk and into the branches and leaves by capillary action. Water molecules, drawn into the tree through tiny root tips, not only bring life-sustaining hydrogen and oxygen into the tree, but they also carry chemical nutrients from the soil. Exactly how a tree manages to lift gallon after gallon of water hundreds of feet into the air against the pull of gravity is a feat of hydraulics that has puzzled naturalists and engineers for centuries, and is still not understood completely by today's scientists.

By summer, xylem cells diminish in size and develop thicker skins, but they still retain their capacity to carry water. In time the innermost xylem cells become clogged with

Cracked and vine-hung bark protects a healthy loblolly pine (*left*) in Congaree Swamp National Park, South Carolina. The magnified section of a single pine stem (*inset*) reveals the hollow phloem through which life-giving carbohydrates flow.

A tree breathes through microscopic pores, or stomata, in its leaves. The tiny oval stomata, dyed yellow in the magnified view at right of an ash leaf, transfer essential carbon dioxide in the air to the tree's vascular system, seen here as red and green bands. The ash leaf is shown in the inset.

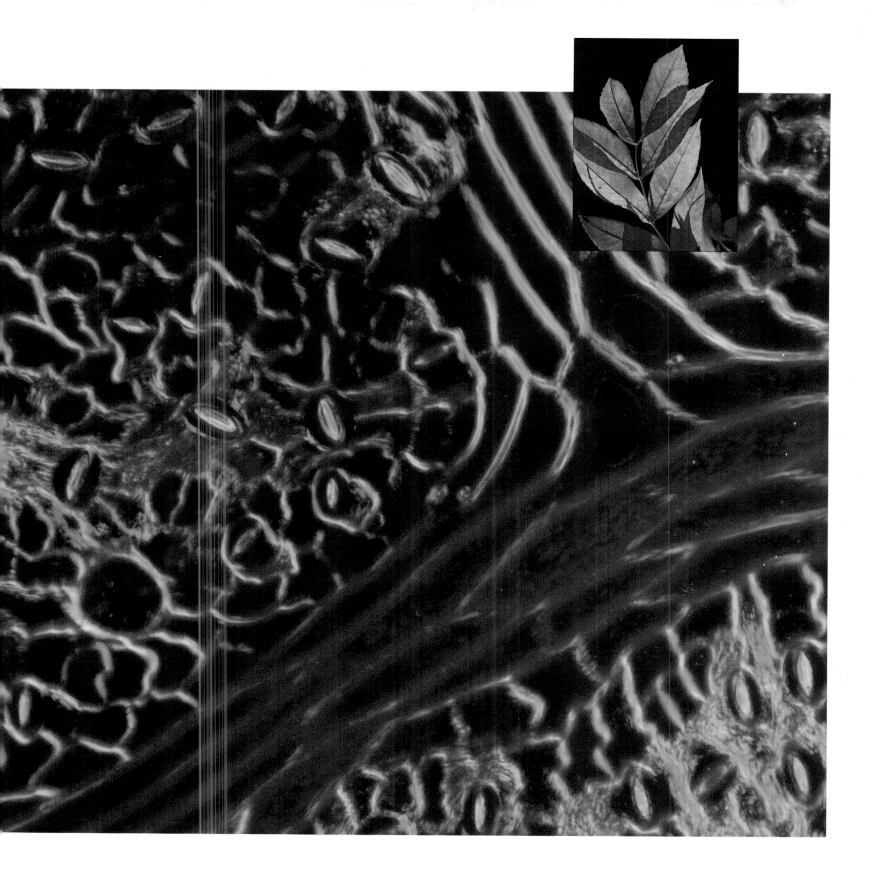

In the Berkshire Mountains, a forester uses a hollow auger to take a sample core from a living tree. Using the sample, no thicker than a pencil, a scientist can deduce the tree's history as well as the region's climatic past.

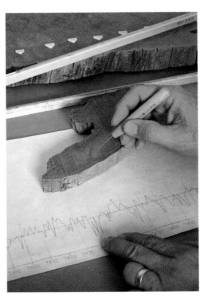

Because tree rings reveal environmental changes on earth, scientists can compare tree ring data (*right*) to records of sunspot activity, to see if solar events influence terrestrial climate.

hard or gummy waste products and can no longer transport fluids. This can be compared to the clogging of arteries in an aging human body. But since the vascular cambium manufactures healthy new xylem cells during each growing season, the death of the old cells does not mean the death of the tree. When they cease to function as living sapwood, dead xylem cells still play an essential role, becoming part of the columnar central core of heartwood, the supportive structure of the tree.

The sawed-off stump of a mature tree shows the concentric rings, called growth rings, that mark the annual production of xylem by the vascular cambium. Actually, a single year's growth is represented by two rings: the more porous wood produced in the spring forms a lighter-colored ring, while the denser wood produced in summer makes a thinner, darker ring. In general, the most recent sapwood is paler than the older heartwood near the center of the tree. As the tree ages, the ratio of darker heartwood to lighter sapwood keeps increasing.

At the very center of the heartwood is the pith, a narrow cylinder of food-storage cells that ascends to the top of the trunk. Mysteriously, the pith often decays or is ravaged by fire, leaving a hollow core; yet the tree not only survives but continues to thrive. In growing and mature trees, growth processes take place in very thin layers of the trunk, yet anything that blocks the tree's complex circulation system of phloem and xylem cells can be fatal. Carving a deep ring around the trunk or girdling a tree with a rope or an inflexible metal band—to support a hammock, for example—can literally choke a tree to death by closing off its lifeline.

The rings of this 15-year-old white fir reveal highlights of its brief life. The center, or pith, indicates that growth started in 1966. A narrow ring indicates a drought in 1977, while the incomplete outer ring shows that the tree was cut early in 1981, soon after being damaged by insects. A bulge at lower right indicates a branch trace; the split at left occurred as the trunk section dried after being cut.

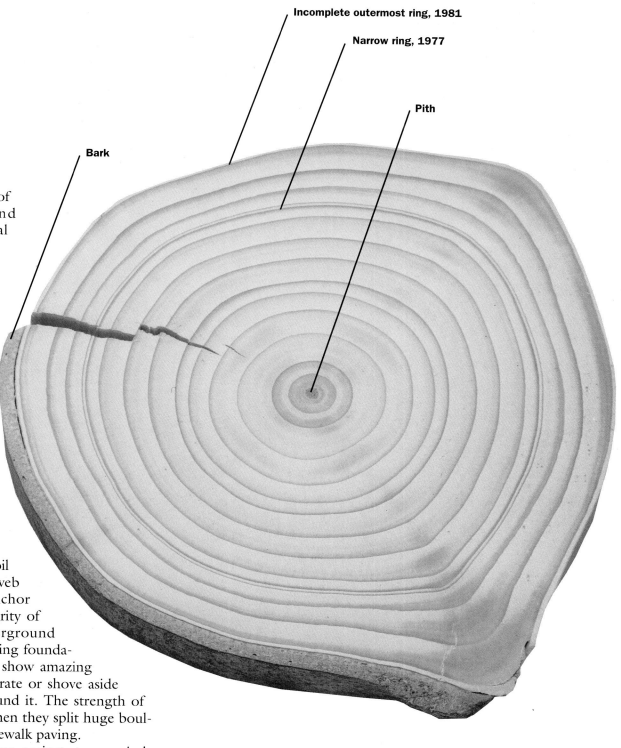

Incomplete outermost ring, 1981

Narrow ring, 1977

Pith

Bark

Many physical features of the tree's trunk and branches are identical in the root system. Mature roots are surrounded by bark, contain vascular cambium and woody centers, and have subterranean extensions of the xylem and phloem pipelines. Beyond these, though, a tree's root system proliferates into a maze of tentacles vastly different in appearance and function from the leaf-bearing branches and the columnar trunk that rises above ground.

Tree roots and the soil in which they grow form an inseparable partnership to promote the survival of the tree. Roots must reach out into the soil in many directions to produce a web of growth strong enough to anchor the massive tree. When the integrity of this web is threatened by underground obstructions, such as rocks, building foundations, or other plants, tree roots show amazing adaptability. If they cannot penetrate or shove aside an obstacle, they will detour around it. The strength of trees in this regard can be seen when they split huge boulders and uproot heavy slabs of sidewalk paving.

In addition to securing the tree against strong winds

and the weight of winter's ice and snow, the root system is responsible for absorbing water and other necessary nutrients from the soil. Except for the deep-plunging taproots of some species like the broom hickory, the root systems of most trees extend horizontally and remain within 4 feet of the surface, which is where most moisture is to be found. Legend has it that a tree's roots extend as far out from the trunk as its branches do. In fact, the spread of roots typically exceeds the spread of the branches, but their depth is nowhere near the height of the tree. One tree scientist has suggested placing a wineglass in the center of a dinner plate to visualize the relative extent of roots and branches. If the glass represents a tree with its rounded crown of branches and leaves, the rim of the plate indicates how much farther the roots will spread in their search for water and nutrients.

When mature, surface roots of a full-grown tree muscle outward to find water and nutrients (*above*). When the tree is upended in a storm (*below*), a suburban pavement is no match for the roots' brute force.

Thirsty trees, such as ancient willows that line streambeds, may drink as much as 50 gallons of water a day. In order to fulfill a maturing tree's ever-increasing need for water while providing firm support for its increasing weight, the root system grows continually except during hard winter freezes. The root tips—soft new fingers of growth that can be less than a quarter of an inch long and as fine as a sewing needle—tunnel through the soil with the help of a diminutive battering ram called a root cap.

The root cap shields the delicate young root tissues

In the intimidating depth of an old-growth forest, it is instinctive for humans to find sanctuary in the embrace of a tree. This massive Sitka spruce has anchored itself solidly in the forest floor of Oregon's Fort Clatsop National Memorial Park.

from injury as they inch their way into uncharted territory. As the root cap itself is bruised by the constant battering, its damaged cells are replaced with new cells. Microscopic root-cell debris that falls by the wayside actually helps to lubricate the forward motion of the root. Behind the root cap microscopically fine hairs branch off from the probing root, dramatically increasing the surface area for water absorption. So fine are these hairs that they take in water one molecule at a time, yet they are responsible for most of the water imbibed by the tree. Special membranes on the root hairs act as filters that let useful nutrients—primarily dissolved minerals—pass through while rejecting substances that might harm the tree.

Because they usually remain in moisture-rich soil within a few feet of the surface, the growing tips of roots are exposed to a wide variety of conditions. Fluctuations in temperature or humidity, as well as the actions of hungry insects, burrowing animals, or humans, can cause wholesale destruction of root hairs. At best, the life expectancy of an individual root hair is a few weeks, but the entire root structure grows in much the same way as branches aboveground. Tiny root tips that survive the perils of underground life eventually mature into woody roots complete with bark and many of the features of branches and twigs that grow above ground.

At the opposite end of the tree from the busy roots are the equally busy leaves, which produce the foodstuffs that nourish the entire plant and provide it with the essentials of growth. Most North American trees fall into one of two categories—evergreen or deciduous—depending on the type of leaf they bear. The leaves of coniferous evergreens—pines, firs, spruces, and redwoods—tend to be narrow and needlelike, whereas most deciduous trees—oaks, maples, birches, and nut trees—have broad, flat leaves. The leaves of deciduous, or broad-leaved, trees can be divided into two categories: simple and compound. Simple leaves consist of a single blade on a stalk; compound leaves have two or more blades or leaflets. Trees with large simple leaves, such as oaks and maples, cast dense shade; compound-leaved trees, like willows and hickories, cast dappled patterns.

Both deciduous and evergreen trees shed their leaves, but deciduous trees typically lose all their foliage at the onset of winter and display naked branches until leaves appear in spring. Conifers and broad-leaved evergreens, such as holly and magnolia, continuously shed and replace their leaves but remain green year round. Pine needles, however, remain on the tree for 3 to 7 years, while the ground around the tree is slowly blanketed with dry, copper-colored dead needles.

Superbly adapted for survival in extremis, the mangrove (*opposite*) has developed an elaborate root structure that withstands salt water and tidal surges, while providing shelter for fish and other aquatic animals. Soil and organic debris that accumulate among these Florida mangroves form the basis of fragile islands that ultimately become the rich swamp forests known as the Everglades.

Given the least toehold, a tree's roots can establish and sustain growth. This weathered, ancient white cedar has flourished for two centuries along Lake Superior's boulder-strewn shore in northern Minnesota.

Sugars

Water

The Tree as Engine

A tree can be seen as a complex engine, converting fuel into energy and manufacturing new products from available resources.

Within every living tree, the roots absorb water and mineral nutrients from the soil and pump them to the farthest branches and leaves. Carbon dioxide, produced by animals and decomposing organisms, is absorbed through the leaves.

Using the water and carbon dioxide in the leaf, sunlight initiates photosynthesis—a chemical process that produces carbohydrates, the sugars that nourish the growing tree.

The tree emits newly manufactured oxygen as waste. This exchange sustains plant and animal interdependence, since oxygen is essential to all animal life, human included.

Oxygen

n dioxide

Photosynthesis

Sunlight

Chlorophyll

Sugars

The complicated but almost instantaneous manufacturing process that takes place inside the leaf employs energy from the sun to convert water and carbon dioxide into sugars and other organic molecules. This process is called photosynthesis, and all tree leaves—whether coniferous or deciduous—carry out the photosynthetic process in basically the same way. The outer skin of the leaf, called the epidermis, incorporates thousands of tiny pores called stomata. These pores, most of which are found on the underside of the leaf, open to take in molecules of carbon dioxide as needed. Meanwhile, water that was absorbed by the roots and transported upward through the sapwood enters the leaf through its stem. Once carbon dioxide and water are present in a leaf that is drenched in sunlight, photosynthesis can begin.

Each leaf gets its green color from chlorophyll, a pigment that is contained in millions of microscopic structures called chloroplasts. When the sunlight shines on a leaf, its energy is absorbed by molecules of chlorophyll; this energy is used to combine water and carbon dioxide molecules to make carbohydrates, or sugars, and other energy-rich organic molecules. In the process, oxygen is released to the outside air through the stomata. At the same time microscopic, threadlike veins in the leaf carry the newly made foodstuffs out through the stem into the twigs and branches, where they begin their journey through the phloem pipeline to be distributed throughout the tree. This process continues all through the growing season, as long as the leaves remain green.

No native North American tree reflects the change of seasons as vividly as the sugar maple: clockwise from top left, in full blossom in late spring; leafed out in summer; aglow with autumn color; and barren through the winter. At center, the familiar symmetrical maple leaf displays its brilliant color.

The life-sustaining role of a leaf is not done when it falls from the tree. Frosted maple and buckthorn leaves in Plumas National Forest, California (*opposite*), will slowly decay into an organic compost, renewing the soil.

The restful atmosphere of this summer tableau with two oaks is deceiving. Intense biological activity takes place throughout the tree. Nutrient-laden water flows steadily from the roots to the leaves, where oxygen and carbon dioxide gasses are continuously being exchanged.

Leaves come in an endless variety of shapes and sizes. Each form, whether long and waxy, needlelike, or broad and wafer-thin, represents an evolutionary compromise between the tree's need to expose its chloroplasts to sufficient sunlight and its need to guard against losing too much moisture to the surrounding air. All living organisms lose moisture through a process known as transpiration. In animals this typically occurs through pores in the skin; trees lose most of their water through the stomata, the pores in their leaves. A large broad-leaved tree can release gallons of moisture into the atmosphere each day.

Trees that grow in dry climates often have thick leaves surrounded by a heavy waxy film called the cuticle, which prevents transpiration or dehydration; the succulent leaves of desert-dwelling aloe or yucca trees are examples. Trees in moister regions do not need such a thick layer of protection. Their leaves may be thinner and broader—in the case of aspen, almost transparent—with a cuticle so fine that leaves dry quickly after rain. And instead of looking glossy, the leaves have a matte surface.

The amount of sunlight needed to keep a tree healthy varies greatly from species to species. Some, like the eastern hemlock, flourish in deep shaded thickets; others, like the Joshua tree and the New Mexican pinyon pine, thrive only in bright sunshine. Among the factors that affect a tree's ability to exploit the sun's energy are the size of the leaves, the length of the individual leaf stalks, and even the way the stalks are attached to the twigs. Held erect by a skeleton of moisture-plumped veins, the leaves of some broadleaved trees can actually move ever so slightly in the course of a day to align their surfaces at right angles to solar rays—the optimal sun-catching position—in a maneuver called heliotropism.

Like variations in bark, variations in leaf size and shape and in the way the leaf stalk is attached to the branch have proved useful markers in helping botanists distinguish one species from another. These variations affect not only the way the tree looks but also the sound it makes when agitated by a breeze. According to naturalists who have kept their ears open, the wind-stirred foliage of an eastern hemlock emits a soft sighing, the fragrant needles of the northern balsam swish gently, spruces whoosh, maples rustle, the heavy leaves of a cottonwood make a noise like rushing water or the patter of applause, the gorgeous fall foliage of a pin oak speaks with a harsh lisp, and the stiff spines of a giant saguaro cactus in the New Mexico desert whisper with a sound like far-off surf.

The extraordinary diversity of today's trees, with each species and subspecies filling a slightly different environmental niche, is the outcome of hundreds of millions of years of reproductive experimentation and adaptation. It is proverbial that "mighty oaks from little acorns grow." But in fact the proverb fails to do justice to the remarkable process that brings together a single-celled grain of pollen and a single-celled egg. This union produces a new organism that may grow, like one of California's coast redwoods, from a kernel a quarter of an inch long into a

Pacific rhododendrons are silhouetted against towering redwoods in California's Del Norte Redwood State Park (*opposite*). The simple alternating leaves of the rhododendrons grow at the end of twisting branches.

On each tiny scale of a single female pine cone (*above*) are two ovules, or egg cells. Pollen from male cones lower on the tree floats upward and fertilizes the eggs, after which the cones dry and harden. A mature tree may have thousands of seed cones, only a few of which will ever germinate into new trees.

leviathan taller than a football field is long. The entire process, which is similar to the sexual reproduction common to animals, is set in motion by the parental reproductive organs that we call flowers or, on coniferous trees, cones.

Despite the analogy to animal reproduction, making generalizations about the gender of trees or their sexual organs can be risky business because so many variations in form and structure occur. It is true that sperm cells, in the form of pollen grains, are produced in a specialized male organ called the stamen; eggs are produced in a specialized female organ called the ovary. In some species all the flowers on an individual tree will produce only pollen or only eggs, and such trees may be referred to as male or female. But there are also species that have flowers of both kinds on the same tree. Many trees, including most of the ornamental varieties, incorporate pollen- and egg-producing structures within the same flower. Such flowers are capable of self-pollination, which means that they can reproduce without any outside intervention.

Since cross-pollination between different individuals leads to greater genetic variability than self-pollination, nature has developed many ingenious mechanisms for transporting pollen from one tree to the egg of another. Springtime allergy sufferers will testify that a vast quantity of plant pollen, much of it from flowering trees, is carried freely on the wind. Like their counterparts in the animal kingdom, only a tiny fraction of these wind-borne grains ever makes contact with waiting eggs to begin the development of new trees.

These tufted blue gum eucalyptus flowers are not only striking to look at, but they are ideally designed for intercepting windblown pollen. After fertilization, the flowers fade and disappear, but the small seeds can develop into trees that tower more than 200 feet in the air.

Some fruits are useful without being edible. The soapberry, for example, is mildly toxic but has had a long and versatile history: ancient Aztecs washed clothes in soapberry suds; today, chemists use the berry to make waxes and varnishes; and advocates of homeopathic medicine treat headaches and rheumatism with it.

By producing showy and fragrant flowers filled with sugary nectar, trees are, in a sense, recruiting animals—insects such as bees and butterflies, as well as some bats and birds—to perform cross-pollination. As a honeybee enters a flower to extract nectar, some pollen grains stick to its fuzzy body; at the same time, pollen grains gathered earlier from nearby flowers fall off. The more flowers the bee visits, the greater the odds that the pollen and eggs from distant trees will be brought together to engender new individuals.

Once an egg is fertilized, an embryo, or seed, develops. In the true flowering trees, or angiosperms, this occurs within the ovary of the blossom. But in the trees called gymnosperms, which include the conifers, embryos develop out in the open, on the naked scale of a cone or similar structure. The maturing ovary, otherwise known as the tree's fruit, not only protects the growing seed but also prepares itself to be the transport apparatus that will carry the seed away from its parent plant. This is necessary because if all the seeds fell to earth directly below the parent tree, competition for light, water, and food would be so fierce that few if any seedlings could survive to maturity.

The dispersal of fruit-encased seeds is accomplished in many ways. The winged fruits of trees like the elm or maple are borne on the wind. Others, like the fruit of the coconut palm, can float for hundreds of miles on water. To exploit the motive power of animals, trees have evolved a variety of ingeniously shaped fruits and nuts, the botanical equivalent of fruits in certain tree species.

Forest animals like the timber wolf pick up seeds in their fur and transport them far afield from the parent tree to start new trees in another part of the forest.

A whole class of burrlike fruits employs tiny spines, hooks, barbs, and similar grappling devices to cling to the hides of furry animals. The aptly named "mule grab," on the other hand, has evolved to fit into the cleft hooves of grazing animals. On some South Pacific islands there are fruits sticky enough to hitch rides to distant islands on the feathers of seabirds.

But the seed-dispersal mechanism that most people are familiar with is the tasty, energy-packed fruit or nut that animals, including human beings, are tempted to eat. In exchange for providing a healthful meal, the tree is rewarded with a free ride for its seeds, which eventually find their way to the ground in a number of ways. Not all the nuts that squirrels hide away for the lean days of winter are retrieved; mighty forests grow from the nuts that germinate in forgotten burial places.

Seeds embedded in the sweet-tasting flesh of ripe fruits may pass unharmed through the digestive tracts of animals; when the seeds are excreted, often far from the parent tree, they will germinate if exposed to favorable soil

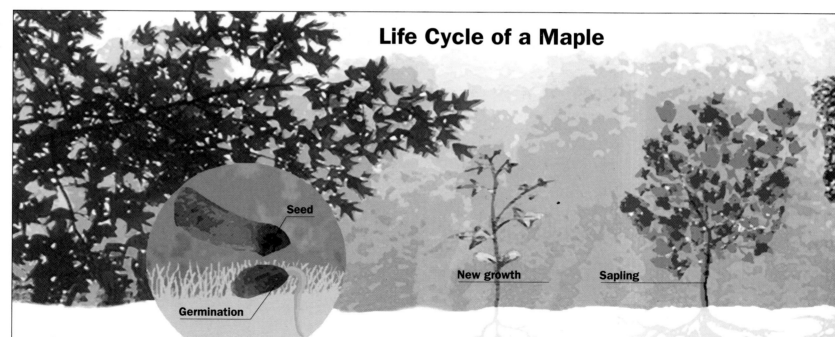

Life Cycle of a Maple

Seed

Germination

New growth

Sapling

The maple begins as a flat **seed** with long, papery, vein-like wings.
Autumn winds carry the seed like a propeller, far from its host tree. After finding the right combination of light, moisture, and soil, a seed **germinates** and sends down a fragile but tenacious root. In early spring, **new growth** beomes apparent. As the young **sapling** develops, it grows as much as several inches a day in a constant search for sun and nutrients.

The tree grows nearly 20 feet in 10 years. Each spring, scarlet flower clusters and new five-lobed leaves brighten the branches. By late spring, winged seeds replace the flowers, remaining on the branches until late autumn.

them on the stem, buds that will eventually become branches appear virtually overnight.

Year after year, in seasonal spurts dependent largely on temperature and water supply, the tree will reach upward and outward, adding billions of new xylem, phloem, cambium, and cork cells not only to its central trunk and its roots but also to all its outstretched branches. Each summer the plant prepares for the next year of growth; by autumn, the youngest branches of most deciduous trees are laden with dormant buds that lie in wait for the following spring's warmth. Some of these buds encase miniature versions of the next season's twigs; a greater number contain minuscule leaves that will unfold to the sun and begin to grow once winter is over.

The growth habits of trees vary greatly from species to species. The shoot growth of dogwood and redbud is limited to three or four weeks in the spring; in maples it proceeds in intermittent bursts throughout the growing season. Hollies and magnolias continue to grow as long as conditions remain favorable. Broad-leaved evergreens, such as bay laurel and eucalyptus, put out new growth buds just as seasonal deciduous trees do. Needle-leaved evergreens—spruces, firs, and most pines—put out new growth only at the tips of their branches, while other conifers, like the fine-needled hemlocks, yews, and arborvitae, send out shoots all along their branches.

The leaves of deciduous trees typically die en masse and drop to the ground as the trees prepare themselves for winter's reduced water supply. But across the temperate zones of the North American continent leaf death is preceded by a unique show of color. The rapidly falling temperatures of autumn trigger a complex chemical reaction: the tree no longer manufactures the green pigment

The fuzzy texture and purple hue of these young white oak leaves barely last a season. When mature, the tree is known for its smooth green leaf.

chlorophyll, and this loss allows the fiery reds, oranges, and yellows of the underlying leaf structure—stored there from spring in pigments called carotenoids—to burst forth before the foliage drops to earth. Then, bare-branched, the trees slow down their internal processes and go dormant until the springtime thaw, just as hibernating animals slow down their metabolic processes during the winter.

As efficient as the inner workings of an individual tree may seem, trees are actually far from self-sufficient. Solitary trees are rarely found in nature; their presence usually signifies human intervention—selective planting, selective removal of adjacent vegetation, or extraordinary efforts at preservation. Whether in a forest grove or on the edge of an open meadow, bordering a lawn or a city playground, trees are involved in a continual give-and-take with other forms of life. Certain bacteria and other microorganisms in the soil, for example, establish symbiotic relationships with tree roots: the microorganisms assist the roots in the absorption of mineral nutrients, while the roots furnish sugars upon which their subterranean partners thrive. Trees also provide essential food and shelter for forest animals, while those same arboreal creatures—from insects to mammals—unwittingly assist the trees by broadcasting pollen grains or enriching the topsoil with excrement.

Such community rapport does not end when trees die. In fact, some scientists argue that a rotting tree trunk is more beneficial to the forest complex than a living tree. When a standing tree succumbs to disease or other ravages of nature, such as fire, wind, or lightning, insects and

microbes soon penetrate the wood. This activity permits air, water, and bacteria to enter the dead but still-standing tree and to facilitate its biochemical decay.

A dead tree is a long-term store-house for water and nutrients that nourish plant and animal life for decades, as these two photographs illustrate. The fallen trunk at left serves as a host for fungi, lichens, mosses, and other forest plants, as well as a primary habitat for insects, birds, and small mammals. The rotting log (*above*) slowly decomposes into the forest floor, releasing valuable organic compounds that make the forest a living, self-sustaining organism.

In time the decomposing tree, no longer able to maintain its own structural integrity, topples over. It then becomes a haven of refuge and nutrition for numerous new species of animals that migrate to it. Roots from other plants and fungal infestations work their way into the rotting log, breaking it down further into what, decades or centuries later, becomes a crumbled mass of spongy particles that eventually return to the soil itself. While some parts of a tree, like the leaves and branches, decompose more quickly than the heartwood of the trunk, all ultimately restore to the ecosystem the useful organic elements that were locked up in the tree during its lifetime.

In terms of quantity, variety, and efficiency of output, trees are without a doubt the dominant members of the forest ecosystem. Although these sovereigns of the forest compete among themselves for light, moisture, nutrients, and ground space, the end result of their competition is an interactive network of organisms in dynamic equilibrium with one another, a vast incubator and nurturer of life whose importance rivals that of the oceans—the original home of all life on Earth. ✳

CHAPTER THREE

An Intimate Partnership

THE FIRST THING THAT EUROPEAN explorers noticed about the forests of North America, even before they set foot on the continent, was the pungent aroma borne to their approaching ships by offshore breezes. Some hopeful sea captains took this pungency as a foretaste of the valuable "Oriental" spices that had prompted the original voyages of exploration. In fact, the agreeable odors came not from spices but from the rich and varied vegetation of New World forests. While their hopes for a trans-Atlantic spice trade were quickly dashed, European traders soon learned to appreciate the real value of these redolent forests.

The aromas of the virgin forests of the new continent arose from the blossoms of numerous trees and from the volatile oils in pine sap: pine trees exude a resinous sap to heal wounds caused by wind, fire, and lightning, and the sap is also a protective coating for otherwise exposed seeds. To sailors, these fragrances hinted at an abundant supply of what were known as naval stores, the pitch and pine tar that kept wooden ships watertight and seaworthy.

Farther south along the Atlantic coast, in what is now Virginia, the Carolinas, and Florida, the air was perfumed by such species as the sassafras tree, which in these warm climates can grow to a height of 80 feet. Powdered sassafras leaves were actually used as spice by the Choctaw Indians, and it is still used to flavor many Creole dishes in the Mississippi Delta region. The strong but pleasant smell of its leaves, bark, wood, and roots—once familiar as the dominant flavoring in root beer—had long recommended sassafras to American Indians as a medicinal panacea. Sassafras tonic was reputed to cure everything from fever to stomachache. In the southeastern part of the continent, sassafras leaves were commonly mixed with native tobacco leaf and smoked, much to the amazement of Europeans.

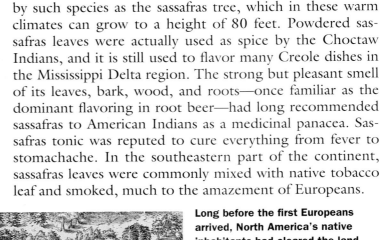

Long before the first Europeans arrived, North America's native inhabitants had cleared the land and put the forest's bounty— including wood, bark, leaves, nuts, and roots—to good use in their dwellings, tools, foods, and medicines. This 16th century engraving shows European explorers arriving at a settlement in Florida.

Fall transforms the leaves of the sassafras (*opposite*) into a panoply of orange and yellow. A member of the laurel family, the aggressively growing sassafras is one of the first trees to reforest abandoned fields and clear-cut land.

Indians used the bitter bark and lemony berries of the prickly ash (*above*) as painkillers and the bark as a poultice for skin ailments. Tribes in the Southeast transformed the aromatic bark of the flowering dogwood (*below*) into a treatment for malaria and extracted a red dye from its roots to color quills and feathers for headdresses.

Word of the miraculous properties of the sassafras reached Europe by way of the French and Spanish colonies of southern Florida. By the start of the 17th century the high price of sassafras on the London market served as a spur to early English expeditions to the New World. Sassafras was one of the first exports from Capt. John Smith's Virginia colony on the James River. The sassafras boom collapsed when the panacea failed to live up to its reputation. Worse yet, the U.S. Food and Drug Administration has deemed sassafras oil—the extract used to flavor root beer and chewing gum until the 1960's—a potential carcinogen, so even Grandma's old-fashioned sassafras tea has become a banned substance. Even so, the belief that American Indians were privy to important lore about the medicinal properties of indigenous plants was founded on hard-won experience and sound reasoning.

When the men of Jacques Cartier's expedition up the St. Lawrence River fell ill of scurvy in the year 1535, a native guide saved their lives by having them drink a

decoction of the bark and leaves of the arborvitae tree; like the limes that were later prescribed for scurvy victims, arborvitae sap is rich in vitamin C. The Indians of the eastern woodlands also put great faith in the painkilling efficacy of certain barks and berries, especially those of the prickly ash, which grateful settlers termed the toothache tree. The name seems less quaint in light of the fact that the formula for aspirin, the most widely used of modern painkillers, is based on an old European folk remedy made from bitter willow bark.

The solar-powered chemical activity within the leaves of trees and other plants manufactures a great number of complex organic molecules that have potent effects on the human body. Along with the gold that the Spanish brought back from their conquests in South America was another bitter brew that the Indians of the Amazon prepared from the bark of the cinchona tree. For more than 3 centuries this bark was the only

Eastern woodland tribes chewed the fragrant, gluelike inner bark of the slippery elm (*above*) into a paste for dressing wounds. Tribes in the Hudson Bay area found the inner bark of the quaking aspen (*left*) soothing to the throat and stomach.

The straight, slender lodgepole pine earned its name by being the perfect support for Indian tipis.
This late 19th-century photograph from the Pine Ridge Reservation in South Dakota,
site of the massacre at Wounded Knee, shows that the Sioux had also learned to use it for fencing.

source of quinine—the first effective treatment for malaria and the forerunner of modern pharmacological medicine. Its active ingredient, a complex alkaloid, was not synthesized until the middle of this century.

It is no exaggeration to say that the trees of North America served the native inhabitants as a rich storehouse of medical drugs. The Cree Indians around Hudson Bay made a cough syrup and laxative out of the inner bark of the quaking aspen. The gummy resins exuded by a number of trees, including the sweet gums of the Southeast, were used to treat skin ailments. Some western tribes mixed the ground bark of the prickly ash with a dollop of bear grease to make a poultice for ulcers and sores. Slippery elm bark, chewed into a viscous paste, was favored for dressing wounds. In the absence of cinchona bark, the Indians of the Southeast treated periodic malarial fevers with the bitter, astringent bark of the flowering dogwood. Today, among the Yavapais of the American Southwest,

women who have just given birth drink a tea made from juniper berries to help relax their muscles.

Although the list of tree-derived medications could be extended almost indefinitely, it represents just one aspect of the intimate partnership that evolved over millennia between the Indians and the trees of North America. Not even the value of the bison to the hunting peoples of the Great Plains can compare with the multiple roles that trees have played in the lives of American Indians.

From the bison, or buffalo, Plains Indians obtained not only food, but dried dung for fuel; horn and bone for tools, utensils, and ornaments; and hides for clothing, blankets, and tipi coverings. But bison hides were typically preserved in solutions of tannin-rich oak bark, and the poles that held up the tipis were the trunks of tall, straight lodgepole pines—native to the Rocky Mountains but bartered far and wide across the Plains. The spears and bows and arrows that the Plains hunters used to bring

down the bison were, of course, made of wood. The wood most prized for bows, because of its supple strength, came from the Osage orange, or *bois d'arc*—bow wood in French. Although native to a limited region where the states of Oklahoma, Arkansas, Louisiana, and Texas meet today, the wood's reputation as the best bow material extended far afield. In the year 1810 a well-made Osage orange bow fetched as much in trade as a horse and a blanket—a high price indeed.

The same trees that provided shelter and weapons for the Plains Indians also eased the burdens of their migratory life. Baskets and carriers woven from the thin branches of willow and other trees were not only utilitarian, but the intricate patterns also identified their tribes and makers. Even before the Spaniards brought horses to North America, dogs were yoked to travois—V-shaped frames made of two lodgepole pines—to drag heavy loads over long distances. This was no small advantage, considering that a Plains family might move their dwelling as often as a hundred times a year.

Lodgepole pines (*left*), like these in Oregon's Cascade Range, grow up to 80 feet tall but only 1 to 3 feet across. The stands are so dense that dead trees may stand for years without falling. Indians collected the dead pines for use as tipi poles and for fuel.

The fruit of the Osage orange (*above*) bears no scientific relation to the common orange, although similarity of shape gives the tree its name. The flexible, durable wood was valued by the Plains Indians for bows used in both hunting and warfare.

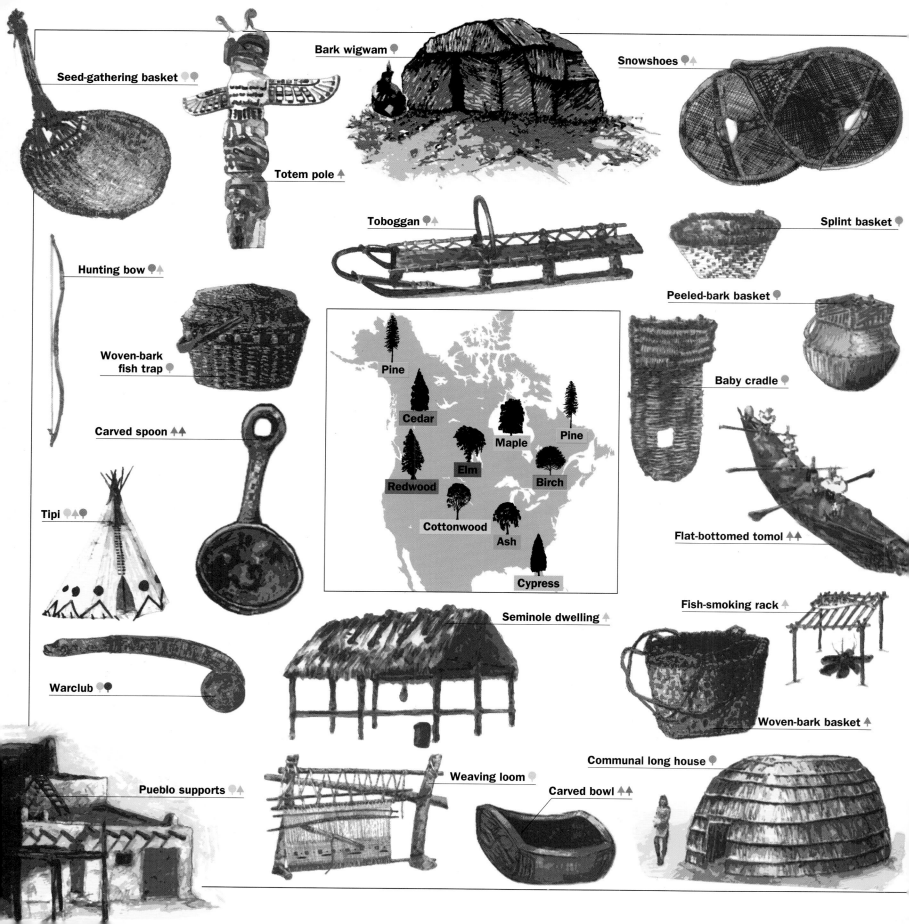

Seed-gathering basket

Bark wigwam

Snowshoes

Totem pole

Splint basket

Toboggan

Hunting bow

Peeled-bark basket

Woven-bark fish trap

Baby cradle

Carved spoon

Tipi

Flat-bottomed tomol

Pine

Cedar

Maple

Pine

Redwood

Elm

Birch

Cottonwood

Ash

Cypress

Warclub

Seminole dwelling

Fish-smoking rack

Woven-bark basket

Communal long house

Pueblo supports

Weaving loom

Carved bowl

Trees in the Native North American Economy, Before 1800

No single resource was more vital to the native people of North America than trees. Besides food in the form of nuts and fruits, maple trees provided sugar from sap, while beverages and medicines were made from the bark and roots of various species.

Before the introduction of metal tools, American Indians tended to use wood in its native state or with minimal processing. Twigs, small branches, bark strips, and roots could be woven into baskets, nets, and containers of distinctive styles.

Flexible branches were worked to fabricate snares, arrows and bows. Solid or split saplings became the framework for objects like looms, snowshoes, and shelters, which were covered with hide or bark.

Strong, stiff pieces of wood were worked into clubs, paddles, bowls and other tools or utensils, often utilizing the natural forks, curves, and bends of the branches. Wooden sticks and poles, their sharpened tips hardened by fire, made eminently serviceable lances and digging implements.

Bark—particularly birch bark in the Northeast and cedar bark in the far Northwest—was an extraordinarily adaptable raw material and was used for everything from clothing to canoes.

Large pieces of wood tended to be used whole, typically as poles and timbers for both temporary and permanent lodgings, as well as for dugout vessels used all along the Atlantic, Gulf, and Pacific coasts.

Making tree trunks and split logs into planks demanded considerable time and effort, but some cultures—with the help of fire and stone tools—laboriously cut, split, shaped, carved, and hollowed wood into objects ranging from utensils and ritual ornaments to huge totem poles.

While life on the almost treeless Plains was more dependent on the bounty of trees than might at first glance seem credible, the inhabitants of the northeastern woodlands structured their entire existence around the resources of the forest, and especially those of a single tree: the birch. So central to the Indians of the Northeast was this tree we know as the white, paper, or canoe birch that anthropologists describe their way of life as the Old Birch Bark Hunting Culture.

The canoe birch is a fast-growing, hardy tree. Often found near running streams, it readily adapts to a variety of soils and growing conditions and may reach a height of 50 feet or more. Its waxy, whitish bark has a smooth surface that peels horizontally into paper-thin sheets, especially in younger trees. Because of its high resin content, birch bark is virtually impervious to moisture; this property, combined with its flexibility and durability, led to its use wherever a lightweight, easily worked, waterproof material was called for.

Birch bark was the Indian's indispensable companion from cradle board to burial shroud. Sheets of bark, cut and folded and secured with thongs of animal hide or sinew, provided household utensils of every shape, size, and function. Formed into storage containers, birch bark helped protect food from vermin and decay. Indians dried newly harvested maize on birch bark sheets spread in the sun and then stored it in birch bark-lined holes in the ground. With resin to seal the seams, birch bark vessels served as cooking pots for boiling water to render tough meats edible in the soups that were the main meals of the Iroquoian peoples. And birch bark imparted no taste of its own to the water or to food it held.

Sheets of birch bark rolled together were fashioned into baskets and backpacks. For larger utensils and containers the Indians reserved the tougher "winter bark," cut from a tree after the second freeze of the season. The winter bark also covered dome-shaped wigwams and multifamily longhouses, either of which had a supporting framework of birch saplings. Shoes were made of birch bark; messages and symbols were written on thin sheets of bark. Shredded birch bark is highly flammable even when wet, so Indians carried bark balls in their backpacks as firestarters and torches; as a bonus, the sweet-smelling smoke from a birch fire helped keep away mosquitoes.

Northeastern Indians fashioned the lightweight, flexible, and waterproof bark of the birch tree into tipi coverings and canoe skins. The painting at left by Canadian Paul Kane shows a mid-19th century encampment on Lake Huron. Indians also believed that the lenticels, or horizontal pores, in the bark (*above*) were eyes through which the spirit of the trees watched over them.

But as ubiquitous as birch bark was in the everyday lives of northeastern Indians, its importance in other applications paled by comparison to its use in the birch bark canoe. Before the arrival of the horse, and for many years afterward, travel on land through the dense forests was slow and cumbersome. The best of trails became overgrown, and danger from wildlife and unfriendly humans was ever-present. Far easier, safer, and quicker were the streams, rivers, and lakes that formed a mazelike network of waterways through the entire region. Although there were places in the network where neighboring waters failed to connect by a few yards or a few miles, the links in general were good enough that a determined man in a light but sturdy canoe could journey hundreds upon hundreds of miles with only a few overland portages.

The extent and effectiveness of this network can be appreciated from the success of the Iroquois League, a federation of tribes based in western New York but linked by waterways well into eastern Canada and as far south as the Delaware River. The birch bark canoe that made

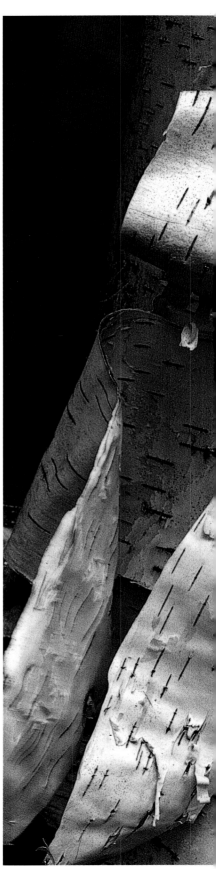

Birch canoes varied greatly in design as well as in decoration, as shown by the watercolors of fur-trade canoes (*above*) painted by Edwin Tappan Adney in the late 1800's. His sketch of a large trade canoe under construction (*below*) reveals the high level of Indian boat-building skills.

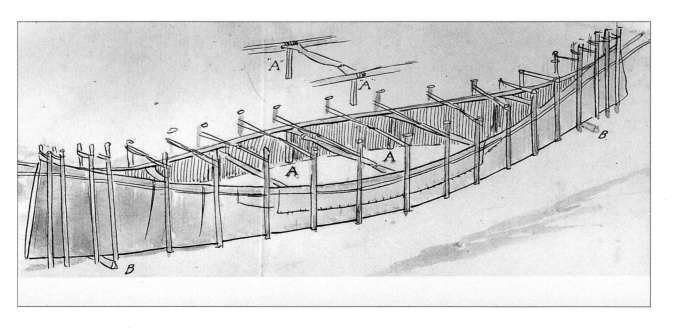

speedy travel possible for the Iroquois was a marvel of Wood and Stone Age engineering. Sheets of birch bark were stretched over frames of birch, white cedar, or arborvitae branches, then stitched together and reinforced with tamarack root. Seams and holes were caulked with pine resin. Propelled by carved hardwood paddles, a birch bark canoe 17 feet long and 4 feet broad at the center might weigh no more than 50 pounds, but it carried up to nine persons—a total payload of half a ton—and was sturdy enough to shoot white-water rapids. Distinctive shapes, dimensions, and construction details varied from tribe to tribe and depended on local conditions. Small streams required narrow, maneuverable craft, but large canoes could be used on wide rivers and open bays. Off the rocky coast of what is now eastern Canada and New England, Indians even hunted whales from huge seagoing birch bark canoes.

In the early 1600's French woodsmen, known as *coureurs de bois*, adapted the birch bark canoe for use in the fur trade. The most valued fur was that of the beaver. Shortly after the European colonization of North America beaver hats became fashionable on both sides of the Atlantic; in the 1660's diarist Samuel Pepys recorded paying £4 for a beaver hat in London, at a time when the annual income of England's leading architect, Christopher

Bark of the white birch (*center*) peels into its characteristic paperlike sheets. A Huron artist decorated this ceremonial birch bark tray (*above*) with a hunting scene.

Rivers, lakes, and streams of Northern Ontario interconnect to form a watery maze (*above*). Indian hunters and European trappers used Northern water routes to penetrate deep into the continent in search of beaver (*right*). The animal's thick, warm pelts were much in demand in the 17th and 18th centuries in England, where they were fashioned into hats.

Wren, was £200. So valuable were beaver pelts that they served as the basic unit of currency over much of what is now Canada and the western United States.

From the early 17th to the early 19th century it was the search for new sources of beaver pelts, more than any other factor, that drove the vanguard of white expansion westward—and the birch bark canoe was the chosen means of transportation for these earliest pioneers. Penetrating to the heart of the continent on the St. Lawrence–Great Lakes system, trappers and traders paddled canoes that were up to 36 feet long and could hold as much as 4 tons of furs. Maintaining a pace of nearly a stroke a second for 16 hours a day, a *coureur de bois* could cover 1,000 miles a month between spring thaw and winter freeze.

The significance of the canoe birch, and its close relative the yellow birch, to woodland culture did not stop with the bark. Flexible birch branches were bent into snowshoes laced with deer or moose hide; a hunter so equipped could literally outrun a moose in deep snow. In addition to fueling campfires, close-grained birchwood was carved into paddles, sleds, bowls, and spoons. Among the Iroquoian peoples, meals were communal, but everyone had his or her own set of wooden utensils. Maize was typically prepared by pounding the kernels in a wooden mortar with a wooden pestle, often of birch. Is it any wonder that the Penobscot and Passamaquoddy Indians of the Northeast believed that a divine ancestor-hero had instructed the birch tree to look after them? To the Indians, the horizontal pores in the bark known to botanists as lenticels were multiple "eyes" with which tree spirits carried on this eternal assignment.

Under the watchful gaze of the birch and other tutelary trees, the Indians of North America sustained themselves through a seasonally determined round of hunting and fishing, food gathering and agriculture. In all these activities trees played a key role—as a source of indispensable tools, as a renewable store of foodstuffs, and even as a hindrance, however temporary, to the raising of crops.

Along with wood-handled spears, axes, and knives, the role of wooden bows and arrows in the hunt—and of pliant saplings and branches as fishing rods and snares for small game—hardly needs explanation. Less well known are the fishhooks shaped from whiplike twigs of the sassafras tree and the large fishing nets—up to 500 feet in length—woven from twisted strands of the inner bark of trees like the arborvitae.

At first hearing, the term "food gathering" may suggest the ultimate in carefree nutrition—as exemplified by the biblical manna that literally fell from the sky. In most situations, however, gathering nuts, fruits, and berries from uncultivated trees takes a great deal of energy and foresight. Unlike domesticated trees, wild trees may grow in inaccessible places with inconveniently high branches; when ripe food starts falling from the trees, gatherers have to be on hand for the harvest if they hope to beat out the fierce competition from birds, bears, squirrels, insects, and other hungry creatures.

Eastern and northern Indians gathered wild plums, grapes, cherries, berries, and crabapples in season; what they did not eat right away they preserved by drying or boiling. Hard-shelled walnuts, hickory nuts, and butternuts, as well as thin-shelled chestnuts, chinkapins, and pecans, provided important sources of protein. The

The workhorse canoes used by fur traders could carry impressive loads of people and cargo. In this painting, eight voyageurs propel a large birch bark canoe carrying officers of the Hudson Bay Company through the Canadian wilderness in the early 1800's. The painting is by Frances Ann Hopkins, a company officer's wife and seasoned canoe traveler, who is pictured amidships.

triangular nuts of the stately American beech were once so abundant that they nourished not only foraging Indians but also the prodigious flocks of the now-extinct passenger pigeon, which were so numerous that they darkened the sky like thunderclouds when they took to the air.

Not all nuts were eaten just as they came from the tree. Some, like the dark-lobed nuts of the shagbark hickory, could be gathered in such numbers that the excess was stored and later processed into an all-purpose food additive. According to William Bartram, the 18th-century American botanist, the Creek Indians of the Gulf Coast broke the hickory nuts into pieces, boiled them, and strained out the "most oily part of the liquid; this they call by a name which signifies hickory milk; it is as sweet and rich as fresh cream, and is an ingredient in most of their cookery, especially hominy and corn cakes."

In some cases, the provender from trees was processed before eating—not for convenience but out of necessity. This was true of most acorns. With the exception of a few species like the basket oak of the Southeast and the valley oak of California, acorns contain bitter tannins that make them indigestible to humans. These ubiquitous fruits of the oak tree must first be boiled or roasted before they can be eaten or ground into a nutritious flour. The fruits of the sweet buckeye, a relative of the horse chestnut, are actually poisonous when raw; peeled, mashed, then leached with water for several days to extract the poison, the starchy pulp makes a tasty and nourishing food.

West of the Great Plains grow several species of pines, whose nuts serve as an important food source, especially in winter when game is scarce. The great sugar pines of the Pacific Northwest produce cones that are almost 2 feet long and more than 3 inches in diameter; their sweet-tasting seeds were much prized as trail food. In the high deserts of New Mexico, Arizona, Utah, and Nevada, gnarled pinyon pines—which rarely grow taller than 20 feet—thrive in natural orchards. Harvesting pinyon nuts is still an occasion for joyful Hopi and Navajo family outings. Sheets and blankets are spread on the ground, and the nut-bearing cones are beaten from the trees with long

Hardy, compact pinyon pines cling to sandstone outcroppings in Utah's Zion National Park (*left*). The tree's sweet, oily seeds are a staple of Paiute Indians, who gather green cones and dry them until they open, releasing the nourishing pine nuts (*above*).

The spiny husk of the American chestnut opens to reveal three edible sections favored by Eastern Indian tribes. In the early 1900's, a blight by a parasitic fungus virtually wiped out this species in North America.

sticks. Some of the tiny nuts are roasted on the spot over aromatic pinyon-wood fires and eaten in the time-honored manner: the entire nut is inserted in the mouth, the shell is cracked between the teeth, the tasty little morsel is extracted with the tongue and eaten, and the empty shell is spit onto the ground. Baskets full of unshelled nuts will stay fresh for a year if they are brought home and stored.

Of all the edible gifts that people receive from trees, the one that perhaps comes closest to fulfilling the biblical promise of manna is maple sugar. No other food of the forest delivers such a jolt of quick energy. The Indians of the northeast woodlands flavored foods with it, from grain dishes to stewed meats. Weary canoe paddlers picked up their stroke, and trailblazers their pace, with traveler's cakes of pounded maize laced with rendered animal fat and maple syrup.

Maple sugar comes from the spring sap of the sugar maple, a long-lived deciduous tree with its familiar three- and occasionally five-lobed leaves. In autumn they put on a brilliant display of yellows, oranges, and scarlets; in the spring they give the gift of sweetness.

When the sap of the sugar maples began to rise in late winter and early spring, Indians drew some of it off by cutting a gash in the bark with a stone blade and allowing the clear liquid to ooze into buckets made of birch bark sewn up with spruce roots. In colonial days the yield was improved with a spout—a hollow reed, a hollowed-out twig, or a bark funnel—inserted deeper in a hole tapped into the tree with a metal bit. Maple sap runs best on warm sunny days that follow freezing nights; at such times the pressure generated in the tree's sapwood can reach 20 pounds per square inch. The sweetness comes from dissolved sugars, mostly sucrose, that make up from 2 to 6 percent of the liquid sap. These sugars are the stored end product of the previous year's photosynthesis, destined to sustain the rush of spring growth that follows sap rise by about 2 months.

A single sugar maple yields from 5 to 40 gallons of sweet sap over a period of several weeks. Making a gallon

Pueblo dwellers used wooden ladders, such as the one shown here at the Taos Pueblo in New Mexico, to reach the upper stories of their multi-level dwellings. Timbers projecting from the roof help support adobe structures, which—with periodic repairs—have survived for almost 1000 years.

Stainless steel buckets have replaced birch bark containers in this Vermont grove, but the ritual of maple sugaring remains a universally appreciated aspect of age-old Indian lore.

of syrup or about 4 pounds of sugar requires more than 30 gallons of maple sap. To concentrate the clear sap into an amber syrup, the Indians poured a large quantity into a hollowed log and brought it to a boil by dropping in hot stones. Alternately, the sap was allowed to freeze at night; skimming the ice sheet off the surface each morning left a crumbly maple sugar that could be stored in bark containers for future use. The nutritional value of concentrated maple sap has been confirmed by modern science; like honey, maple syrup contains phosphates that help to promote calcium retention in bones. As for flavor, those lucky enough to have taken part in "sugaring off" in the woods of New England or eastern Canada insist that nothing comes close to the taste of freshly boiled maple syrup poured over a ball of new-fallen snow and eaten as heaven-sent candy.

Agricultural products formed an important part of the daily diet of woodland Indians. Among the Iroquoian tribes, who lived far from coastal fishing grounds, common crops were maize, beans, and squash. To the Iroquois these were the "three sisters" because they grew side by side in their fields. Lacking domesticated animals, Indian farmers, usually women, prepared the soil with wooden hoes and planted seed in holes dug with a fire-hardened dibble, or sharpened stick.

Since their farming methods depleted nutrients from the soil after a few growing seasons, woodland Indian tribes relocated their villages periodically to be near new fields. These fields were typically natural clearings in the forest opened by fires, windstorms, landslides, insects, or the industrious beaver. Of these, only the beaver could be counted on to maintain a clearing. To keep their fields open for cultivation, Indian farmers—like later colonists and farmers today—had to fight against the constant encroachment of opportunistic seedlings from the forests that surrounded them. One of their weapons in this never-ending battle was fire.

Historians differ on the extent to which Indians intentionally set fires to clear new fields and to improve the soil with nutrient-rich ashes. There is little doubt, however, that long before European colonization, native peoples used controlled burns to clear underbrush and expand the boundaries of arable cropland. Short of resorting to fire, small trees could be pulled from the ground or laboriously chopped down with stone axes. The only way to down a large tree was by girdling—gashing a wound through the bark all around the trunk. The wound stopped circulation in the sapwood and eventually killed the tree, and a dead tree is far easier to fell than a living one. A girdled tree, moreover, is likely to provide sound, strong timber for houses and boats, unlike trees that have been felled by disease, lightning strikes, or old age.

The first European settlers not only took over Native American food crops and slash-and-burn farming methods, they often took over the same clearings that the Indians had farmed. With metal axes capable of felling even the largest trees, and by using horses and oxen to pull out the stumps, colonists soon made inroads in the virgin forests that were far beyond the means of Wood and Stone

Age farmers. Even so, it meant years—sometimes generations—of hard work: wresting a sizable farm from persistent woodland might take 50 years or more.

From the beginning, the colonists adopted a very different attitude toward the wilderness than did the native inhabitants. In the lands the European settlers had left behind, most forests were under the protection of kings and noblemen who controlled hunting and timber rights, while exacting severe penalties from subjects who cut more wood for their own needs than law and custom allowed. Legends and story cycles like the tales of Robin Hood and his outlaw band were the result of widespread resentment against absentee ownership of forests. Yet the rationale behind many of the unpopular laws was to conserve a scarce resource. By the end of the 16th century some German states were practicing systematic forest management. In England and Scotland tree plantations that raised desired species from seeds and cuttings had become profitable investments.

By contrast the extent of and accessibility to the North American forests overwhelmed settlers arriving from the Old World. On one hand, they could not imagine that such a resource could ever be exhausted; on the other hand, they felt intimidated, even oppressed, by the towering vegetation that limited the advance of their settlements while providing a refuge for their often hostile neighbors. From testimony left by the early settlers, it is apparent that cutting or clearing space in the apparently endless woodlands was considered an act of virtue for its own sake, quite aside from the value of the lumber and other products from the felled trees.

Nothing could be further from this attitude than the down-to-earth reverence that Indians showed toward the trees on which their lives depended. While traditions and religious beliefs differed widely among Indian cultures, there was universal acceptance that everything—living things like animals and trees as well as inanimate objects like stones, streams, and the sky—were embodied with active spirits.

To the Papago Indians of the Southwest, the thorny mesquite tree was a benign presence whose bounty never ended. The dome-shaped hogans of the Papago were built around a framework of slender mesquite poles bound together with branches and fibers from other desert plants, such as the saguaro cactus, the soapweed bush, and the ocotillo. The podlike fruits or beans of the mesquite, which may be up to 30 percent sugar, can be eaten raw or boiled, or fermented to make a mildly alcoholic drink. The mottled seeds inside the beans can be ground into flour for cakes and mush. Bees attracted to the fragrant, creamy-yellow flowers make a clear amber honey. A small tree, rarely reaching 50 feet, the mesquite can thrive in arid soil because its roots can drive down 60 feet or more to tap ground water. On the open range, despite its 2-inch-long

Although trees were sparse on the northern plains, wood still figured prominently in the lives of Plains Indians. A 1915 photograph (*opposite*) shows a rack used by the Hidatsas of North Dakota to dry squash and other foods.

Blessed with an abundance of trees, eastern tribes could make more liberal use of wood. In this 16th-century drawing of an Algonquin encampment at left, spacious wood-framed longhouses are protected by a palisade of poles.

With a stick rigged like a pruning device, a Papago woman collects edible fruit from a saguaro cactus. The saguaro also contributed fibers to bind together wood and branches to make the framework for the Papago's dwellings, known as hogans.

thorns, mesquite provides forage for deer and antelope, cattle and horses, besides being a bulwark against erosion during violent desert cloudbursts.

The mesquite exudes a gum from its trunk that Indians chewed and put to good use as a dressing for wounds, as a black dye for pottery and hides, and as glue for broken pots. They shaped their new pots from wet clay using paddles made from mesquite, and they worked their plantings of maize with mesquite digging sticks. They also used mesquite bark for tanning hides and the strikingly figured wood for long-lasting fence posts and reliable bows. Papago children spent their infancy in cradles crafted of mesquite roots and later played games of kickball with spheres of mesquite wood. The long underground stems of the mesquite, often mistaken for roots, burn with a slow, intense heat and give off a pungent smoke that imparts a welcome flavor to grilled meat, poultry, and fish.

With all its inherent virtues to indigenous people, the mesquite is viewed differently by modern ranchers and farmers. The hated mesquite readily colonizes overgrazed rangeland and untended farmland with impenetrably thorny thickets; because of its extensive roots and below-ground stem system, the only way to kill a mature mesquite is to cut it off at the ground and poison the stump. Yet hardy mesquite trees—and their spirit—survive.

Seeking protection from both enemies and the elements, Anasazi perched their village of Betatakin high atop a cliff inside a natural sandstone alcove. Timbers supported the walls and roofs of this remarkable

13th-century masonry apartment dwelling, which contained 135 rooms and housed up to 25 families. The village is now preserved within Navajo National Monument in Arizona.

Papago Indians of the Southwest enjoyed the sweet, podlike fruit of the honey mesquite (*left*). The tree also furnished wood for the frames and walls of the Papagos' dome-shaped hogans (*above*). Like pueblos, hogans are one of the few forms of traditional Indian architecture still in use today.

The soaring, straight-trunked western red cedar was one of the trees favored by canoe makers of the Pacific Northwest. One of these giant conifers supplied enough durable, rot-resistant softwood to produce two to four mammoth 65-foot-long dugout canoes.

What the canoe birch was to the Indians of the Northeast and the mesquite was to the Indians of the Southwest, the red cedar was to the Indians of what is now Oregon, Washington, and British Columbia. Western red cedar is often called the canoe cedar because this giant conifer supplied the natives of the western coast of the continent, from the southern tip of Alaska to the southern tip of Puget Sound, with the raw material for their seagoing dugout canoes. These extraordinary craft, as much as 65 feet in length, were fashioned from a single tree trunk; they carried as many as 40 people on coastal journeys or on fishing and whaling expeditions into the open ocean. When a British mariner visited the west coast of Canada in 1791, his trading ship was surrounded by 600 native canoes. According to some accounts, the lines of the larger dugouts were so trim, so perfectly attuned to wind and wave, that their hull lines were admired—and closely imitated—by the designers of the famed Yankee clipper ships of the 19th century.

The peoples of the Pacific Northwest lived in what is known as a temperate rain forest. Between the peaks of the Coastal and Cascade ranges, moisture-laden ocean air drops up to 160 inches of rain a year, and temperatures rarely fall below freezing. Under these conditions trees like the red cedar grow arrow-straight trunks 8 feet thick at the base and 200 feet high.

The Haida people, who come from the Queen Charlotte Islands off British Columbia, were especially noted for their skill in canoe making. After felling a giant tree with controlled burning, they split the log with stone wedges into lengthwise sections. After burning away some

Some of the most splendid conifer forests in the world are found along the northwest coast of the United States and Canada, where growing conditions are nearly ideal. Warm ocean currents moderate the climate, producing warm summers and winters that are mild enough for the trees to continue to carry on photosynthesis all year round. The cove above is along the Oregon coast.

of the heartwood with smoldering fires, they gouged out more with stone adzes attached to handles of wood, bone, or antler, leaving a rough but strong cedar shell. To finish the hull, they drilled holes of carefully determined depth into the trunk from the outside, then shaved away wood from the inside until they reached the holes; this allowed them to shape a hull systematically and accurately, with the thickest and heaviest sections below the waterline where the extra weight helped keep the canoe upright in stormy seas. The holes were later filled with watertight wooden plugs.

To further enhance the canoe's stability, the hull, supported in a wooden frame much like a dry dock, was filled with water. With the water heated to boiling by hot stones dropped into it, the wood was rendered temporarily flexible. At this point the sides of the hull were forced apart and held with stout wooden thwarts, which were left in place to serve as both cross braces and seats. Light but strong paddles carved from the wood of the yellow cedar, another giant of the temperate rain forest, provided motive power.

Farther down the coast, where nature was less profligate with big trees, the Chumash Indians of southern California built a different kind of seagoing vessel, the tomol, out of driftwood. Using stone wedges, the Chumashes split long planks from redwood logs that drifted south with the ocean currents. They lashed these planks together with red milkweed fiber, which was preferred over animal sinew because it would not rot, and caulked the hulls with asphaltum, which occurred naturally in blocky deposits. The flat-bottomed tomols ranged from 8 to 30 feet long and, like the Haida dugouts, were elaborately decorated and painted.

Making their living primarily from the sea, coastal tribes of the Pacific Northwest raised canoe building to a high art, creating dugout canoes that were swift, stable, and seaworthy enough to use for whaling (*below*). The boats were often painted with elaborate designs (*left*) that may have represented tribal spirits.

The Haida Indians from the Queen Charlotte Islands of British Columbia designed canoes of such beauty and utility that neighboring tribes were willing to exchange quantities of hides, meats, and oils for a Haida canoe, represented at right in a 19th-century model. These graceful canoes became the island-living tribe's chief item of export.

In their staunch vessels, which could carry up to 5 tons, the Indians of the Northwest were able to take full advantage of the cornucopia of food and other riches provided by the sea. With harpoons of yew wood, baited hooks crafted from red cedar wood or shell, and lines of twisted and braided bark fibers, they fished for cod, sturgeon, and halibut, and hunted whales, seals, and sea otters. Big fish and game animals, weighing up to 500 pounds, had to be stunned with wooden clubs before they were dragged aboard for fear that their thrashing would capsize the canoe.

The Indians also took shelter from the rainy Northwest winters in communal dwellings of red cedar. The fragrant wood, impregnated with a natural preservative oil, is soft enough to be worked easily but strong for its weight and highly resistant to decay. Because of its straight-grained texture, planks 40 feet long, 3 feet wide, and 4 inches thick can be split from a standing tree with simple stone tools. Large houses were the rule, shared by several Indian families. Cedar planks made up the siding; cedar logs, notched and fitted together without pegs, formed the main pillars and beams; the roof consisted of

The Makah were an ocean-going tribe from the Olympic Peninsula of Washington. In this miniature 19th-century model, a Makah canoe maneuvers within striking distance of a whale. The canoe represented here would have been about 30 feet long and carried a crew of eight: a harpooner, a steersman, and six paddlers. The model maker erred in proportioning the whale, however; even the smallest minke whale would be larger than the whale shown here.

Using wooden stilts as housing supports, the Ukivok turned an otherwise uninhabitable granite slope on King Island, off the Alaskan coast at the entrance to the Bering Sea, into a vertical village that provided hunters with quick access to the water when prey was sighted (*left*). The houses were plank-framed boxes anchored to the rock face with tall wooden tree trunks, towed from the mainland in skin boats. Extending above the houses, these wooden poles supported platforms for drying skins and food.

overlapping slabs of cedar bark. When an entire village decamped each spring to harvest the salmon that made their way upstream to spawn, the people stripped the cedar planks from their homes and used them to build temporary shelters near the spawning grounds. On the return trip, lashed horizontally between two canoes with ropes of twisted bark, the planks formed a kind of cargo deck for the heaps of smoked salmon that served as a staple of the Indians' winter diet.

The inner fibers of red cedar bark were literally woven into all aspects of the lives of the Northwest Indians. Shredded, twisted, and plaited in various ways, the bark served—sometimes in combination with the soft wool of mountain goats—to make blankets, hats, aprons, cloaks, belts, and all manner of household baskets and boxes. The nets that fishermen deployed to catch the spawning salmon were crafted from cedar bark and branches. Strips of cedar bark went into cradle bindings, tourniquets, and bandages.

Living in a land so blessed with natural resources, the Indians of the Northwest Coast had time, especially during the rainy winters, to pursue interests not immediately related to survival. Of the many arts they practiced, the most highly developed, not surprisingly, was wood carving. Fine utensils and boxes, elaborately detailed masks, huge ceremonial bowls, canoe figureheads, chiefs' furniture, shamans' rattles and staffs, and spirit effigies of all kinds were carved from red and yellow cedar. Many of these beautiful objects figured prominently in the rituals of competitive gift-giving, politicking, and consumption—and occasionally sacrificial destruction—known as potlatches.

On the North Pacific Rim, functional objects of daily life and symbolic ritual were closely linked. An Eskimo hunter might have worn this carved wooden mask as a seal decoy to mimic the animal's spirit. Masks combining human and animal features expressed the culture's intricate ecological dependencies.

But the outstanding achievements of the wood carvers of the Pacific Northwest were undoubtedly the towering, mysterious creations of red cedar that we know as totem poles. These finely crafted examples of folk art probably began as decorations added to the structural pillars that flanked the entrances to the dwellings of high-ranking families. Over time the pillars evolved into free-standing monuments on which master artists, wielding tools of jadeite and shell, carved the ancestral histories and achievements of the wealthy chiefs who commissioned the work.

Even red cedar eventually decays when exposed to the elements, so virtually no totem poles more than a century old remain. It seems clear, however, that the art enjoyed a brief golden age in the second half of the 19th century. This was when steel axes, saws, knives, and other woodworking tools became widely available to Indian carvers. With more efficient tools, Inuit and Tlingit craftsmen made gigantic poles that literally dwarfed the houses they adorned. They covered great cedar logs with full-relief images

Totem poles reached their highest level of development among the Tlingit and Haida tribes of the Canadian Pacific coast (*above*), along the range of the western red cedar from which they were carved. The fanciful animal-like and mythological figures carved into totem poles (*opposite*) served as valuable collective memory devices for tribes that lacked written language, recording ancestral histories, personal experiences, and tribal folklore.

of hook-beaked owls, shaggy-haired bears, pop-eyed frogs, and other figures out of both myth and the natural world. Mortuary poles supported boxes of human ashes; potlatch poles, some as high as 80 feet, celebrated memorable feasts; there were even poles designed to mock enemies and shame debtors into paying their debts. Every pole told a story of some kind—a symbolic story that could be read by anyone familiar with the imagery of a particular tribe or clan.

But in the early decades of the 20th century, a collision with white culture precipitated a crisis in Indian culture that virtually decimated the peoples of the Pacific Northwest. After a long period of decline, the art of totem pole carving has recently been revived, with the aid of public and private institutions and the enthusiastic support of tribal authorities. Once again, Indians of the Northwest are rediscovering their ancient heritage through the form of a red cedar tree trunk. They are seeking, in its fresh-scented, reddish-brown interior, the liberating self-images that artists the world over have sought and discovered in the heart of nature. ✦

Tim Paul, a Vancouver Indian carver, begins work on a seasoned red cedar log, using a traditional handmade adz. The finished totem pole is intended for permanent display at the National Museum of Man in Ottawa, Ontario.

An Exploitable Resource

THE MOMENTOUS CHANGES THAT Europeans brought to North America were, as much as anything else, a matter of technology. Until the arrival of Columbus, iron was entirely unknown in the Americas, and metalworking in copper, gold, and silver was common among only a few advanced cultures of Central and South America. Elsewhere, most native people were at the stage of development we now call Neolithic, or New Stone Age. Iron tools and weapons, together with mastery of the wheel and of domesticated animals like the horse, gave the Europeans an insuperable advantage in all their dealings with the people they chose to call Indians.

But this advantage did not mean that the Europeans had less use for the forests of North America than the native inhabitants did. The opposite was true. Wood had been one of the primary construction materials in both the Old and New Worlds for some 9,000 years, ever since the advent of stone tools. With a flint ax and adz—tools with their cutting edges in line with and at right angles to their handles, respectively—people could not only fell trees but also strip wood from raw logs and work it into beams, utensils, and furniture.

The Ages of Metals—first the Ages of Copper and Bronze, then of Iron and Steel—introduced a new kind of material: malleable when hot but capable of holding a useful shape when cold. Metalworking skills developed in different places at different times, but by 3000 B.C. the use of bronze had spread from the Near East to Europe. People soon found that bronze axes, while not as sharp as the best flint, were easier to handle and could be readily

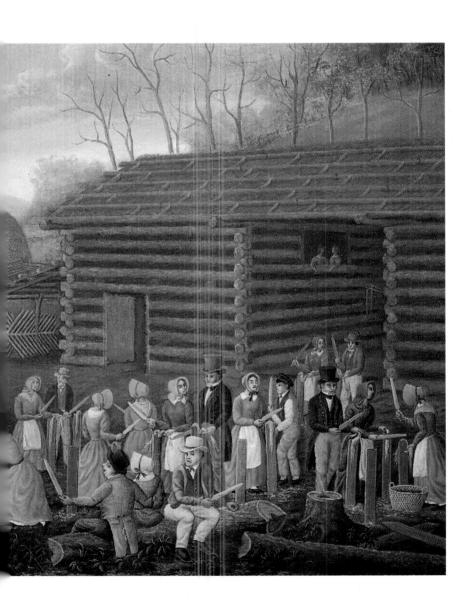

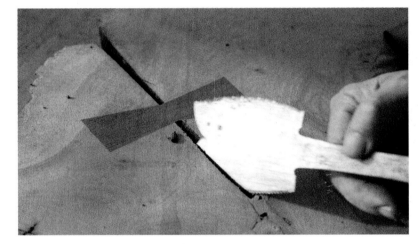

In capturing the exuberance of a community scutching bee—a gathering to separate flax strands from other parts of the plant—this 1885 painting by Linton Park illustrates how prominently wood figured in everyday life, from log buildings and fences, to ox yokes, baskets, drying racks, fuel, and flax beaters.

The tradition of fine woodworking extends from ancient times to the present. The hand of master furniture maker George Nakashima uses a Japanese azibiki saw to fashion a tabletop featuring his signature butterfly wedge.

Crafting wagon wheels required specialized skills and a knowledge of different woods. The drawing above shows a wheelwright hammering a hickory spoke into an oak hub. An apprentice turns the wheel that powers a belt-driven lathe, as a journeyman turns a new hub. Another craftsman planes one of the oak felloes that make up the rim.

Wooden casks and barrels (*opposite*) once served as the basic means of storing and shipping items of every description. Coopers were skilled in shaping oak staves into sturdy, watertight containers for cider, whisky, salted meat, and countless other comestibles.

resharpened instead of discarded. Between 1500 and 1000 B.C. bronze implements were gradually being replaced by more durable and effective iron tools; as a direct result, woodworking attained new heights of efficiency and sophistication. Until the Industrial Revolution of the late 18th century, when machines began to replace hand tools, one of the primary values of metal was its superiority for tools used in working wood.

Using their iron and steel axes and adzes—as well as knives, hammers, saws, chisels, drills, gouges, and planes—the European colonists who came to North America turned raw logs into everything imaginable: boards and beams, shakes and shingles, chairs and tables, looms and spindles, barrels and boxes, wheels and wagons. Like 10th-century Viking longboats and the caravels of 15th-century explorers, the square-rigged sailing ship that carried 101 Pilgrims to the coast of New England in the fall of 1620 was built of wood. Although no detailed description of the *Mayflower* exists today, her hull, like those of most English vessels of the day, was probably made of oak, her three masts fashioned of pine, her sides and decks caulked with pitch extracted from pine resin. Without such waterproofing and wood-preserving products as pitch, tar, and turpentine—known collectively as naval stores—no wooden ship could have long survived its launching, much less ventured across an ocean.

Not only were iron and steel tools used to fashion wood into everyday necessities, but wood in the form of charcoal was indispensable to forging those metal tools. The production of charcoal, one of the earliest chemical processes known to humankind, has been traced back at least 6,000 years. In one traditional European method adapted to North America, charcoal burners, or colliers, set hardwood logs on end in a circle with the tops leaning together to form a huge inverted cone and covered the sides with wet leaves or earth. Inside the cone a fire was kindled with twigs and straw, its purpose not to consume the wood, but to transform it. The secret of making charcoal lies in smothering the fire to deprive it of sufficient oxygen to burn the wood completely. Instead, long days of slow, controlled combustion reduce the wood inside to highly concentrated carbon. When charcoal itself is burned again in the presence of abundant oxygen—such as a jet of air from a blacksmith's bellows—it sustains a much hotter flame than can be obtained from wood alone.

The best charcoal comes from hardwoods like oak and willow. Coke, made in a similar way from bituminous coal, was a critical factor in the Industrial Revolution of Europe, where hardwood forests had been depleted long

before. But charcoal is superior for metallurgy and remained the fuel of choice in the eastern industrial centers of North America, where large stands of hardwood abounded, at least until the mid-19th century.

With charcoal to fuel forges, metallic iron can be separated from iron ore and heated sufficiently to allow it to be beaten and cast into useful shapes. More important, with charcoal to supply a carbon-rich vapor, iron is carbonized and becomes steel—harder and more durable than iron, and capable of taking and holding a sharp edge. Steel-bladed swords and axes, far superior to the stone, bronze, and iron implements that preceded them, became the tools that subdued a continent.

As for cast-iron cannons and wrought-iron muskets that brought to the new continent a distinctive new kind of weaponry, their iron balls and lead shot were propelled by another chemical wonder derived from wood—gunpowder. The recipe for black powder, used universally until a century ago, called for 75 percent saltpeter—itself extracted from hardwood ashes—10 percent sulfur, and 15 percent charcoal. The smokeless gunpowder used today, as well as other explosive compounds, is also made from cellulose, another product derived from wood.

When the Stone Age people of North America were confronted with the sophisticated tools and ideas of the advanced Iron Age, the abrupt cultural invasion changed the relationship between people and trees on the continent. Symbolized by the tree-felling pioneer with his steel ax, the change went far deeper. As odd as it may seem, a well-made, carefully polished flint ax can actually hold a sharper edge than all but the finest steel tools. Yet a stone ax is far more brittle than a metal one, harder to make, harder to use, and harder to resharpen once dulled. The superior flexibility and versatility of metal becomes even more apparent in the blades wielded so effectively by soldiers, and in the saws, drills, planes, and other woodworking tools that were entirely unknown in the Stone Age.

Chopping down trees is hard work with any kind of tool—which is why Europeans preferred taking over land that had already been cleared by Indians for their own fields. But however arduous it may be, chopping down trees does not entail much inherent skill; anyone with a strong back can learn to swing an ax effectively enough to fell a tree.

In the traditional charcoal process (*top*), colliers stacked hardwood logs to form a central wooden "chimney." Sealed under wet leaves or earth, the wood burned slowly until reduced to concentrated carbon. By 1900 permanent brick beehive charcoal kilns (*bottom*) became commonplace; today charcoal is made in sophisticated factories.

Slow-burning hardwoods were preferred for charcoal production because of their high carbon content. These young oaks and hickories have taken over formerly cleared land at Hopewell Furnace, New Jersey, once the site of a thriving ironworks that burned tons of charcoal a year in the 1700's.

Converting that tree into useful lumber for houses, furniture, and utensils is something else again; such work calls for special skills and special tools. A woodcutter's felling ax, for example, was ground on both sides of the blade to a tapered cutting edge. For splitting logs into fence rails and firewood, the woodsman used steel wedges, driven by a heavy two-handed hammer, or maul, never an ax.

Once the tree was down, a different tool—the broad ax—was used for hewing the felled logs into square-sided house beams. To square a beam with an ax was an exacting, time-consuming job. First, the woodcutter chalked a series of straight guidelines on top of the debarked log and made deep vertical cuts with a felling ax right up to the chalk mark; this was called "scoring to the line." Then, a carpenter with a broad ax went to work. The broad ax was shorter than the felling ax, and its heavy blade was flat on one edge, beveled on the other. The offset handle allowed the carpenter to walk backward alongside the log, "hewing to the line" and leaving a more or less straight edge. Where looks were important, an adz with a single-beveled edge was used to smooth any visible ax marks. When a log was destined to become a gutter, water trough, dugout canoe, or coffin, a round-bladed adz could gouge a hollow down the middle.

European settlers wasted no time in importing their technological know-how to North America and applying it to the forests around them. The continent's first recorded metal-working forge, wood-fueled, of course, was built in Virginia in 1620. By the 1640's the Massachusetts Bay Colony was operating an ironworks on the Saugus River north of Boston; under the supervision of an English ironmaster, it turned out wrought-iron bars to be worked into carpenters' tools and other implements by local blacksmiths. Meanwhile, logging and sawmill operations were well under way.

The saw—a flat, flexible blade with uniformly shaped and sharpened teeth—is one of humankind's great inventions, and one that far surpasses the ax and adz in its capacity to reduce living trees to usable timber. Handsaws had been perfected over centuries, and by colonial times two-handled, two-man pit saws were in common use.

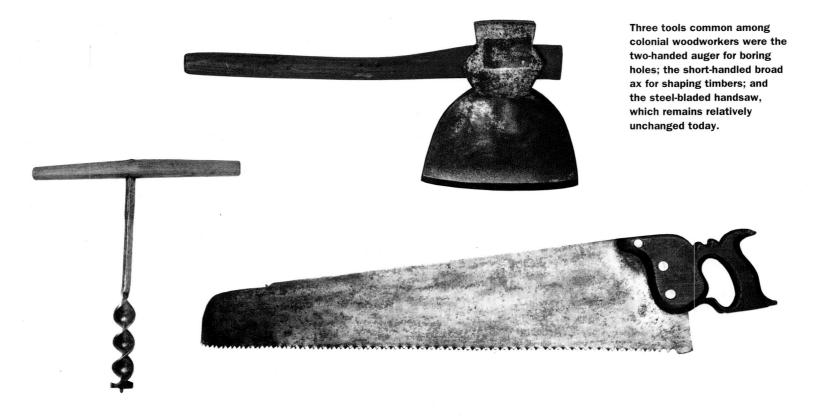

Three tools common among colonial woodworkers were the two-handed auger for boring holes; the short-handled broad ax for shaping timbers; and the steel-bladed handsaw, which remains relatively unchanged today.

The pit saw required the log to be hauled into position over an open pit or trench; one man stood on top of the log and pulled the saw upward, while the unfortunate pit man stood below, providing the powerful downstroke that ripped logs into boards suitable for building.

Where fast-running streams were at hand—as they were along the Atlantic seaboard from Newfoundland to the Virginia colony—sawmills harnessed water power to perform the same basic function, increasing efficiency considerably over manually operated saws. To encourage development, expanding towns offered entrepreneurs hundreds of acres of free timberland and free sites for water-powered mills. Sawmills in Maine were converting pine logs into construction timbers in the 1630's, and by the 1660's there were hundreds of sawmills throughout New England, reducing logs from countless old-growth trees to the timbers that framed a new continent.

Iron and steel tools, plus an insatiable appetite for wood products, allowed early settlers to tap freely the forest resources of North America. There were so many trees that no one thought about cutting down too many. Quite

Commerce in native timber (*above*) of the northeast colonies—now Maine and the Maritime Provinces—started early. The logging boom reached the Machias River in northern Maine (*below*) around 1810, where a bustling mill town quickly sprang up. Colonial exports included pine masts and naval stores to seafaring Britain; oak barrels for rum and molasses producers in the West Indies; and casks of dried fish wherever cargo space allowed.

The simple but strong technique of "saddle notching" made quick work of buildings like soldiers' quarters (*above*) at Valley Forge, Pennsylvania, in the winter of 1777. Nothing but an ax was needed to fell trees and cut notches that held the green timbers in place.

the contrary: unlike the first wave of fur trappers and traders, who were just as dependent on the forest for their livelihood as the Indians were, later settlers who came to farm the land looked on the "wilderness" more as an impediment than an asset. They took what they needed from the wilderness, but they also delighted in pushing it back, taming it, and overcoming it.

The old-growth forests of North America were an oppressing prospect to pioneer farmers. To hack farmland out of mature forests with rudimentary hand tools—and maybe an ox or a mule to help pull stumps—required herculean effort. If stumps could not be pulled out, crops were often planted between them, the same slash-and-burn agriculture still practiced in developing countries. Land stripped of trees was seen as land gained for farming, even though this equation did not always hold in actuality. Some newly cleared fields turned out to be unsuitable for agriculture, but a few species of trees—in particular beech, sycamore, wild black cherry, and the tulip tree—were reputed to flourish on the best agricultural soil. As a result, stands of those trees were hunted down by homesteaders, who eliminated them to make room for new farms. To the typical settler, a tree was good to the extent that it was useful, and the most useful trees were felled logs ready to be turned into homes, barns, and fences.

Modern reconstructions of colonial settlements include rustic cabins with familiar walls of rounded logs laid up horizontally. Despite scholarship to debunk it, the log cabin myth will not die. The first English colonists actually built clapboard houses, a bit like ship hulls turned upside down on corner posts. The log cabin came to America with Swedes who settled the Delaware River in 1638, but the style did not spread elsewhere until the 18th century. As settlers pushed westward, however, the log cabin became the architecture of choice. Settlers could build cabins with nothing more than an ax for notching and fitting the logs, and because the work went rapidly, most of their energy could go into clearing land and planting crops. On the Great Plains, sod houses prevailed, but as soon as sawed timbers became commonplace, wood frame houses replaced both log and sod cabins.

Oiled pine paneling and massive stairways, featuring treads of split oak logs nearly 8 feet wide, have delighted guests in the rustically ornate lobby of Old Faithful Inn, Yellowstone National Park, since 1904.

Wharton Esherick, a virtuoso sculptor-craftsman who worked from the 1920's through the 1960's, combined fine craftsmanship with innovative explorations of wood's innate artistic possibilities. The spiral staircase, banister, and paneling in his studio, now the Wharton Esherick Museum in Paoli, Pennsylvania, celebrate both the functional and aesthetic qualities of natural wood.

Every colonist was aware that there were different woods for different purposes. Men and women of that time would no more have mistaken a board of light-weight, pale, white pine for a board of heavy, yellowish, white oak than someone today would mistake a cast-iron skillet for a ceramic microwave dish. In fact, far more subtle distinctions were made. A traditional Windsor chair, for example, required several kinds of wood—oak or elm for the seat, ash for the legs, hickory for the arched back, and maple for the spindles—each kind of wood selected for a specific purpose because of its unique, inherent qualities.

Given the vast supply available, such selectivity now seems downright wasteful. While the wood of the white oak was preferred above all others for waterproof barrels and ships' hulls, huge logs of the closely related chestnut oak were left to rot on the forest floor—but only after being stripped of their bark. Chestnut oak was more difficult to season than white oak and was not highly valued as

In a Long Island, New York, luthier's shop (*below*), spruce soundboards and darker maple backs are ready to become mandolins. Lightweight and strong, spruce has long been prized in stringed instruments for its inherent tonal qualities.

Young green pines and brightly hued hardwoods make a classic fall land-scape (*right*). Along the northeast-ern continent, such trees quickly generate second-growth forests wherever clearcuts and abandoned farmland permit.

timber, but its tannin-rich bark was prized for another reason altogether: crushed and pressed, the bark yielded an acidic juice that was used by tanneries to process raw hides into fine leather.

As every child knows who has slapped together a rough wooden box and watched it warp out of shape, working with wood is an exacting and somewhat mysterious craft. Any task that requires joining two or more pieces of wood must take into account the fact that, unlike metal or plastic, wood starts as a living organism. Even though its cells die after a tree is felled, a piece of wood is never completely at rest. It continues to move, often frustrating attempts to transform it into an inert table or chair. The cause of this constant movement is water: both in the walls of the woody cells and in the spaces between the cells.

Modern materials notwithstanding, the dependability of a stout wooden hull in heavy seas cannot be denied. In a Rockland, Maine, boatyard, the oak-framed schooner *Mattie* undergoes a complete overhaul for more years of yeoman service.

A vast circle of pulpwood logs dwarfs the semi-trailers arriving to unload their cargo at an Alabama paper mill. The unending demand for paper products consumes acres of forest annually for every North American citizen.

Drying side by side in the sun, debarked Douglas fir logs (*below*) suggest an oversized rustic fence. Depending on their girth, the logs season from 6 months to a year before being turned into furniture by a small Seattle manufacturer.

> *"Working a rough piece of wood into a complete useful object is the welding together of man and material."*
>
> — SAM MALOOF

Freshly cut, or green, wood feels heavy, cold, and wet. This is because water makes up about a third of the weight of freshly cut softwoods like firs and cedars, and as much as two-thirds of the weight of freshly cut hardwoods like oak and cherry. If the wood is left exposed to the air, much of the water evaporates over time until the moisture level of the wood achieves equilibrium with the moisture, or humidity, of the air around it. The time required for seasoning varies according to the type of wood, the climate, and the ultimate use to which the wood will be put. Freshly cut pine boards stacked outdoors under a tarpaulin in New England typically stabilize at 12 to 15 percent moisture content in a month or two, while hardwoods may take several years. This process of seasoning, or air-drying, was the standard treatment for green wood until kiln- or oven-drying came into widespread use at commercial sawmills in the 19th century. Kiln-drying can achieve more consistent results than air-drying, and can do it in a matter of days rather than months.

Properly seasoned wood weighs anywhere from a quarter to a third less than green wood, is more resistant to rot, and is less likely to warp or split from shrinkage. But that is hardly the end of the story. Seasoned wood retains the capacity to reabsorb all the moisture it has lost—and then some—if the humidity of the outside air rises or if it comes into contact with water. Whenever wood absorbs moisture, it swells; whenever it loses moisture, it shrinks. Since changes in humidity are inevitable, wood is constantly expanding and contracting. Because its cells are arranged in long vertical chains, wood swells primarily in one direction—across the grain—when it gets wet. If its freedom to move in this direction is restrained by glue, nails, screws, or another piece of wood, the buildup of pressure can make the wood warp; likewise, unseasoned, moisture-laden wood will inevitably crack and split when it dries.

Since wood is capable of absorbing as much as three times its weight in moisture, the forces involved can become intense. Stonecutters have long taken advantage of this property of wood by driving long, dry stakes into narrow fissures in stone blocks, then wetting the stakes and waiting until the wood swells enough to split the stone apart. Conversely, green wood allowed to dry too fast may split with a sound like a gunshot.

This 8-foot-tall pendulum clock (*above*), elaborately carved and inlaid with animals and flowers, was handcrafted in 1815 of maple, pine, ash, and tulipwood. The classic Chippendale style pediment (*right*), with carved cherry embellishments on a mahogany panel, embodies the height of artistry in wood.

As they piece together a table or a chair or a chest of drawers, furniture makers must try to anticipate how different kinds of wood will behave under different conditions. But there are limits to human foresight. Age has no effect on the moisture-absorbing capacity of wood; a piece of bone-dry sandalwood buried 4,000 years in an Egyptian tomb will still swell if moved to a high-humidity environment. And early in this century, when central heating became common and drastically reduced the ambient moisture levels in American homes, some cherished colonial antiques literally self-destructed. To keep up with the times, today's cabinetmakers favor wood that has been kiln dried to below 10 percent moisture content.

Because green hardwood tends to contain more water than softwood does, hardwoods are more susceptible to shrinking and swelling unless properly seasoned. Nevertheless, their strength, the beauty of their grain, and their ability to take a lasting finish have recommended hardwoods to the makers of fine furniture for centuries. Black walnut, highly figured maple, and black cherry were

Colonial frame maker Elisha Babcock fashioned this looking glass in the early 1790's. The frame is mahogany veneer over white pine and tulipwood. The glass plate was likely imported, as American artisanship stopped short of high-quality glassmaking until the late 1800's.

among the favored native cabinet woods in the colonial period; high-quality American black walnut was being exported to England as early as 1610.

Initially, the appeal of hardwood furniture lay not so much in its natural beauty—it was often painted or inlaid according to the fashion of the day—but in its strength and durability. Much colonial furniture was painted, even by the Shakers, whose style is associated today with simple, clear finishes. While their neighbors painted wood furniture to make it more "beautiful," the Shakers apparently worried that the look and feel of natural wood would be too distracting, too sensuous.

Oak, which was the construction wood of choice in Elizabethan England, was more likely to be found in well-made, utilitarian furniture during the late 17th century—solid gateleg tables, stools, benches, and cupboards—sometimes carved in the ponderous style now known as Jacobean. Cheaper pieces were often made from the easily worked white pine, but few of those have survived.

When the vogue for mahogany reached the colonies in the mid-1700's, customers who couldn't afford the real thing from the West Indies made do with native maple and cherry that was stained or even painted to imitate mahogany. So prevalent was this practice that some Yankees referred to cherry as New England mahogany. But among the wealthy in such coastal cities as Boston, Philadelphia, Baltimore, and New York, there was a growing demand for the work of fine craftsmen who could re-create, and sometimes creatively reinterpret, the classic furnishings of the home country. In Newport, Rhode Island, for example, cabinetmakers developed a local version of Chippendale rococo in which matched panels of highly figured veneer served as decoration instead of the usual carving or inlay work.

When cabinetmakers want to emphasize the beauty of wood grain, they typically rely on a technique called veneering. Although known since Egyptian and Roman times, this technique came into special prominence in the walnut and mahogany furniture of the 18th century. Veneer is a thin piece of wood cut, sawed, or peeled from a larger block; the advantage of veneer is that it offers maximum use of a valuable commodity. Small pieces of veneer can be inlaid into contrasting wood panels, a technique known as marquetry. Large sheets of veneer glued to an underlayer of solid wood or modern plywood give the effect of solid wood. In colonial days the finest veneers, about 1/8 inch thick, were laboriously sawed from carefully selected wood blocks, using wide-bladed, fine-toothed saws. Today endless sheets of veneer up to 1/32 inch thick can be mechanically shaved from a debarked hardwood log.

The appearance of veneer depends on two factors: the quality of the natural wood grain and the angle of the cut relative to that grain. Curlicues and stripes, feathers and clouds, flames and butterfly wings are some of the designs that careful veneer cutting can bring out. In a sense, the veneer maker faces a challenge similar to that of the sculptor as defined by Michelangelo: to lay bare the figure buried in the natural material. Once cut, different pieces of veneer can be matched or combined to form an endless variety of patterns. Knots, which indicate the base of a branch, are considered defects in some circumstances, but marks of beauty in others. Compression stress or other distortions in the living tree produce some of the most highly figured wood veneer.

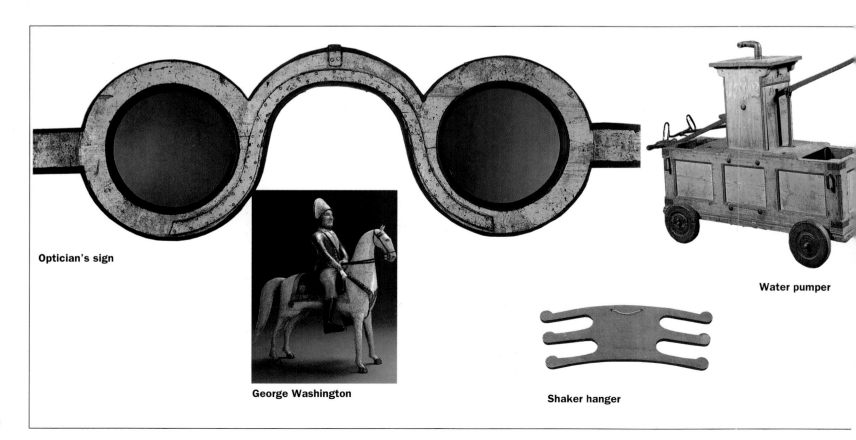

Optician's sign

George Washington

Water pumper

Shaker hanger

Ash- and beech-handled gouges, chisels, and carving knives (*below*) remain essential tools for a modern-day furniture maker putting the finishing touches on a classic oak rocker (*right*).

In the hands of a master woodworker, a razor-sharp bench plane (*above*) makes oak shavings fly. The bench top and vise jaws are seasoned beechwood, traditional material that does not go out of style.

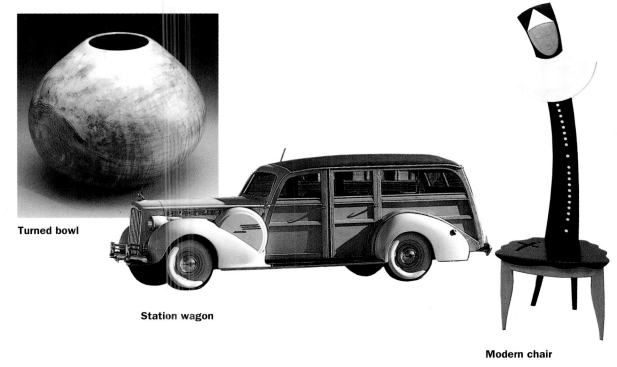

Turned bowl

Station wagon

Modern chair

The Craft of the Woodworker

Over the decades, the versatile properties of wood have inspired designers and artisans to blend beauty with utility. From left to right: an antique gilded wood and glass optician's sign; a period replica of George Washington carved in his lifetime; a Shaker triple clothes hanger made in the 1850's; a 19th-century firefighters' hand-powered pumper; a contemporary bowl turned from myrtle wood; a classic 1940's Packard "woodie" station wagon; and a whimsical contemporary chair of walnut, curly maple, and pear.

Black walnut

The fine art of veneering also has a practical side: a well-laid veneer is less likely to warp or crack with changes in humidity than is a thick slab of wood. Along with native walnut, ash, cherry, and hard maple, woods favored for veneers in colonial days included imported mahogany and ebony. Usually the carcass, or structural framework of a piece of furniture, was of a different, less desirable wood. But in some 18th-century colonial furniture, selected mahogany veneer might actually have been applied to a carcass of sound but inferior quality mahogany.

The finer the work, the more important it was to have the right tool for each job; an 18th-century cabinetmaker's toolbox contained scores of specialized planes, chisels, gouges, and scrapers. Since sandpaper was unknown, smooth surfaces were achieved by meticulous scraping. Light-colored woods like maple, beech, and pine could be stained or dyed with a variety of homemade potions,

Cherry

White oak

such as boiled walnut shells, mild acids, alum, tannin, and ferrous sulfate from iron rust.

When it came to finishing a piece of furniture, the colonial workman had a number of choices. Milk-based paints were tinted with dyes from various plant extracts and widely used on household items, while varnishes compounded from oil and resin might be used on fine work. By the early 1800's, spirit-based varnish, as well as shellac imported from the Orient, became popular but never cheap. If they could afford it, householders preferred a shiny finish that reflected the meager candlelight of the period and that resisted discoloration from the ever-present fireplace soot.

Common, utilitarian finishes included beeswax, walnut oil, poppy seed oil, and linseed oil, processed from flaxseed. One of the cabinetmaker's rules of thumb called for a light application of oil once a day for a week, once a week for a month, once a month for a year, and once a year

Fiddleback maple

Native hardwoods vary widely in color, texture, grain and figure. To the woodworker, each has its own characteristic properties. Black walnut (*top left*) is the traditional choice for gunstocks, fine furniture, and carved or lathe-turned objects. White oak (*top right*) is one of the most versatile species, straight grained, strong, and water resistant. Cherry (*bottom left*) has straight grain and fine texture, ideal for musical instruments and furniture. Maple (*bottom right*) varies from straight to highly figured and is valued for marquetry and cabinetry. A 500-year-old white oak (*opposite*) represents the solidity and dignity inherent in a mature, healthy tree.

forever. The oil made the wood glow, protected the surface against nicks and scratches, and afforded some protection against moisture. An oil finish could never seal off the piece entirely from environmental changes, to which each type of wood responded with restless, almost lifelike, movements of its own.

In the days before clear-cutting and large-scale pulp mills, logging in North America was a selective trade, geared to serve a selective market. Spotters, also known as land lookers, tramped the New England wilderness, looking for high-value hardwoods or commercially exploitable groves of white pine. The most sought-after trees were those found near streams that ran full in the spring. The trees were felled during the winter by ax-wielding lumberjacks and bucked—stripped of branches and cut, if necessary, into manageable sections. The logs were then skidded individually along the still-icy ground or pulled on ox-drawn sledges to rivers and streams to begin their journey to the sawmill.

Colonists in New England and eastern Canada considered white pine a staple commodity. At home it was used for everything from covered bridges to cupboards, from bobsleds to looms, from exterior siding and roof shingles to interior paneling, doors, and window sashes—not to mention firewood, turpentine, resin, tar, paints, lamp black, tanbark, and pitch. Its appeal soon extended to overseas markets. By 1650 New England was exporting significant amounts of white pine, along with oak barrel staves and beams and cedar shingles, to the Caribbean and Africa, although high shipping costs made a regular timber trade with the home country less profitable.

But starting in 1653 the Royal Navy began importing North American white pines—unrivaled for ship masts because of their height, strength, and lightness—on an annual basis. To keep this valuable asset out of the hands of the Spanish and Portuguese navies, the British Crown acted to reserve the majestic white pines for its own use. According to the Royal Charter granted to Massachusetts in 1691, all trees 24 inches or more in diameter found outside townships on land not previously included in grants henceforward belonged to the Crown. Poachers were subject to severe penalties.

But the long arm of the law had trouble enforcing its writ across an entire ocean. The White Pine Acts of 1705, 1722, and 1729 repeated the ban against cutting down

Trees in the Pre-Industrial American Economy, 1500-1850

To survive and prosper in the New World, European settlers—whether they came from England, Spain, France, or elsewhere—depended on wood for houses, vehicles, furniture, and utensils. At first, wooden objects reflected Old World traditions of design and workmanship, but after a few generations new styles appeared, combining the best elements of the past with ingenious adaptations that could only be called "American."

Wood from different trees found favor for specific uses, at first by trial and error but eventually using logical and scientific principles. To a shipwright, rot-resistant white oak was essential for framing and planking, straight white pine for masts and spars, bendable hickory and ash for mast hoops, and wear-resistant chestnut for block sheaves and other fittings.

To a wheelwright, only tough elm would suffice for the hub, springy ash or hickory for spokes, and sturdy oak for the rims. For fence posts and rails, nothing beat locust and cedar for resistance to decay. Ax handles and ramrods demanded the elasticity of hickory, while smooth, hard hornbeam was preferred for the soles of the cabinetmaker's plane. Custom eventually demanded hard, highly figured maple for the stocks of hunting rifles and sturdy, straight-grained walnut for military muskets.

Material for dwellings varied widely. Traditionalists preferred oak beams and cedar siding, but eventually houses for common folk were framed in easily worked pine and fir in the East—or redwood and cedar in the West. The same softwoods sufficed for everyday furnishings, while native hardwoods like beech, walnut, cherry, and maple were crafted into fine furniture.

Styles in woodworking ranged from heavy European-inspired Jacobean furniture in the 1600's to local variations on Queen Anne and Chippendale in the 19th century, as well as Spanish-influenced mission furniture in the South and West. During the Industrial Revolution of the mid-1800's, much woodworking moved from the artisan's workshop to the factory. Even so, the craft of the individual woodworker has survived to modern times.

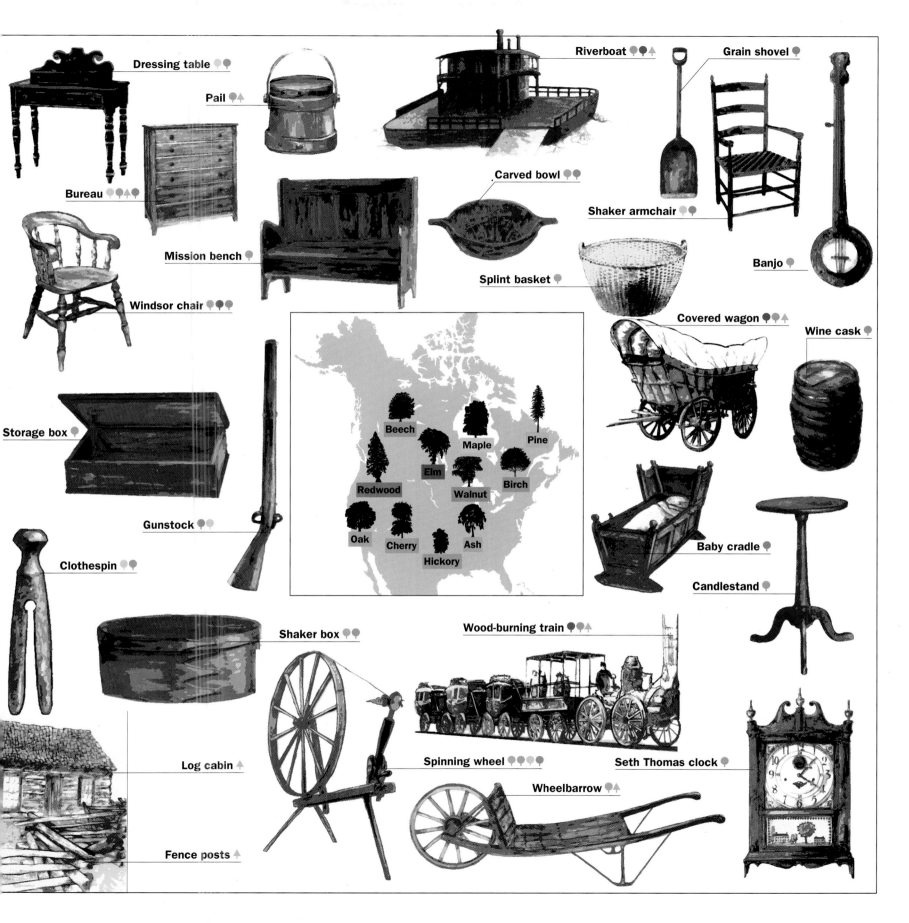

Dressing table

Pail

Riverboat

Grain shovel

Bureau

Carved bowl

Shaker armchair

Mission bench

Banjo

Splint basket

Windsor chair

Covered wagon

Wine cask

Storage box

Beech

Maple

Pine

Elm

Redwood

Walnut

Birch

Baby cradle

Gunstock

Oak

Cherry

Ash

Candlestand

Hickory

Clothespin

Shaker box

Wood-burning train

Log cabin

Spinning wheel

Seth Thomas clock

Wheelbarrow

Fence posts

Of all the oaken-planked, pine-masted ships that have plied the seven seas, the U.S. Frigate *Constitution*—"Old Ironsides"—may be the most famous. In this painting by J. G. Evans, she wears full dress, celebrating Washington's birthday, 1837, off the former British island of Malta in the Mediterranean.

Celebration of "Washington's Birth Da[...]

His Majesty's mast trees and extended it to all ungranted lands from New Jersey to Nova Scotia. At the same time, to encourage a transatlantic trade in naval stores, which England had previously been buying from Sweden, the Crown forbade shipping tar and pitch from the colonies to any foreign nation and prohibited the destruction of pitch- and tar-producing pines on ungranted lands from Maine to New Jersey.

But the more the Crown tried to interfere with what the colonists saw as their business, in every sense of that word, the more resistance grew. A decree threatening law-breakers with flogging had no perceptible effect. Lawsuits challenged the validity of the White Pine Acts; attempts to enforce the prohibitions were met with noncooperation and, here and there, violence. Royal agents went into the forests of the region to mark every tall pine with a triangular blaze known as the "King's broad arrow." It is documented that loggers disguised as Indians chopped down trees with this hated insignia in the middle of the night and floated them downriver before the king's agents got wind of the deed. In retaliation, British agents accompanied by troops burned down sawmills and drove loggers from their camps.

It is no exaggeration to say that British attempts to control the supply of North American white pine sparked grievances among colonists akin to those incited by the British taxes on stamps and tea, feeding the flames of rebellion that culminated in the American Revolution. With war on the horizon, the colonists turned the tables, reserving the great white pines for their own ships and those of their French allies. Capt. John Paul Jones's

A on board the U.S.S. CONSTITUTION. Comm. J.D. ELLIOT. 1837.

Set out in rank and file on a tree plantation in southwestern Pennsylvania, young white pines stand in readiness for service as ship masts, construction timbers, or other commercial uses.

Ranger, commissioned in 1777 and flying the newly adopted Stars and Stripes, was fitted with what have been described as "three of the tallest white pine masts that ever went to sea."

Indeed, the trees of North America went to war on every front. Swamp cedar from the gloomy bogs of southern New Jersey was burned to a fine charcoal that went into gunpowder for General Washington's troops. From the same area of New Jersey came so-called bog iron for Revolutionary cannons; local furnaces and forges were fed with charcoal made from the abundant pitch pines. For the stocks of shoulder arms, black walnut had, and has, no peer. When seasoned, it is an extremely stable wood, little given to warping or splintering. Musket stocks of American black walnut served with such distinction during and after the Revolutionary War that "to shoulder walnut" came to be synonymous with serving in the army.

To anyone with a scientific turn of mind, the trans-Appalachian wilderness that the United States of America took claim to after the Revolutionary War offered a particularly exciting challenge. Here was a vast expanse of trees, containing innumerable species unknown to European science, with as-yet-untested properties that might be of great benefit to the new country and its people. Thomas Jefferson, the drafter of the Declaration of Independence and the third President of the United States, was a devoted botanist. When he left public service in the spring of 1809 to return to his estate at Monticello, it was his dream, along with founding the University of

In his orchard at Monticello near Charlottesville, Virginia, amateur botanist Thomas Jefferson imported and experimented with native and exotic trees. Today, newly planted silver maples flourish, as other trees did under Jefferson's guidance two centuries ago.

Virginia, to spend more time in "the care of the garden, and culture of curious plants, uniting beauty and utility."

As a younger man, while serving on diplomatic missions for the new government in France after the American Revolution, Jefferson had pursued botanical interests, collecting specimens and sending seeds from Europe to be planted in America. One of his pet projects, repeatedly frustrated, was to introduce the European cork oak to the American South. During his first term as President, Jefferson negotiated the acquisition from Napoleonic France of the Louisiana Territory, which nearly doubled the size of the United States. By the time the purchase was completed, in 1803, Jefferson had already spent 2 years grooming his private secretary, a young army captain named Meriwether Lewis, to lead an expedition to explore the western part of the continent. As part of his preparations Lewis studied celestial navigation, zoology, and botany in Philadelphia.

Both Jefferson and Lewis were familiar with the efforts that previous plant explorers had made to catalogue and comprehend the botanical riches of North America. The first printed record of indigenous plant life in Virginia, published in England at the turn of the 18th century, reflected the labors of John Banister, an English clergyman who had been sent to America in the 1670's by the Bishop of London. The first volume exclusively about American trees in English was published by Mark Catesby in 1737. Catesby had spent many years collecting seeds in North America and sending them back to English nurseries. His *Natural History of Carolina, Florida and the Bahama Islands* featured exceptionally beautiful color-

119

John Bartram's meticulously researched and exquisitely detailed painting of *Franklinia alatamaha*—named after Benjamin Franklin—typified the seriousness of purpose among 18th century botanists in their quest for knowledge about the trees being discovered as new regions of the continent were being explored.

FRANKLINIA *alatamaha. Bart. Journ.*

plates depicting native plant and animal life, drawn and engraved by Catesby himself.

John Bartram, who was born on a farm near Darby, Pennsylvania, in 1699, not only exchanged seeds, specimens, and information with leading European botanists, but he established America's first botanical garden, in Philadelphia, and helped educate an entire generation of plant explorers and investigators. One of his correspondents, the eminent Swedish botanist Carolus Linnaeus, whose system of classifying plants is still in use, acclaimed Bartram "the greatest natural Botanist in the world." The Quaker Bartram was appointed Royal Botanist for the colonies; at the age of 70, he used the stipend of £50 to underwrite a botanical expedition to South Carolina, Georgia, and Florida in the company of his son William. He brought specimens and seedlings back to his botanical garden, naming one of his discoveries after Benjamin Franklin. This act turned out to be an inadvertent example of rescuing a botanical species. The tree has since spread widely, but no wild stand of *Franklinia alatamaha* has ever been found. It is said that concern over the fate of his botanical garden led to John Bartram's death, after the British army threatened Philadelphia in 1777. Yet Bartram's home and garden survived; they may be visited today along the Schuylkill River in Fairmont Park.

One of the elder Bartram's botanizing excursions included Jane Colden, a young botanist from near Albany, New York. Like Bartram and other amateur colonial botanists, Colden corresponded widely with her European counterparts, winning their respect and filling their collections

From 1806 to 1809, botanist François Michaux documented trees in the French and British colonies. His graceful depiction of the white pine (*above*) belies the intense commercial and political importance of the tree at the time.

with New World specimens. During the Revolution, Hessian troops overran the Colden family property. Her collections and research were taken to Germany and finally came to rest in the British Museum. Jane Colden died at age 42 of complications following childbirth, and it was not until 1963 that her work was published.

One enthusiastic visitor to John Bartram's garden in Philadelphia was André Michaux, a French botanist who had traveled extensively in the Near East before coming to America in 1785. He had been commissioned by his government to look for trees, especially oaks, that would grow well in France, where the forests had been nearly depleted to stock the French navy. From his plantation near Charleston, South Carolina, André Michaux and his son François nurtured thousands of seedlings and mounted extensive tree-hunting expeditions through the Carolinas, southern Appalachia, Spanish Florida, and the Bahamas, and as far north as Hudson's Bay. The elder Michaux also introduced several tree species to the United States, including the mimosa, ginkgo, and sweet olive. He died of a tropical fever in 1802, but not before producing a major illustrated study of North American oaks. His book, the world's first systematic treatment of a North American tree species, was published posthumously.

André's son François extended his father's work and wrote compellingly about it. His best-known work was written in French between 1810 and 1813; a complete English translation appeared in 1819 under the title *The North American Sylva; or, a*

Between 1730 and 1747, Mark Catesby published *Natural History of Carolina*, featuring his own colored copper-plate engravings, like this one of a water tupelo with a hooded titmouse in its branches. While he sometimes combined plants and animals in unreal ways, his illustration is stunning.

Description of the Forest Trees of the United States, Canada, and Nova Scotia, Considered Particularly with Respect to the Uses in the Arts and their Introduction into Commerce. In this book, which remained the most comprehensive study of North American forests until after its author's death in 1855, François Michaux sought to educate Americans about managing their vast but finite forest resources. His was one of the earliest voices to make a rational case for what would come to be known in the 19th century as conservation.

William Bartram also wrote about the wilderness. His illustrated travel

diaries, which have become classics of the genre, are filled with vivid reportage of life in the wild, inspiring Samuel Taylor Coleridge to borrow some of Bartram's descriptions of Florida for his poetic fantasy "Kubla Khan." Despite some harrowing experiences—such as spending an entire day and night trapped in a small boat by a herd of enraged bull alligators—William Bartram never lost his appreciation for what we would now consider a balanced ecosystem: an environment in which plants, animals, and the Indians who had long inhabited the North American woodlands each had a necessary role to play. ✦

William Bartram had an appreciation, uncharacteristic of his day, for a wilderness in which wild animals, colonists and Indians coexisted peacefully.

Despite harrowing experiences, William Bartram never lost enthusiasm for the wilderness. Blundering into an alligator breeding area, he spent 24 hours trapped in a small boat by bellowing, bellicose bulls (*above*) with only a paddle to fend them off. Alligators played in his nightmares ever after. The beauty and serenity of the wilderness Bartram explored is still around us, as in this cypress grove (*opposite*) in Merchants Millpond State Park, North Carolina.

CHAPTER FIVE

Mining the Forest

Two legendary 19th-century superheroes, Johnny Appleseed and Paul Bunyan, shared a belief: North America's woodlands are enormously valuable to human beings. Where they differed was in their methods for realizing that value. Appleseed, the orchardist, wanted to farm the land; Bunyan, the logger, wanted to mine it. Until well into the 20th century, North American lumber interests listened to the logger.

Paul Bunyan is the mythical embodiment of the North American logger. Stories about Paul and Babe, his faithful Blue Ox, began circulating through the upper Midwest in the late 1800's, and no child who ever heard the tall tales can forget them. The huge griddle in Paul's logging camp was greased by boys skating over it on sides of bacon. Babe was so heavy that his footprints filled with water to form Minnesota's 10,000 lakes, and the tips of his horns were so far apart that they were hinged so he could walk through the woods. Paul hitched Babe to the Mississippi River to straighten it. Paul and Babe cleared the trees from North and South Dakota to open the land for farming, and eventually they dug Puget Sound.

Such tall tales spun around wood stoves in logging camps became part of our folklore, but the legend of Paul Bunyan reflected reality—the boisterous braggadocio of rough-hewn, hard-working men whose goal was not to husband the forests but to exploit them, to exhaust them the way a gold or coal mine is exhausted, and then move on.

Johnny Appleseed was born John Chapman in 1774—a few months before British soldiers charged up Bunker Hill. In 1801, when he was 26 years old, Chapman was wandering the sparsely populated "western country" that was still 2 years away from becoming the state of Ohio. His

Paul Bunyan, forest legend and folk hero, was conceived from tall tales spun in logging camps and was later adopted as a larger-than-life symbol of the timber industry. Eben Giben's lithograph of him (*right*) dates from 1930.

This trio of Washington State loggers felling a Douglas fir (*opposite*) posed for photographer Darius Kinsey in 1906. One sawyer lies down on the job, nestled in the notch that determines the direction of the tree's fall. This giant fir measured 51 feet in diameter.

Winter Pearmain

129—

SheepNose *or* Bullock's pippin

125—

Apple trees were one of the first plant varieties imported to the New World. Varieties like the Winter Pearmain (*top*) and Bullock's Pippin (*bottom*) painted by Elizabeth Coxe McMurtrie, were an important part of colonial life. Fresh from the tree or dried for the winter—in apple pies, apple sauce, and apple butter—they enlivened and improved the rural diet.

purpose was simple: he planted seeds salvaged from rural cider presses wherever he found suitable soil.

To frontier settlers, this man had "a thick bark of queerness on him." He wore strange clothes and went barefoot in the coldest weather. He treated settlers and Indians alike with respect that was returned in kind. A pacifist in a time of frontier warfare and brutality, he killed no animals, ate no meat, and even opposed grafting and pruning his beloved apple trees so as not to cause them pain.

Chapman spent almost 4 decades wandering by foot and canoe through Ohio and Indiana planting apple seeds; raising, selling, and giving away apple saplings; exchanging medicinal plant lore with Indians and settlers; and gently proselytizing for his own brand of frontier religion.

During his years of "apple seeding," Chapman stayed ahead of large settlements. His notion was to prepare the way for farms and towns—planting apple seeds in grassy clearings alongside rivers, girdling large trees that might shade seedlings, and building simple wooden fences to keep animals out of his rudimentary orchards. Chapman died in 1845, but it took the country many years to catch up with his ideas.

Dressed in homemade garb, John Chapman wandered the Northwest frontier preaching and planting apple trees. This engraving appeared in *Harper's Weekly* in 1871, by which time Chapman was better known as Johnny Appleseed.

Making the forest bloom by clearing it was a long-standing Old World tradition. A thousand years earlier an Anglo-Saxon chronicler described the stalwart English farmer as "the grey enemy of the wood." Benjamin Franklin spoke approvingly of "scouring" America of woods, and Thomas Jefferson imperiously wrote in approval of "an immensity of land courting the industry of the husbandman." President Andrew Jackson, representing more common frontier sentiments, equated woods with wilderness and clearing with civilization: "What good man would prefer a country covered with forests, and ranged by a few thousand savages to our extensive Republic, studded with cities, towns, and prosperous farms . . . and filled with all the blessings of liberty, civilization, and religion?"

The agricultural development that Franklin, Jefferson, Jackson, and Chapman anticipated was in fact marching across the eastern half of the United States and Canada at an ever-increasing pace—with predictable consequences for the continent's forests.

The land area of the contiguous United States and Canada is just over 4.8 billion acres. When the Europeans arrived, nearly one-third of that area was covered with forests. When settlers from western Pennsylvania began to arrive in John Chapman's chosen territory of Ohio, for example, some 90 percent of the land was still thick with elm and ash, beech and maple, oak and hickory. The rise in the state's population was explosive—from 45,000 in 1800 to nearly 2 million in 1850—and they cut down trees at a fearsome rate. By mid-century more than 40 percent of the land in Ohio was "improved," meaning cleared of trees and converted to farms. And what one pioneer called "the war on the woods" did not abate until after 1880, when fully three-quarters of the state had been cleared.

The same relentless war was waged throughout the continent. An estimated 100 million acres of forest were cleared by the sweat of pioneer farmers in the 2 centuries

of settlement up to 1850, and in the next decade alone, another 40 million acres. Technological innovations, like John Deere's steel plow in 1837, made life a little easier for pioneers once the land was opened up. But it still took a full month of one person's labor, with the help of controlled fires or a team of oxen, to cut trees and remove stumps from an acre of forest.

Newspaperman Horace Greeley, who advised, "Go west, young man," also urged caution: "I would advise no one over forty years of age to undertake to dig a farm out of the dense forest, where great trees must be cut down and cut up, rolled into log-heaps and burned to ashes where they grew. Digging a farm out of the high woods is, to any but a man of wealth, a slow, hard task."

Despite such admonitions, there were plenty of volunteers. With the official population of the United States, excluding Indians and slaves, increasing nearly fourteen-fold during the century—from 5.8 million to 76 million—and rising from 300,000 to 5.4 million in Canada, prime farmland was at a premium. And except for the treeless prairies, which began to come under extensive cultivation after the Civil War, the land for new farms came almost exclusively from old forests.

This devastated Michigan land-scape (*left*) gives grim testimony to the unregulated logging common in the last century. Today, clear-cut terrain near

La Push, Washington, (*above*) appears equally stark, yet this land will be replanted for another carefully managed tree harvest in a few decades.

Of course, clearing land for cultivation was by no means the only front in the war on the woods. Of the 54,000 dwellings constructed in the United States by 1839—from log cabins to clapboard cottages—more than four out of five were built mainly of wood, and most were roofed with wooden shingles. All were filled with wooden furniture, and many were heated by open fireplaces, which sent as much as 80 percent of their heat up the chimney. According to one estimate, it took from 10 to 20 acres of woodland to keep a single fireplace burning for a year. Wood and wood products were so much a part of everyday life that an American writing in 1836 declared: "Well may ours be called a wooden country."

Even as towns and cities grew in importance—the proportion of North Americans classified as urban rose from just over 7 percent to nearly 20 percent between 1810 and 1860—the demand for wood continued to increase. One reason was that the early years of the Industrial Revolution in North America were fueled and shaped by the continent's abundance of wood.

Long after the British iron industry had begun firing its furnaces with coal or coke, North American ironmasters relied on charcoal. Since it took 8 tons of wood to make 2 tons of charcoal to smelt 1 ton of pig iron—and even more wood to feed the forges of the blacksmiths who worked the iron—the toll on the forests was high. Countless acres of woodland were felled during the first half of the 19th century to stoke furnaces and forges; the acreage lost to out-of-control fires, for which the charcoal burners were notorious, cannot be calculated.

The river steamboats and "iron horses" that came into operation after 1830 had an even more voracious appetite for wood, particularly clean-burning hardwood. To hold down their running weight and still keep their paddle wheels turning, steamboats typically took on fuel twice a day. The wood was supplied by thousands of itinerant "wood hawks" who lined the banks of such major rivers as the Ohio and the Mississippi with piles of cut firewood, some of which, despite precautions, was occasionally swept away in floods. The larger and faster steamboats saved time by towing flatboats of cordwood upstream to assure a ready supply; when empty, the flatboats were cut loose to float back downriver to the wooding stations.

"As long as our forests stand, as long as trees march down to the sea or climb the wind-swept ridges...the strong, pitchy odor of its groves and the heavy chant of the wind in them will stand for something that is wild and untamable."
—Donald Culross Peattie

After the American Civil War, railroads linked the industrial Northeast with remote territories rich in natural resources. This wood-burning logging train was still chugging through the forests of southern Georgia in 1903, carrying softwood logs to the mills.

Flat-bottomed barges called arks were first used to transport timber by water around 1800. The practice continued into the 1930's, allowing celebrated American photographer Dorothea Lange to record this shipment of pulpwood destined for Mobile, Alabama.

On the rivers, coal came into use slowly, partly because wood-burning boilers required extensive refitting to handle coal, and partly because the steamboat operators, a conservative lot, resisted innovation. Annual consumption of wood on riverboats neared 1 million cords by 1839 and continued to increase up to the end of the Civil War in 1865. As a result, river valleys that saw the heaviest steamboat traffic were virtually stripped of their forests by mid-century.

Acceptance of coal also came slowly on the railroads. In 1864 one calculation put annual consumption of firewood by the railroads at 6.5 million cords, which would have required cutting more than 215,000 acres of woodland a year just to keep the locomotives rolling. Clean-burning hardwood not only remained the fuel of choice on North American railroads, but enormous amounts of strong oak and black locust went into the manufacture of ties, cars, bridges, trestles, fencing, and telegraph poles. In the decade from the end of the Civil War to 1875, the United States almost tripled the nationwide rail system, adding 58,000 miles of new track. Track length doubled in the next decade and again in the next.

Canadian railroads also stretched from coast to coast by 1885. Each additional mile meant at least 2 more miles of fencing and more than 2,500 ties. And the ties, like the bridges and trestles, had to be replaced every 6 or 7 years.

Is it any wonder that an observer in 1866 noted: "Even where railroads have penetrated regions abundantly supplied, we soon find all along its track timber soon becomes scarce"?

For all their profligate use of firewood, however, railroads and steamboats were not the principal consumers of forest products in the 19th century. This honor went to homeowners. In 1870 a third of a million acres of forest went into the wood-burning boilers of trains and boats to keep people on the move. Yet this was only a fraction of the 4.5 million acres that went up in smoke to heat the continent's homes that year. Two-thirds of all households in North America burned wood; as late as 1920 the figure was no less than 25 percent. And land cleared for farms averaged between 2 and 3 million acres a year throughout the century.

The devastation caused by this unrelenting assault on the forests did not go unnoticed. A few sensitive travelers, especially those from Britain, were shocked by the "bleak, hopeless" aspect of the cleared land. "The trees are cut over at the height of three or four feet from the ground and the stumps are left for many years till the roots rot," one Englishman wrote in the 1820's. "The houses, which are made from logs, lie scattered about at long intervals; while the snake fences, constructed of the split trees, placed in a zig-zag form, disfigure the landscape."

Choking the St. Croix River between Minnesota and Wisconsin, a log drive in 1905 sent thousands of free-floating logs drifting toward the Mississippi River and on to St. Louis.

But for sheer concentrated exploitation of North America's forests, nothing done by the farmers or the charcoal burners or the riverbank wood hawks or the railroad ax gangs could match the sustained onslaught by the lumber industry itself. During the entire 19th century this industry was absolutely central to the North American experience—supplying the single most valuable raw material for a rapidly expanding nation while changing forever the face of the continent. Long before the range-riding cowboy became the mythical embodiment of manly independence, the lumberjack loomed large in the popular imagination. From Yankee log drivers to the Midwestern prototypes of Paul Bunyan to the hard-working, hard-drinking "skid-road" loggers of Washington State and British Columbia, the story of lumbering in the 19th century is one of impatient men determined to wrest livelihoods from living forests without pausing to reckon the consequences.

The first of the great log drives on the streams of the Northeast came tumbling down the Schroon River, a tributary of the Hudson, in the spring of 1813, headed for the sawmills at Glens Falls and other New York river towns. With an ever-expanding market to serve, the felling of trees had become much less selective. Instead of searching for flawless white pines for ship masts and planking, the new breed of commercial loggers spent the winter cutting all trees within 6 miles of the major streams. Logs were stacked by the water's edge and, with the coming of the spring thaw, were launched downriver in one unruly jumble. To ride herd on this mass, lumberjacks donned spiked boots, hefted sharp-spiked harpoons called peaveys, and became log drivers.

It was a dangerous occupation. A man was lucky to escape with the loss of a foot or an arm if he lost his footing on a slippery peeler—a hemlock log peeled of its valuable tannin-rich bark, whose smooth nakedness helped break up logjams in rock-strewn white-water channels.

The resemblance between lumberjack and cowboy, between log drive and cattle drive, held through every phase of the operation. As more and more lumber companies added their logs to the great spring drives, loggers cut or burned a registered mark or brand into each log so that mill operators downriver could credit the right company for lumber delivered. Log lifting, or lumber rustling, became common, despite the threat of fines or worse for anyone caught red-handed with someone else's logs. State legislatures declared the rivers of New England, New York, and Pennsylvania "public highways," with special consideration given to the "floating of sawn logs and timber" during spring drives.

To keep pace with the increased volume of lumber, sawmills improved significantly in the early 1800's.

Although still water-powered—steam did not become a common power source until after 1850—many mills installed efficient transfer wheels and lighter, faster-moving saws, some with multiple blades, some with circular blades. Such improvements doubled or tripled the amount of lumber that could be milled in a day. Machines for planing, joining, shingle-making, and lathe-turning further boosted production. By 1840 there were 31,649 sawmills in the United States, an average of 25 per county. While most such sawmills were one-person, part-time operations, the biggest commercial mills employed as many as 100 people.

Hardwood trees, showing their autumn regalia, have reclaimed this old river bed, surrounded by stands of evergreens. Before New England industry turned to coal, these forests fueled Rhode Island's iron-smelting and casting mills.

and 1859, annual production of lumber jumped an incredible five-thousandfold—from 1.6 million to 8 billion board feet. This would have been impossible without the widespread application of steam power; wood-fueled steam engines meant that sawmills could be built far from riverbanks. At advanced mills workers hardly touched raw lumber: machines moved and barked the logs, finished the boards, and even took sawdust from the sawing and milling lines back to fuel the boilers.

In addition, it was now possible to build railroad lines right into the forests, so that felled logs could be shipped to market at any time of the year. This did not by any means spell the end of seasonal log drives and rafting; on the contrary, logjams 10 miles long were not uncommon in the 1860's. But by providing efficient transportation far from rivers, railroads in time revolutionized the economics of the lumber business.

Inevitably, the relentless logging took its toll on forests that had once seemed inexhaustible. As the finite nature of the Northeast woodlands became apparent, lumbermen began to fight over the choicest pineries. One such battle, the so-called Aroostook War of the 1830's, nearly precipitated an international incident over the vaguely defined border between the state of Maine and the Canadian province of New Brunswick.

At issue were valuable stands of virgin white pine on wilderness land drained by the Aroostook River. Timber interests in Bangor claimed them all and accused their counterparts in New Brunswick of poaching. To resolve matters before skirmishes between armed loggers triggered a full-scale war, U.S. Secretary of State Daniel Webster met with Lord Ashburton, who represented the British Crown. The 1842 Webster-Ashburton Treaty that settled the conflict also established a permanent boundary between the northeastern United States and Canada, which remains in effect to this day.

But no act of diplomacy could mitigate the ever-accelerating war on the woods. Between 1840

A log-driving crew stands with poles at the ready, near Tonawanda, N.Y., in 1870. The man on the far right holds an auger for boring holes in the ends of logs, which were then lashed together into rafts instead of drifting out of control.

These innovations had their greatest impact not in the Northeast, where the best pine and hardwood forests had already been exploited, but in the Great Lakes region of the United States and Canada. Settlement was booming on newly cleared farmland that had once been covered by hardwood forests; much of the original oak, hickory, cherry, and beech was gone, but extensive stands of white pine had hardly been touched.

In every way, lumbering in the Great Lakes region was carried out on a far grander scale than in the Northeast. The log drives were longer, the logging camps and sawmills were bigger, the logging companies even when financed with Eastern capital were richer and more powerful. Frederick Weyerhaeuser and his partners built a massive holding and sorting boom at the mouth of Wisconsin's Chippewa River where it flows into the Mississippi. Once he had established control over lumber supplies to burgeoning prairie settlements, Weyerhaeuser bought up vast tracts of timberlands in the Midwest, the South, and the Pacific Northwest, giving him a major stake in the industry for the remainder of the century and beyond.

Although Weyerhaeuser came from Chicago, many of the key entrepreneurs, operators, and workmen in the Great Lakes lumber industry were transplanted Easterners, so it is not surprising that the lumber industry in the Midwest resembled that of the Northeast. Both U.S. and Canadian logging camps employed thousands of men during the peak felling seasons. The typical camp had a bunkhouse, a kitchen and eating area, stables and storehouses, an office, and a blacksmith's shop, all made of logs felled, trimmed, notched, and fitted together on the spot. Since loggers were continually moving to new stands of timber, these camps were necessarily transient; some buildings were even set on wheels or skids and hauled from one camp to the next.

Lumberjacks, many of whom were farmers trying to earn hard cash over the winter months, worked 10 hours or more a day, 6 days a week. According to legend, these rugged individualists shrugged off the 30-below-zero temperatures of the North Woods winters. Gloves were for sissies; to keep warm the lumberjacks relied on red woolen underwear—which they removed only for infrequent baths—lots of food, and a plentiful supply of homemade whiskey. At day's end they piled into bunkhouses, open dormitories for scores of men, where a single wood stove provided heat. Lice, laughingly referred to as sawdust with legs, were so common that some men claimed they could get to sleep only by turning their underwear inside out and dozing off before the lice worked their way back inside. Sundays were for haircuts and shaves, washing clothes, writing home for those who could write, playing cards, visiting other camps, and hunting game to offset a diet often short on fresh meat.

For the energy to fell and buck 100-foot-tall trees, loggers ate prodigious amounts—sometimes four or five meals a day, amounting to an estimated 7,000 to 9,000 calories. In a well run

Intended as temporary quarters for poorly paid men far from home, logging-camp bunkhouses were designed for business, not comfort. In 1899 this midwestern crew gathered around the stove of Ole Emerson's Logging Camp, with their sodden boots and gaiters hung up to dry for another day's labor.

A two-man crosscut saw (*left*) was as essential a piece of equipment to a lumberman as a saddle was to a cowboy. While other members of his crew broke for an *al fresco* lunch in the winter of 1904 (*below*), one diligent Wisconsin logger used the time to sharpen his saw.

The lumber industry spurred employment for countless other trades. Workers in a wooden-timbered factory in the 1880's made commercial-size bandsaw blades destined for sawmills throughout the Midwest. Compact and durable, the bandsaw was a popular alternative to the massive circular saw.

camp, breakfast—served at 5:30 a.m.—might include steak, half a dozen fried eggs, bacon, fried potatoes, pancakes, oatmeal, doughnuts, stewed prunes, and coffee. In remote wilderness camps, however, fresh meat, fruit, and vegetables were scarce. There, cookhouse menus relied on beans, salt pork, and bread, supplemented by such treats as dried codfish, pickled beef, molasses, sourdough biscuits, and tea so strong that loggers reputedly could float their axes in it.

The foremen who hired and bossed these unruly and undisciplined logging crews had to keep order by knocking heads together and hauling these back-country fighters and boozers out of the notorious saloons of the north country. But the logging bosses also had to be able to cruise knowledgeably through a forest of mixed conifers and hardwoods and come out with an accurate estimate of how much the felled lumber would be worth when it arrived at the sawmills.

In general, life in the logging camps was governed by strict protocols that laid out what was proper and what was not. Everyone had his own place to sit at table and his own nail to hang his hat on; trespassing on someone else's space was a sure way to provoke a fight. Meals tended to be all business; no one spoke except to ask for more food. Such rules were necessary to keep the peace in a closed society that brought strangers together to perform back-breaking, dangerous labor under harsh, crowded conditions for poor pay.

Gazing into a personal crystal ball in 1851, journalist Ben Eastman assured his faithful readers that the green and growing treasures of the Midwestern pine forests were beyond the ability even of Americans to deplete: "Upon the rivers which are tributary to the

Mississippi, and also those which empty themselves into Lake Michigan, there are interminable forests of pines, sufficient to supply all the wants of the citizens for all time to come." Like-minded Canadian entrepreneurs echoed similar sentiments.

By the 1890's it was clear that the new technologies and economic imperatives of the Great Lakes lumber industry had triumphed over the natural abundance of the forests. When the best pines had been cut, the loggers turned to lesser softwoods. New processes for turning the soft-fibered hemlock and spruce into pulp for paper created new incentives for clear-cutting. Rail transport encouraged inroads into hardwood species that did not float well. Even so, annual production in the Midwest fell steadily after 1892.

In 1906 the great log boom that Weyerhaeuser had built on the Mississippi River was dismantled because of the steadily dwindling supply of logs. In that year, however, the United States' total lumber production reached an all-time high of 45 billion board feet. By then the focus of the lumber industry had shifted ahead to the rich timberlands of the Southern and Western states, where Weyerhaeuser and other farsighted lumber companies had invested heavily.

What remained in the Great Lakes region struck many observers as nothing less than a tragedy. When the wood ran out, camps and mills closed, leaving entire towns and counties destitute. Where forests once stood, entrepreneurs attracted homesteaders with low-priced, clear-cut stump lands, but poor soil and short growing seasons left

Then as now, advertisers could make grueling work look easy—as long as a fellow used the right tools. This ad for an Indianapolis saw manufacturer made life in the woods look like child's play.

many farmers bankrupt, and only large-scale dairy operations moderately successful.

But the really tragic legacy of the Great Lakes lumber boom was the succession of fires that raged where mountains of tinder-dry slash had been piled between stumps of felled trees. Year after year, as farmers set small blazes to remove stumps from their new farmland, uncontrollable fires of almost inconceivable proportions were ignited. While the great Chicago fire of 1871 made worldwide headlines, an uncontrolled wildfire near forgotten Peshtigo in northeastern Wisconsin devastated 1.3 million acres—an inferno so intense that bricks melted and more than 1,500 people died, many suffocated as the oxygen in the air burst into flame and burned.

Meanwhile, the lumber boom had moved south. What historian Michael Williams calls "the assault on the southern forest" was largely organized and financed by Northern interests. In the depressed economy of the post-Civil

Forest Succession—Natural Growth Over 3 Centuries

Mature pine forest (1700)
Old-growth lodgepole pines dominate other varieties, absorbing much of the water supply with their vast root systems. Their spreading branches let little sunlight filter to the forest floor, suppressing undergrowth.

Fire (1720)
Lightning causes a forest fire that consumes standing trees, undergrowth, and everything that lies on the forest floor. After being heated by fire, fallen cones from the lodgepole pines open and release their seeds, which begin to germinate.

New growth (1722)
New varieties of plant life sprout among the burned stumps and snags. Roots that survived the fire sprout new growth. Lichens and mosses break down the charred timber, while microorganisms stimulate decomposition, releasing nitrogen and other valuable nutrients to the soil.

Mixed plant growth (1725)
Without the forest canopy, sun-loving ferns, grasses, wildflowers, herbaceous plants, and berry patches flourish rapidly. Trees like beech, aspen, and pine are in the seedling stage, their seeds having been carried by the wind or dropped by birds.

War South, undeveloped—meaning uncleared—land was a bargain. A Pennsylvania lumber syndicate, facing the rapid decline of their industry at home, bought a half million acres in east Texas and Louisiana at 50 cents an acre. Saw manufacturer Henry Disston headed a logging syndicate that bought 4 million acres in the state of Florida in 1881 at half that price. The state of Texas sold or gave away 32 million acres—the equivalent of 15 Yellowstone National Parks—by 1885.

Large-scale felling of southern forests was well under way by 1880, using techniques perfected in the Great Lakes and adapted to a new environment. In the South there was no snow to smooth the way downslope for felled trees, and many streams flowed too slowly for log drives. The trees in these remote southern forests were unfamiliar species growing in terrain that no Yankee or Midwestern lumberjack had ever encountered: coarse-grained longleaf, shortleaf, loblolly, and slash pines.

**ense second growth
1735-1740)**
round-cover vegetation gives ay to hardy scrub oak, arrow- ood, and juniper. Pine saplings ontinue to thrive, while young ardwoods—primarily beeches, ut also alders, birches, aspens, nd elms—form stands 10 times ore dense than the forest was efore the fire.

**Mature hardwood forest
(1870)**
Broadleafed trees mature steadily, sharing sunlight, water, and soil nutrients. Beneath a towering stand of white elms are alders and beeches. Below that are dogwoods, hawthorns, hollies, and immature softwoods. Rot and leaf decay continually enrich the soil.

**Intense hardwood logging
(1920)**
Shorter-lived alders, willows, and birches have matured and died. To satisfy commercial demand, other mature hardwoods—elms and beeches—are logged. The absence of hardwoods opens the way for hardy, slow-growing lodgepole to flourish once again.

**Mature pine forest
(2000)**
As the lodgepole pines grow tall and their root systems spread out, they deprive other plants of sunlight and water. Low-growth vegetation eventually fails, and the pines resume their former dominance. The forest has come full cycle.

In the swamps and bayous where bald cypress thrives, standard logging practices were out of the question. The ground was too boggy for teams of oxen, and fresh-cut trees heavy with sap tended to sink into the mud. For years local loggers simply girdled selected trees and waited until they lost enough sap to become buoyant. Then during the wet season loggers floated logs out of the swamp, guided by pole-wielding swampers who stood waist-deep in water during the entire operation.

About 1890 high technology came to bald-cypress logging. The pull boat—a shallow-draft scow or barge mounted with a steam-powered winch—was securely anchored to nearby trees or pilings. Radiating from this pull boat were channels dug or blasted with dynamite more than half a mile into the bald-cypress stands. The steam winch hauled the great logs through the channels by cable. When one channel was cleared, the process was repeated in the next until the pull boat was in the center of a large circle of downed cypress trees. Then the boat itself was moved to a new part of the swamp. By 1905 the annual production of bald cypress had risen to a billion board feet—a level that was sustained for 8 years. Yields began to slip after 1913 as supplies dwindled, but the last of the bald-cypress mills survived well into the 1950's.

After Nathaniel Spaulding of Sacramento, California, devised removable, easily replaceable teeth for circular sawblades in 1859, giant cut-off saws could cut logs to the sawyer's specifications, almost non-stop.

Trees cut along major rivers were rafted downstream to steam-powered sawmills that sprang up virtually overnight. Logging trains were integral to the southern logging industry from the beginning; in the pineries themselves temporary narrow-gauge spur lines snaked through the woods to serve as skidders, loaders, and all-purpose haulers. From the sawmills, main-line railroads then carried the cut lumber north and west to the most lucrative markets.

The major technological advance of the southern loggers was a method of pulling logs from the felling site on overhead cables. This system came into its own in the bald-cypress swamps of the lower Mississippi valley and the half-flooded bottomlands of Georgia, South Carolina, and Florida. A water-loving conifer, the bald cypress grows on a tapering trunk whose broad base is buttressed by ridges and projections called knees. Cypress wood, easily worked yet resistant to termites and rot, was prized for roof shingles, water tanks, and cisterns.

The exploitation of the bald cypress is emblematic of the entire Southern logging boom. Large-scale organization, modern technology, and the urge to turn a fast profit picked the forests of the South clean in a few decades. Even producers who might have preferred to cut at a slower rate were driven by the need to meet rapidly mounting state tax bills and to pay off large debts incurred in the laying of railroad track. Not until most of the old-growth forests were gone and tax laws were changed to favor uncut forests did a few enlightened companies begin experiments in reforestation.

Because the climate is wetter, the clear-cut forest lands of the South were not subject to the uncontrollable fires that ravaged parts of the Midwest and Canada in the wake of their lumber booms. But in some ways, devastation in Southern forests was even greater. Dragging felled logs through rivers by pull boats, power skidding them out of forests with tractors, and grappling them out with cables mounted on tall trees or railroad cars—all these methods uprooted or fatally skinned dozens of young trees for every merchantable log harvested successfully. One early proponent of reforestation compared the results of power skidding in Texas to the shell-ravaged European battlefields of World War I. As in the Great Lakes region, initial hopes that the cleared land would be suitable for farming, with few exceptions, came to nothing.

Because logging in the South was never as rigidly seasonal as in the North, the logging camps in the southern pineries and bald-cypress swamps often developed into towns where the loggers lived with their families year-round. In many cases, when nearby forests gave out, a town that had grown to a population of thousands in a few short years faded quickly, leaving behind nothing but empty streets, deserted buildings, stacks of unsold lumber, and mountainous piles of moldering sawdust.

At first glance, the story of logging on North America's Pacific Coast sounds like a rerun of what happened in the other timber-rich regions of the continent. Even the towering redwoods and Douglas firs—many more than 200 feet tall, with trunks as much as 17 feet in diameter—were indiscriminately felled by men and axes. Early in the 19th

In the 1890's, floating pull boats extracted bald cypress from Louisiana swamps. Steam engines and steel cable gave the shallow-draft barges the power to drag ancient trees out of places inaccessible to mere men with saws and axes.

century, before Pacific Coast urbanization, these big trees along with lesser sugar pines and white pines were shipped from the Pacific Coast to markets in Latin America and across the Pacific.

Ironically, demand for timber sparked the Gold Rush of 1849. Intending to cut sugar pine for the overseas trade, the ambitious John Sutter built a sawmill in the Sierra foothills of central California. A carpenter working for Sutter discovered flakes of the precious metal, and the rush was on. Although the influx of gold seekers brought ruin to Sutter, other lumbermen soon got rich supplying the gold panners with pine boards for sluice mining, to say nothing of boards, beams, and shingles to house the exploding population.

The second half of the century saw the development of new technologies that made it possible to exploit more fully the resources of the temperate rain forest in the western United States and Canada. Pacific Coast lumberjacks hauled logs from the felling sites on skid roads—small trees trimmed and laid in a corduroy pattern for miles into the forest. In the 1880's double-drummed "steam donkeys," dry-land cousins of the pull boat of the bald-cypress swamps, replaced horses as the primary motive power on the skid roads. Railroad spur lines brought logs from the forest to sawmills along the coast. Around the turn of the century, another variant on pull-boat technology—known variously as high-lead yarding, overhead cabling, or skyline logging—literally left the skid roads in the dirt. Intrepid high-riggers linked trimmed spar trees together with huge pulleys and steel cable hundreds of feet in the air. With the help of these cables, 50-ton logs could be hoisted and carried to skid roads or railroad tracks, a distinct advantage in the steep terrain of the Northwest forests and less destructive to uncut trees.

A real logging boom began on the Pacific Coast in the early 1900's, financed by capital from the East and Midwest. Some eastern lumber companies, having cut the last of the worthwhile timber in their home forests, not only moved west but brought their best logging crews and latest milling equipment with them.

Darius Kinsey was a Missouri-born photographer who documented western America's turn-of-the-century forests. In 1918, Kinsey produced this photograph of his family car halfway through a cedar stump in Washington State. Also present were the photographer's wife, Tabitha, and Darius junior.

Branch lines of the Canadian railways created instant "build while you wait" towns. One town, of many in which the building frenzy fed on itself, was Mirror, Alberta. In the first 12 hours after land was open to buyers, nearly 600 lots were sold—a rate of nearly one per minute. Within the first month the town had five stores, three lumberyards, three restaurants, two banks, two pool rooms, a hotel, a newspaper, and a sash and door factory.

Frederick Weyerhaeuser and his partners began buying millions of acres of prime timberland in the state of Washington, and Weyerhaeuser's company eventually controlled 4.3 percent of all the privately held forest lands in the United States. As it turned out, the very size of the Weyerhaeuser holdings led the management of the company to champion farsighted conservation measures, such as fire control and reforestation. In 1909, George S. Long, manager of the Weyerhaeuser Timber Company,

American ingenuity knew no limits when figuring out how to harvest timber. In Washington State, a system of pulleys and cables was used to hoist logs up and over living growth (*left*) and into water-filled flumes (*above*) that carried logs to far-away rivers.

proclaimed, "Timber is a crop," meaning a sustainable resource as opposed to a one-time asset like a vein of ore to be mined and abandoned. But before such a concept could be widely applied, areas of northwestern forests were subjected to ruthless clear-cutting.

Not even the venerable sequoias, the largest living things on the Earth—and some of the oldest—were spared the bite of the lumberman's ax. In the shade of these giant trees, lumberjacks looked more like Lilliputians than real-life descendants of Paul Bunyan, but they knew their jobs well. To bring down a tree having the girth of a house, they first chopped away the flaring buttresses of the trunk to a height of 6 feet. Then two axmen standing on a wooden platform opened a 10-foot-deep notch in the tree's side. Two sawyers, hefting a 20-foot blade, attacked the tree from a platform on the other side. After several days of dragging the greased saw through the cut, into which wedges were repeatedly driven to keep the tree from settling and trapping the blade, a few well-placed iron "gluts" were pounded home. A tree that may have been growing for more than a thousand years toppled to the ground with a tremor that could be heard and felt a mile away.

Two loggers use double-bit felling axes to make an undercut in a fir tree on Snoqualmie Pass near Seattle in 1940. The logger on the left stands on a flexible springboard notched into the tree that raises him to the level of his partner.

The felling of these age-old giant sequoias ended after lumbermen discovered that their wood, though highly resistant to rotting, was less well suited for construction purposes than that of western pines, coast redwoods, and Douglas firs.

It took a series of conflagrations in the forests of Washington and Oregon in the fall of 1902 to alert both lumber companies and the public to the danger of indiscriminate cutting. The fires started in clear-cut areas, but spread through 700,000 acres of valuable forest, claiming 35 lives in the process. They were among the first recorded fires to devastate the Northwest forests, but hardly the last; terrible blazes struck the same region in 1910, 1933, 1939, 1945, and 1951. The introduction during this period of the gasoline-powered chain saw, the logging truck, and the belted-tread tractor made it possible to cut and clear trees in areas previously inaccessible. Yet the great fires of the early 1900's helped generate support for policies of protection and conservation that eventually reversed several centuries of laissez-faire attitudes and brought about a deeper and more realistic appreciation of the forests of North America. ★

A once-towering fir, felled by a logger's chainsaw (*right*), crashes through a stand of commercially owned timber. A lonely logger (*opposite*) prepares to top a Noble fir in Washington's Cascade Range.

CHAPTER SIX

Trees–Present and Future

IF IT IS SOMETIMES hard to see the forest for the trees, the reverse is also true. According to recent estimates, there are 245 billion trees on the continent of North America—a daunting number. The fact that the total averages out to roughly 900 trees for every inhabitant brings it a little closer to home. But 900 trees is still a *statistical* forest, an abstraction far removed from the down-to-earth specifics of leaf, trunk, and root.

To make sense out of this census we have to keep in mind the diverse reality behind the numbers—a reality that stretches from a stand of giant sequoias rising from a fog-bound hillside overlooking the Pacific Ocean to a clump of fan-leaved ginkgos thriving in the soot and smog of a downtown city park; from a grove of dusty cottonwoods huddled around a muddy water hole on a ranch in the Southwest to a row of stricken elms struggling through one more summer along a New England main street; from the spindly oaks and maples peeping over the fences of a raw new subdivision to the geometrically spaced ranks of Scotch pines in a Christmas tree plantation waiting for the next holiday season to roll around.

What all these different sites and species have in common is that someone has found them to be valuable in one

A lone tree breaches the symmetry of a plowed Wisconsin field (*above*). Why the tree has survived the ax and the plow is a secret known only to the farmer who spared it.

The splendor of high timber hardly gets better than the view toward The Garden Wall from Going-to-Sun Road (*opposite*), a winding, 50-mile highway that spans the Continental Divide in Waterton/Glacier International Peace Park, bridging British Columbia, Alberta, and Montana.

way or another. The very concept of "value" as applied to trees has been greatly broadened in this century. During the second half of the 19th century, unrestricted exploitation of North America's forests led to the fear—at least on the part of a few farsighted preservationists—of a potential "timber famine."

Faced with the prospect of living in a world without trees, a broad coalition of concerned citizens began agitating for new laws and new attitudes; they argued that there would be enough trees to go around, for all purposes, if only our forests were managed on a rational, scientific basis. This save-the-forest crusade was the beginning of the modern environmental movement. Among its first fruits was a continent-wide network of national parks and national forests, in which trees were viewed not just as isolated economic assets but as integral parts of a complex whole we now call the ecosystem.

The once-controversial assertion of the save-the-forest crusaders—that despoiling the environment is bad for the soul, bad for the body, and bad for the pocketbook—is now universally accepted, at least in principle. Forest management today is a full-fledged professional discipline, practiced by governments and private industry alike. No one seriously doubts the wisdom of treating trees as a renewable resource. After more than 3 centuries of unrelenting exploitation, we have begun to replenish the stock of trees in North America. Each year, despite expanding markets for forest products, the total of new growth on the continent exceeds the number of trees removed by as much as a third.

Some of this new growth occurs naturally, as abandoned farms and other types of open land are colonized by seedlings that serve as the vanguard of new forests. But the vast majority of new growth comes from tree-planting programs. More than 4 million acres are planted with seedling trees every year in the United States and Canada.

A modern tree farm, like this one under cultivation in northern California, is more like a field of corn destined for harvest than a forest. Ninety-five percent of the ancient spruce-fir-hemlock forests of the Pacific Northwest have been felled, most replaced with second-growth woodlands, and a small percentage with tree farms.

A Forest Service employee carries out an increasingly essential routine, planting a seedling pine on a recent burn-over in the remote reaches of federally owned forest in Idaho.

Fully one-tenth of the timberland in North America has been reseeded in this manner. Most of this planting is carried out by private industry, often with government incentives. On commercial tree plantations mechanized planters can put a thousand seedlings in the ground in an hour, at a cost of $100 to $200 an acre. Of each thousand seedlings planted, however, only about 20 percent survive to maturity. Tree plantations are especially prevalent in the South, where such fast-growing conifers as loblolly and slash pine, destined for the sawmill or pulp mill, can be profitably harvested after 15 or 20 years.

At the other end of the scale are the trees planted, one by one, by individuals who, usually unknowingly, are following in the footsteps of Johnny Appleseed. Even homeowners concerned with enhancing the present value of their homes are likely to be awed by the realization that the tree planted today may outlive them. Two thousand years ago the Roman orator Cicero noted that those who plant trees benefit not just themselves but succeeding generations. Is it any wonder that so many people get sentimental about "their" trees? Gardeners may pull up flower beds and even rose bushes without a second thought, but

Extent of North American Old-Growth Forests

○ Old growth
○ New growth

1620-1820

1850

1880

1920

1620-1820
The first two centuries of colonization had almost no effect on the vast forests blanketing the continent. A small population, concentrated along the coasts and inland rivers, barely touched the fringes of old-growth forest. Even westward expansion that started in the late 1700's and early 1800's left the wilderness largely untouched and unspoiled.

1850
Industry and agriculture blossomed in the first half of the 19th Century. As settlers moved across the Appalachians, into the Great Lakes and Mississippi basins, and up the West Coast, demand soared for farmland and timber. By 1850, more than 100 million acres of old-growth forest had been cut or burned off in New England, the Southeast, the Great Lakes region and along Canada's St. Lawrence River.

1880
As immigration and westward expansion surged after the American Civil War, railroads, steel plows, and mechanical harvesters swept over the land. Logging moved into the Appalachians and the Northwest, leveling another 125 million acres of forests. Coal replaced wood as a primary fuel, and the difficulty of transportation spared remote stands of virgin hard- and softwoods.

1920
The population of the U.S. and Canada topped 100 million, and nearly half the primal old-growth forest was gone. The southeastern U.S. had been virtually clear cut. While the timber trade intensified in the Pacific Northwest and British Columbia, forests in the Northeast, mid-Atlantic and Great Lakes regions began to return. Protective conservation laws were enacted.

the decision to cut down a tree, even one that is old and sickly and in the wrong place, is never made lightly.

Scientific research has confirmed the age-old intuition that trees are good for the environment. The most obvious benefit is shade. Any overheated dog or cat can appreciate the relief provided by a mature shade tree on a sunny day. While all living things need sunlight, too much of it can be oppressive, even damaging to animal life. The densest foliage, and so the densest shade, is found under the broad leaves of deciduous trees like oaks and maples. The narrower, compound leaves of trees like willows and mimosa provide a dappled shade, which may be more beneficial to lawns and garden plants. By cooling the surrounding air, they also reduce the demand for air-conditioning in nearby homes—which translates into reduced emissions of carbon dioxide from oil- or coal-fired electrical generators.

Studies in California's scorching inland valleys show that walls of houses shaded by trees are generally 15 degrees cooler than comparable unshaded walls. To the

Planting a tree (*left*) calls for planning and forethought. Before making a commitment to the tree's future, the wise consumer learns about a tree's characteristics and growth habit from an agricultural extension service or a nursery professional.

The large, simple leaves of an American chestnut provide welcome shade for a father and daughter swinging in its dense shadow. This majestic tree in Sherwood, Oregon—the largest known chestnut in the United States—is one of the few not ravaged by the dreaded chestnut blight.

owner of an air-conditioned house, this difference translates into significant savings in monthly electrical bills. Three good-sized trees placed around the west and south sides of a house in the temperate zone can lower the air-conditioning costs by anywhere from 10 to 50 percent. According to some estimates, a concerted effort to take advantage of the cooling properties of trees will save more than $2 billion a year in energy bills.

Evergreen trees planted in the right places can also have a significant impact on energy use in winter. In regions of North America subject to strong winds, houses screened by windbreaks of evergreens can be heated to comfortable temperatures with 25 percent less fuel than unprotected houses.

In addition to providing shade and cooling through evaporation, trees filter noise, dust, and chemical pollutants from the air. Curiously enough, one of the greatest benefits that trees can provide for human populations is being realized by extending and improving what today's foresters call the "urban forest." This includes all the trees in city parks as well as all the trees planted along city streets and highways, and the trees in people's yards. The extent of this forest is surprising. About one-third of the surface area of the average city is given over to streets and structures; the rest is covered by grass and trees.

The concept of a tree-lined town common or village green has a long ancestry, but one of North America's first public parks planned and created as a unified project was New York City's Central Park. Designed by landscape architects Frederick Law Olmsted and Calvert Vaux in the late 1800's, its inspiration came from the picturesque gardens of European estates and reflected the romantic landscape paintings of the Hudson River School, a popular artistic movement of the mid 1800's.

The site for the park was an 843-acre rectangle in the middle of Manhattan Island. It had once been forested, but the trees were long gone. Since the soil was too poor for farming, the area had been used as common pasture and eventually deteriorated into a kind of wasteland on the outskirts of the city, dotted with garbage dumps and squatters' shacks.

To transform this wasteland into a semblance of its original appearance, with rolling hills, grassy meadows, and woody thickets, laborers moved mountains of earth and rock, and planted thousands of trees. The result of

New York City's Central Park (*left*) is an island of green where trees serve as counterpoints to skyscraping concrete and glass. Created by landscape architects Frederick Law Olmsted and Calvert Vaux, the park countered relentless urban mechanization with open space, plenteous trees, and Thomas Jefferson's vision of rural simplicity.

The deep-seated human urge for trees cannot be denied. Even where brick, concrete, and asphalt force out real trees (*above*), people will find ways to keep them in their collective consciousness.

In a city long since stripped of its old-growth trees, architects find ways to plant new ones. Reflected in steel and glass, leafy Bradford pear trees grace the terraced heights of Trump Tower along Manhattan's Fifth Avenue (*right*).

"We thought of New York as a hemlock forest that had been overlogged."

— Murray Gell-Mann

While all living plants add oxygen to the air, not even the hardiest can withstand the extreme assaults of chemical pollutants. Industrial fumes and auto exhaust in a city like Los Angeles (*left*) slowly stifle urban trees, robbing city dwellers of their life-giving function.

Orange trees, palms, and other specimen trees flourish year round in Sun City, Arizona (*above*), an irrigated oasis in one of the nation's most arid places. Besides offering comfort for the eyes and soul, such trees help to moderate the extreme desert temperature.

Olmsted's vision was a man-made oasis in a setting of steel and stone, a green respite for the eye, a haven of cool breezes and open spaces that has since been acclaimed as "the city's lung" and imitated in other cities throughout the continent.

In recent years, however, hard-pressed city governments have cut back spending on tree planting and maintenance, with predictable results. Compared to their country cousins, city trees have predictably short life spans. Trees on downtown streets, which share the least hospitable surroundings, live an average of only 13 years. One problem is the soil, which may be so compacted that air and water—both vital requirements for the tree's survival—are literally squeezed out. In addition, city soil is often contaminated with salt, lime leached from building foundations, as well as a noxious brew of petroleum and other potentially harmful wastes.

A recent survey of 20 cities found healthy trees in fewer than half of the planting spaces available. Dead trees are not being replaced; in some cities they are not even removed until they become a hazard to pedestrians and motorists. Just to halt the decline of the urban forest would require planting 4 times as many trees each year as current plans call for, in cities already struggling to manage their over-extended budgets.

And in a number of cities, concerned citizens have been working to help restore the urban forest. Global ReLeaf, a program funded by the American Forestry Association, supports tree-planting efforts in both urban and rural areas. Inspired by this approach, a grass-roots organization in Portland, Oregon, brought together neighborhood groups, local businesses, and government agencies for a similar purpose. Called Friends of Trees, the coalition has planted hundreds of street trees and thousands of seedlings.

In Los Angeles, an organization called TreePeople got its start through the determination of a high-school student named Andy Lipkis. In 1970 Lipkis learned that the forest where he spent his summers outside the city was being slowly obliterated by industrial smog. Unable to reverse that process, he got together with some friends and decided to "save" an abandoned parking lot in town. "Instead of sitting around figuring out what to do for entertainment," he wrote later, "we swung picks at rock-hard ground and shoveled cow manure." The smog-tolerant trees they planted on the transformed lot are still flourishing, as is the organization. TreePeople remains active not only in tree planting but in a broad range of other ecologically motivated community projects aimed at repairing what Lipkis calls "an environmentally- and socially-damaged world."

Activism on behalf of tree preservation, such as this protest on Earth Day 1991 in Washington, D.C., has become a recognized part of the political process. Ultimately, the fate of the continent's forests rests in the hands of federal legislators.

Despite the increasing sophistication of ecological science, making informed decisions about the environment remains a daunting task. For example, it is clear that trees play a key role in regulating the amount of carbon dioxide in the atmosphere; yet evaluating the net impact of trees on carbon dioxide (CO_2) levels is not easy. Trees remove carbon dioxide from the air during photosynthesis and store the carbon in their tissues. When these same tissues burn or decompose, the carbon is released as carbon dioxide. Due in part to the burning of fossil fuels like coal and oil and the clearing and torching of vast areas of tropical forests, the amount of carbon dioxide in the Earth's atmosphere has more than quadrupled over the last half century.

This causes concern because carbon dioxide is the most important of the eight gases that contribute to the worldwide "greenhouse effect." The fear is that the so-called greenhouse gases will cause a buildup of heat within the 7-mile thick envelope of the Earth's atmosphere.

According to some experts, the greenhouse effect is already responsible for raising temperatures around the world. Eight of the hottest years of the 20th century were recorded in the late 1980's and early 1990's. If this trend continues, global warming could theoretically melt a large part of the polar ice caps, flooding low-lying coastal areas from Florida to Bangladesh and wiping out, according to some estimates, 15 percent of the Earth's existing species.

Not every scientist who has studied the greenhouse effect, however, believes that it is implicated in the current warming trend. Statistical variations are to be expected; the recent run of hotter-than-normal years may be followed by a cooler-than-normal period, as has happened in

North American Forests, 2000 A.D.

The map below shows the natural distribution of native trees, which has not changed significantly as new growth replaces old. Commercial and federal forest management, as well as heightened public awareness about conservation, have enabled extensive refor- estation on federal and privately owned land. Since the 1920's, nearly 150 million acres have been replanted or have been allowed to reforest themselves. Additional millions of acres have been designated as national parks, national forests and wildlife refuges in both the United States and Canada. Reversing a 300-year trend, per capita timber consump- tion has declined throughout the 20th centu- ry, mainly because rising lumber costs have made other products more competitive.

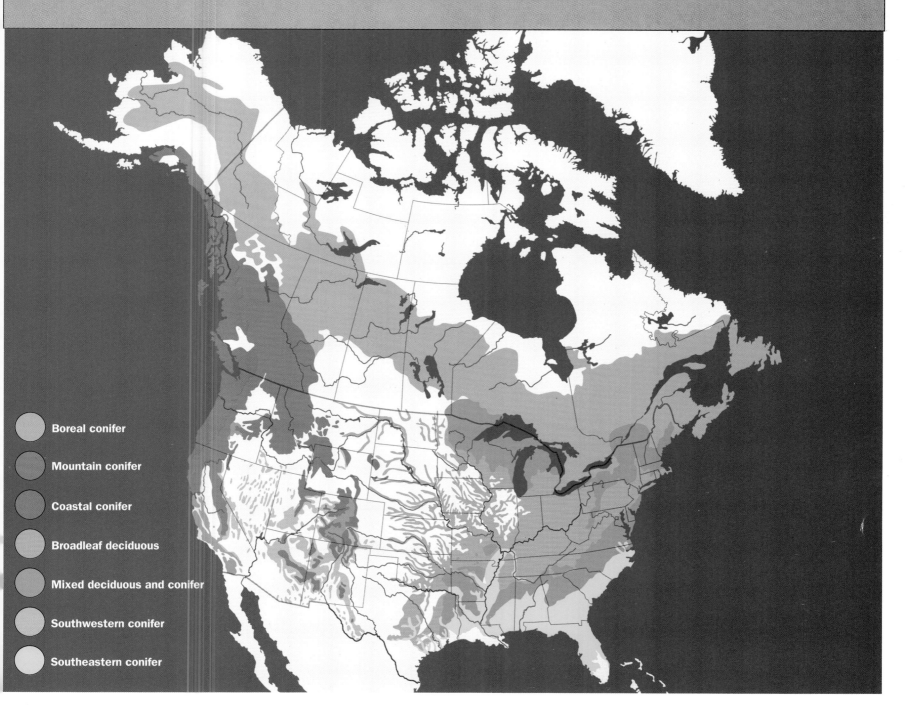

- Boreal conifer
- Mountain conifer
- Coastal conifer
- Broadleaf deciduous
- Mixed deciduous and conifer
- Southwestern conifer
- Southeastern conifer

"*The more highly developed our culture has become, the greater our appreciation of wilderness has grown.*"

—HOWARD ZAHNISER

the past. But no one doubts that further increases in greenhouse gases like carbon dioxide would pose a serious threat. Only two natural mechanisms are available for taking carbon dioxide out of the air. The oceans absorb some, but far more is removed by trees and other forms of plant life through photosynthesis.

Measurements of the impact of trees on atmospheric gases are difficult, even controversial: results vary by region, by the age of the trees, and by species—hardwoods, for example, tend to be richer in carbon than softwoods. But studies by Canadian researchers have confirmed that forests can be an important line of defense against global warming since they absorb and store significantly more molecular carbon, in the form of carbon dioxide, than they release each year.

A single tree can absorb as much as 26 pounds of carbon dioxide a year. The world currently generates some 5 to 7 billion tons of carbon dioxide annually. By preserving existing trees and by planting new trees on land that is now treeless, enormous amounts of carbon could be withdrawn from the atmosphere each year. Expanding the urban forest would have the greatest impact.

A tree standing alone is almost always a sign of human intervention, either in the planting or the sparing. The sight of a majestic specimen oak on an Ohio hilltop in spring is ample justification for either course of action.

The main reason, however, that people go to the trouble and expense of planting and maintaining specimen trees is the pleasure derived from looking at them. Deciduous trees that drop their leaves each autumn offer no protection against winter winds, but the natural calligraphy of their bare branches silhouetted against the sky can lift the heart on an overcast day. While beauty is certainly in the eye of the beholder, it would take a weary spirit not to respond to the unfolding each spring of new foliage from apparently lifeless wood.

Some trees, like cherries and magnolias, offer spectacular displays of blossoms in the spring; others, such as the holly and the Japanese maple, are prized for the distinctive shape and color of their foliage. And still others, like the

The Tree as Host

A healthy tree, whether deep in a forest or in a suburban yard, helps to support or sustain many kinds of life. In the growing season, it emits a steady supply of oxygen, which is essential for all forms of animal life.

Many animals are adapted to the annual growth cycles of broadleaf deciduous trees *(left)*. Insects find food in tree leaves, bark, and shoots; flowering trees also provide nourishment in the form of nectar. Many insect species have become adapted to living in specific trees, establishing a symbiotic relationship.

Birds not only nest in trees, but thrive on fruits and insects that they find there. Large mammals like deer eat fruit, nuts, bark, and leaves. Small mammals like squirrels, raccoons, and opossums live and raise their young in trees. Bees build hives on high limbs and in hollow trunks.

Fallen trees provide the ideal habitat for worms and insect larvae, and support other plant species like fungi, mosses, and lichens.

Gypsy moth larvae (*left*) began their invasion of North American hardwoods more than a century ago; in 1981 alone they defoliated 13 million acres of trees. Although they prefer aspen, poplar, and oak, experiments show them to have diverse tastes.

Engraved beneath the bark of a lodgepole pine (*above*) is the intricate yet deadly pattern of the lodgepole pine beetle. As they feed, the beetles eventually girdle the tree and block the flow of nutrients.

Combating arboreal pests by efficient aerial spraying (*right*) introduces another controversy about the safety of chemical incursions on other plants, wildlife, and human populations.

With the demise of the chestnuts, squirrels and other animals that had relied on these trees for food had nothing to eat but acorns—a far less dependable source since early-blooming oak trees are susceptible to frosts that can inhibit acorn production from year to year.

Hopes for restocking the streets and forests of North America with chestnut trees rest on attempts to introduce strains that have been exposed to the fungus and developed resistance to it. Efforts are also being made to hybridize American chestnuts with Asian varieties that resist the blight.

Dutch elm disease, first noted around 1930, has been even more devastating to the American white elm—a tree of no commercial value but one that has been cherished from early colonial days for its majestic beauty. Another fungal infestation, Dutch elm disease is spread by elm bark beetles. Since there is no known cure, infected trees must be felled and burned as soon as possible.

Other imported pests that have wreaked havoc among North American trees include the balsam woolly aphid, a wingless insect that attacks the Fraser fir forests of the Smokies. In the eastern part of the continent and moving steadily westward, the European gypsy moth has defoliated millions of acres of trees from Maine to Texas and into Canada. A more recent arrival is the Asian gypsy moth, which is spreading east from the Pacific coast.

Defending the continent's trees against invading pests and pathogens is just one of the missions of modern tree and forest management. Besides combating the tangible threats of fire and disease, foresters are engaged in the larger battle against such global challenges as acid rain. To complicate matters, these challenges are interrelated in ways not fully understood.

A case in point is fire protection. In the early years of this century, following a devastating series of blazes that swept through millions of acres of timberland in the West, a fire-fighting effort was organized by the Forest Service on a national scale. Symbolized by Smokey the Bear warning campers, "Only *you* can prevent forest fires," this effort involved hiring legions of fire-spotters, constructing networks of mountaintop lookout stations, bulldozing firebreaks and access roads through remote forestlands, and organizing quick-response teams ready on short notice to be ferried to blazes by trucks, airplanes, and helicopters.

The cooperative effort succeeded in cutting losses due to fire from a high of 53 million acres in 1931 to fewer than 5 million. Without this success, the net increase in trees recorded throughout North America in the past 50 years would have been impossible. Yet some unexpected consequences of this fire-fighting effort placed large forest tracts in peril until modern-day foresters rediscovered what American Indians had long known: that periodic fires are *good* for the forest.

When a disastrous fire in 1955 threatened a cherished grove of giant sequoias in California, observers noted that the flames were fed by dead wood and highly combustible debris that had accumulated on the forest floor over years of fire suppression. This matted debris had prevented the diminutive seeds of the giant trees from making contact with bare soil—a prerequisite to their germination. By contrast, periodic low-level fires ignited by lightning strikes not only keep the ground free of combustible litter but actually induce the sequoia cones to open and release their seeds for germination.

Even the great height of the sequoias can be seen as an adaptation to fire that gives them a competitive edge over the white pines that share their habitat. Occasional blazes set by lightning kill off nearby pines without pushing flames high enough to damage the sequoias' food-producing foliage, which typically begins 75 to 100 feet above the forest floor. And mature sequoias, with their trunks insulated with thick, spongy, tannin-rich bark, have evolved to withstand even the most intense fires.

While the public typically reacts with horror to media accounts of raging wildfires, research shows that forests go through natural fire cycles measured in centuries. Tree-ring studies, for example, suggest that lodgepole pines and giant sequoias have evolved with fire being part of their normal life process; examining the scars left in wood by fires of the past, researchers have concluded that renewal of the lodgepole forest requires one major burn every 300 years or so. The piney woods of the southeastern United States may also owe their existence to fire. Without periodic blazes, shade-tolerant hardwoods soon begin to intrude on stands of commercially valuable softwood species like the longleaf pine.

Periodic fires are necessary to remove nutrients from standing trees and return them to the earth, where they become available to the root systems of new trees. This is especially important in thin soils on high slopes. In the absence of fire, the sparse nutrients lie locked in forest litter and duff. Fire not only releases nutrients to the soil, it opens the forest canopy overhead to sunlight.

Fire can also control insect infestations, such as those caused by larvae of the mountain pine beetle. Feeding on the inner bark of a lodgepole pine, these larvae eventually girdle the tree and block the flow of nutrients through the

> "To plant a pine, one need
> be neither God nor poet, one need only
> to own a shovel."
>
> — JOHN MUIR

trunk. Eventually the trees die, their strangled foliage appearing as patches of orange in an otherwise evergreen landscape.

These open patches, whether caused by diseased trees or by fires, make temporary openings in the tree cover that actually benefit a variety of wildlife and enhance the diversity of the predominantly pine forest. When the dead trees burn during periodic outbreaks of fire, the heat kills off great numbers of beetles and larvae, providing a natural, self-regulating method of population control.

One of the unwanted consequences of overzealous fire suppression in the West has been the transformation of two insect pests, the spruce budworm and the Douglas-fir bark beetle, from intermittent nuisances into an endemic plague. Despite their names, the two species actually attack a broad range of conifers, working in tandem to complete the systematic destruction of trees.

With fire towers now largely replaced by surveillance satellites, today's policy is to allow natural fires to burn under close observation and to set "prescribed" fires under carefully controlled conditions. In Florida's

Highrock Lookout on Washington State's Mount Rainier, once a fire-spotting station, affords splendid views of the surrounding forest. Today, satellite scanning has made the need for fire spotters in such remote places largely obsolete.

Among the trees introduced to North America in the 1700's by French botanist François Michaux, the ginkgo (*opposite*) may be the most unusual. An evolutionary survivor from the early Carboniferous era 200 million years ago, the ginkgo is one of the few trees that thrive in the polluted air of industrial cities.

Acid rain damage to evergreens on Clingman's Dome, North Carolina, gives new meaning to the name Smoky Mountains. Smoke-borne sulfuric acid from copper smelters was noticed in Tennessee in 1865 and in British Columbia in 1896, and has since become an increasing menace to wild places.

Apalachicola National Forest, to keep savanna lands open and to reduce the growth of saw palmettos that would otherwise crowd out other species, prescribed burns are carried out every 3 to 5 years. A natural cycle of wildfire that sweeps Florida's Everglades every 3 to 7 years has been found to maintain the pineries there against competition from hardwoods. The judicious use of fire as a tool of forest management has markedly improved the health of California's sequoia groves and other stands of protected trees.

Maintaining a dynamic balance between fire, insect pests, and the ups and downs of climatic cycles is made even more difficult by assaults on trees that cross international borders. One such assault is acid rain. When wood and fossil fuels burn, the products of combustion contain chemicals that turn into dilute sulfuric or nitric acid on contact with water vapor. Any precipitation that contains a heavy dose of these corrosive compounds is called acid rain—whether it reaches the ground as snow, sleet, hail, or fog.

Some acid rain occurs naturally, as the result of forest fires and volcanic eruptions. But emissions from automobile tailpipes and factory smokestacks have raised concentrations of acid rain to previously unheard-of levels all over North America, poisoning fish, birds, and other wildlife and affecting large areas of forest. There are some days in the Great Smoky Mountains of North Carolina and Tennessee when the rain gently pattering on the leaves has an effect comparable to sprinkling house plants with lemon juice instead of with tap water.

Conifer trees are especially vulnerable to acid rain. Affected conifers produce fewer and fewer needles, and those produced often turn yellow and drop prematurely. Despite their weakened condition, dying trees may put out an abundance of cones as if trying to reproduce themselves before their demise. Local treatment with lime, which neutralizes acidity, may restore some trees to health. But acid rain is not just a localized problem. Although most of it is generated in industrialized areas and in urban centers where large numbers of people drive cars, even a mild breeze can propel an acidic cloud 200 miles in a day, until atmospheric conditions trigger rain, snow, sleet, and fog containing anywhere from 10 to 1,000 times the normal concentration of acid.

The international nature of the acid-rain problem in North America was acknowledged in 1979, when representatives of the United States and Canada called for a joint 10-year program to cut in half the level of acid-forming pollutants in the atmosphere. The potential benefits of this international effort are promising, but in the meantime millions of tons of

A man-made mountain of softwood logs feeds a pulpmill near Baie Verte, Newfoundland. A professionally managed renewable resource, pulpwood provides essential paper and related products to consumers across the continent.

acid pollution still blow across the northern border of the United States into Canada, causing Canadian sugar maples drenched in acid rain to cease producing syrup. Ultimately, the only way to control such far-reaching pollution is at its source, through stringently enforced emission controls for automobiles and industries.

Poet Walt Whitman once cautioned that too much knowledge about "birds and trees and flowers" could interfere with our innocent enjoyment of nature. But in this day and age, the danger usually comes from too little knowledge. If urban tree planting programs are ultimately going to succeed, the selection of seedlings must take into account the reality of local pollutants.

One tree that handles all kinds of urban pollution well is the ginkgo, also known as the maidenhair tree. Surprisingly, this tree is a living fossil; it is the only representative of a once widespread group of gymnosperms that flourished some 200 million years ago. The ginkgo itself is no longer found growing wild; it avoided extinction only because it was kept under cultivation in Buddhist temple gardens in China and Japan many centuries ago.

While most gymnosperms, like pines and spruces, cannot long tolerate polluted air in major urban centers, the ginkgo is unaffected. It is also fungus- and insect-resistant, tolerates cold weather as far north as Minnesota, and thrives even in poor soil, so long as there is room above and below ground to accommodate its spreading habit.

While individuals affect the environment by planting trees one at a time, it is also true that North America remains both the world's largest supplier and the world's largest consumer of wood and wood products. The average North American uses more than 600 pounds of paper products every year—the equivalent of a 100-foot-tall tree. This does not take into account the consumption of wood for its own sake.

Meeting the needs of a rising population without depleting the continent's stock of trees will require ever more efficient forest management. In Canada, which contains 10 percent of the world's forestland, a cooperative endeavor initiated in 1981 by federal and provincial governments has demonstrated some of the benefits, as well as the difficulties, of scientific forest management.

Canadian foresters each year calculate the volume of wood that can be harvested without threatening the sustainability of the nation's forest resources. This figure, the annual allowable cut, takes into account such intangible factors as the need to maintain wilderness areas. While the annual harvest has increased steadily over the last 2 decades, it remains well within the guidelines set to ensure the productive capacity of Canadian forests.

North America's forests are now maintained, in part, by a vigorous program of replanting and reseeding. In 1990 alone nearly 1 billion trees were planted in Canada and nearly twice that number in the United States. Not all these trees will grow to maturity, of course. And many environmentalists warn against equating an artificially planted tree farm with the natural growth it replaces. By design, tree farms lack the diversity of vegetation and wildlife that marks old-growth forests. Since the great majority of trees are of the same age and the same species, tree farms are more susceptible to opportunistic insect pests and diseases that can sweep through large areas before remedial steps can be taken.

The simplest, and certainly the least expensive, way to conserve forests is to cut down fewer trees. For this reason innovations have been embraced that make wood-intensive manufacturing processes more efficient. The goal is to turn out the same finished product with less wood. Canada's pulp and paper industry offers an encouraging model. While production has doubled over the last 30 years, the burden on forestland has been reduced by a quiet revolution in technology. In the 1960's sawdust and other "wastes" from

sawmilling—which were historically discarded or burned—made up 25 percent of the raw fibers used in pulp and paper production; by the end of the 1980's this figure had more than doubled. In addition, new pulping processes make possible across-the-board improvements in fiber recovery of another 15 percent. As Canada phases out its older and smaller mills, the efficiency of its pulp and paper industry should continue to increase.

Further savings in felled trees are being realized by the use of recycled paper. The bulk of Canada's output of newsprint ends up in the United States, where more and more states are passing laws that require newsprint to contain a certain percentage of recycled fibers from old newspapers. Canadian manufacturers must import old newspapers from the United States to assure their supply and install special de-inking machines to prepare the newspapers for processing. The recycling laws were actually passed to lessen the burden on landfills in U.S. population centers; their effect on Canadian forests is a beneficial by-product common to many environmental initiatives.

A continuing source of controversy is the practice of clear-cutting, or felling all the trees in a designated tract. Some environmentalists oppose clear-cutting on principle because it is patently "unnatural" and leaves ugly scars on the land that take years to heal. Because of the combustible slash left behind and because of the drying effects of sun and wind, clear-cut land is also prone to fires.

But managers of wood products companies compare the effects of clear-cutting to the positive effects of wildfires. They point out that reforestation of species like Douglas fir, whose seedlings thrive in open sun, is actually speeded by a modified form of clear-cutting in which clear-cut strips of land are alternated with unlogged stands of timber. The trees left standing stabilize the soil, moderate the effects of sun and wind, and provide a source of seeds for the next crop, while supplying local wildlife with food and space for dens and nests. Since many species of hardwood trees will sprout naturally from stumps, clear-cut stands of hardwood—so goes the argument—can be expected to regenerate themselves spontaneously in time.

Planting a tree is an act of faith in the future. On

Snowshoers under soaring redwoods in Yosemite National Park leave only their tracks behind them. National parks and forests are committed to a dual-use policy: conserving natural resources while offering recreational opportunities to millions.

the evidence, it appears that many people still believe in "tomorrow." Arbor Day, the brainchild of Nebraska farmer and newspaperman J. Sterling Morton in the late 19th century, is now observed with tree-planting ceremonies throughout the world. The National Arbor Day Foundation, with a dues-paying membership of 800,000, calls itself the world's largest tree-planting environmental organization. Its projects range from the planting of maples, pears, and ginkgos in Brooklyn, New York, to the beautification of Macon, Georgia, with 69,000 cherry trees raised from donated cuttings and distributed free to interested homeowners.

On a larger scale, the American Tree Farm System, funded by the forest products industry, mobilizes professional foresters to teach private landowners to manage and maintain their tree-covered property using the latest scientific methods. The Tree Farm System, with locations in all 50 states, now covers a combined area bigger than the total land mass of Japan.

The extraordinary capacity of forestland to restore itself, given sufficient time, is exemplified by New York State's Adirondack Park and Preserve, which was established in 1892. Although an easy half-day's drive from New York City, the park is larger than Yellowstone, Yosemite, Grand Canyon, and Olympic national parks combined, yet is easily accessible to millions in the Boston–Washington corridor.

The outer limits of the Adirondacks are defined by a "blue line" that encloses 9,400 square miles designat-

ed as mixed-use land. Within the park itself, development is controlled by a crazy quilt of public and private jurisdictions. Some of these tracts have been given over to clusters of vacation homes; others are designated "forever wild" by the state constitution.

The park's boundaries were fixed in 1894, by which time much of the land was despoiled. Still, by the turn of the century the Adirondacks served as a summer playground for America's wealthy elite—the Rockefellers and Vanderbilts and Morgans—who arrived from stifling Eastern cities with armies of servants to "rough it" in oversized log cabins called "great camps." The once-abundant beavers, wolves, wolverines, moose, lynx, and cougars were gone. Even the prolific white-tailed deer were in severe decline.

Since then, an unending battle has been waged over what kinds of activities should be allowed within the park. Today, a thousand new homes a year are being built; current regulations allow for 400,000 in all. Elsewhere, logging companies are permitted to engage in clear-cutting. Yet more than two-fifths of the land remains wilderness; white-tailed deer are everywhere, the moose have returned, and 15,000 beavers are now trapped annually. The greatest immediate threat to the park is acknowledged not to be logging but acid rain; hundreds of lakes have been poisoned by fallout from factory smokestacks a thousand miles to the west. The ultimate survival of this rich, albeit largely second-growth, wilderness is now recognized as a major test case for environmentalists facing the 21st century.

Seedling firs replanted on an Oregon tree farm (*right*) are destined for commercial use in the 21st century. In the meantime, they perform a small but essential role in maintaining global ecological balance.

Lake Colden (*opposite*) nourishes the Flowed Land region near Algonquin Peak in Adirondack Park, New York. Formerly a haven for brook-trout fishing, acid rain has rendered the lake fishless since the early 1960's.

> *"I like trees because they seem more resigned to the way they have to live than other things do."*
>
> — WILLA CATHER

From the beginning of history, trees have inspired respect, admiration, emulation, and reverence. "In the woods," wrote Thoreau, "we return to reason and faith." Now modern science has confirmed that the fate of human beings and the fate of trees are intimately connected. Trees created, and continue to maintain, the breathable atmosphere we need to live. The legacy that has been handed down to us in the forests of North America can only be appreciated as a dynamic system of give and take that functions like some macro-organism of wondrous complexity. But the give and take does not stop at the forest's edge. It encompasses the trees we plant in our backyards and on the streets of our cities. We may speak of a particular tree as "our" tree; but the closer we look, the clearer it becomes that the relationship between people and trees is reciprocal and that it extends far beyond our backyard or our neighborhood.

Trees affect our living space just as we affect theirs. The oxygen we breathe in is the waste product of some tree's photosynthesis. The carbon dioxide we breathe out is the raw material for some tree's new growth. For a true picture of this interrelationship, we have to see ourselves and our trees—all trees—as sharing a single environment, indivisible and without boundaries. To know something about trees—about even one tree—is to know something important, something fundamental, something profound about the nature of the world and our place in it. ❧

A solitary walker on a tree-lined country road exemplifies a principle: a healthy environment is enduring testimony to the benefits of peaceful coexistence with the natural world.

Acacia (*Acacia*)

Acacia is a tropical and subtropical group of some 1,000 species, ranging from 5-foot shrubs to 90-foot trees. These trees have round to flat-topped crowns and feathery, usually evergreen leaves, often with a silvery cast. Fuzzy clusters of fragrant yellow flowers blossom in spring and are followed by dry pods. Acacias are fast-growing and may sprout 4 feet or more in a year. They are fine ornamentals and are often used as street or accent trees. They require ample water, full sun, and a warm, dry climate. Cool summer nights and relatively dry winters are best for flowering.

Sweet acacia (*Acacia farnesiana*) is a shrubby tree that may grow to 10 feet in height. It has thorny branches bearing compound leaves composed of tiny leaflets less than $1/2$ inch long. Bright golden-yellow flower clusters blossom very early in spring. Although it is a North American native, sweet acacia is cultivated in France, where its fragrant floral oils are in demand by the perfume industry. Sweet acacia also is cultivated and naturalized throughout the tropics. In the wild, its seeds are an important food source for large

The trees described in this guide represent a cross section of the many types of trees found throughout the United States, Canada, and Mexico. Some are native to North America, and others are well-established imports. Some are listed because they fill an ecological niche, others because of their economic, historical, or cultural significance.

Entries begin with the common name of the tree, followed by the scientific name of the genus to which it belongs and a general description of the genus. Detailed information is then given about one or more species within each genus.

birds. In North America sweet acacia is encountered in Florida, Louisiana, and California.

Alder (*Alnus*)

Alders are deciduous large shrubs or trees reaching 40 to 70 feet high, and sometimes over 100 feet. In spring their flowers emerge from delicate hanging clusters called catkins and are followed by toothed leaves and small conelike fruits. Three features of alders place them firmly among the species of great value to forest ecology: (1) They are fast growing and are therefore important pioneer species that fill in quickly to recover land after burning or logging; (2) they grow in dense thickets and so are useful in erosion control; (3) their roots bear nodules that house nitrogen-fixing bacteria, which improve the fertility of the soil by adding valuable nitrogen, thus helping to make the area more habitable for their environmental successors. Alders grow in full sun or partial shade, and thrive in wet or moist soil.

Red alder, or **Oregon alder,** (*Alnus rubra*) has a round crown and spreading, often drooping branches. Egg-shaped leaves are some 6 inches long and 2 inches wide, with coarsely toothed margins. This species prefers wet areas along rivers, streams, ponds, and swamps, where it often forms dense thickets.

The red alder is one of the most prominent broadleaf trees in the Pacific Northwest and is the single most important hardwood in that region. The tree may provide logs as much as 30 inches in diameter. The lumber is whitish when cut and light reddish brown when dry. Because it is lightweight and soft but strong, it is widely used for inexpensive furniture, cabinetwork, pulp, and woodenware. Alder wood withstands constant wetting and drying, and so has been used in the construction of canal locks and bulkheads.

Apple and Crabapple (*Malus*)

Apples, crabapples, and pears are regarded by many botanists as members of the same genus, *Malus*, while others separate the pears into their own genus, *Pyrus*. Apples and crabapples are ornamental or fruit-bearing trees that grow 15 to 65 feet tall, with rounded crowns. They produce abundant clusters of fragrant white to rosy-pink flowers, and

Sweet acacia (*Acacia farnesiana*)

Red alder (*Alnus rubra*)

green, yellow, orange, or red fruit. Native species of crabapples have spines on their branches and usually bear apples less than 2 inches across.

The **common cultivated apple** (*Malus pumila* and its hybrids) is now naturalized over much of North America. It grows up to 40 feet tall, with a short trunk and stout branches. Dark green leaves have fine teeth along the margins and a fuzzy underside. Flowers are on fuzzy stalks and are 1 to 3 inches across. The apple fruit is 1 to 3 inches in diameter. Apples are considered to be one of the oldest cultivated fruits. It is believed that the first apple tree was brought to North America by John Endicott, one of the early governors of the Massachusetts Bay Colony. Today the annual harvest of apples in the United States is about 239 million bushels, and half of this total is produced by Washington State.

The **southern crabapple,** or **narrowleaf crabapple,** (*Malus angustifolia*) is a small tree with stout branches and cinnamon-colored bark. Its leaves are between 1 and 1½ inches long and only about ½ inch wide, being widest toward the base. Although they are hairy when they first unfold, the leaves become smooth, thick, glossy, and dark green. Flowers are fragrant and have a rosy-pink blush. The hard greenish fruits are about 1 inch across, with a very tart flavor. This species grows in coastal areas from Maryland to Texas. The fruit of the southern crabapple is eaten by whitetail deer, foxes, raccoons, skunks, squirrels, quail, turkeys, and small birds.

Crabapples gathered from the wild are used for making tangy jellies and cider. As cultivated plants, crabapples are the easiest to grow and most cold-hardy of all flowering fruit trees. They need full sun to flower and bear fruit, and do best in well-drained, moist, acid soil.

Araucaria (*Araucaria*)

Araucarias are native to the Southern Hemisphere. In North America they are used as ornamentals, both indoors and out. Of major interest are the monkey puzzle tree, native to South America, and the Norfolk Island pine of New Zealand. Both are tall, cone-shaped, evergreen conifers that grow to 70 feet or more, depending on the species. Araucarias have airy, spreading, whorled branches.

Monkey puzzle (*Araucaria araucana*) grows to 90 feet, with upward-reaching, twisted, ropelike branches. This tree often sprouts new stems from the roots near the base of its trunk. Its needles are large, sharp scales that cover the branches. As an ornamental, the monkey puzzle makes a bold landscape statement. It prefers full sun and moist but not soggy soil. In North America it is well-established along the west coast in British Columbia and the Olympic Peninsula in Washington State.

Norfolk Island pine (*Araucaria heterophylla*) grows to 70 feet or more, with branches in regular whorls. Its soft, bright green needles are about ½ inch long and overlap on the branches. Cones are almost round and 4 to 6 inches wide. Norfolk Island pine is grown outdoors in the southern United States and indoors elsewhere as a houseplant. It does best in partial shade and adapts to a variety of soil conditions.

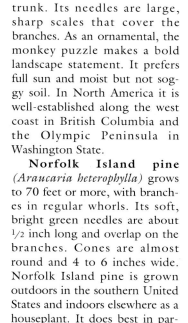

Arborvitae see Cedar

Ash (*Fraxinus*)

The ash is a fast-growing shrub or a round-crowned tree that grows as tall as 80 feet. Clusters of small flowers appear in early spring, followed by groups of paddle-shaped, winged seeds that are released in autumn. A single ash leaf is composed of one to five pairs of leaflets along a central stalk and one leaflet at the end. Ashes are excellent shade trees, and most species are adaptable to a variety of conditions if they get full sun.

White ash (*Fraxinus americana*) grows 50 to 80 feet tall. Its leaves usually are composed of seven leaflets; each leaflet is 2½ to 6 inches long and 1½ to 3 inches wide and broadest near the base or middle. Foliage of the white ash turns orange to reddish purple in the fall. The narrow, winged seeds are 1 to 2½ inches long and hang in dense clusters.

White ash is a valuable timber tree. The wood is strong, pliant, resilient, and lightweight. It is popular for sporting goods, such as hockey sticks, baseball bats, skis, oars, and tennis rackets, as well as for tool handles, furniture, and paneling. Quarter-sawn

Common cultivated apple
(*Malus pumila*)

Monkey puzzle
(*Araucaria araucana*)

Norfolk Island pine
(*Araucaria heterophylla*)

White ash (*Fraxinus americana*)

boards have a fine figure that is popular as a veneer.

Aspen see Poplar

Avocado see Persea

Azalea see Rhododendron

Basswood see Linden

Bayberry *(Myrica)*

Bayberries are shrubs or small trees with leathery, paddle-shaped, aromatic leaves. Their tiny round berries have a waxlike outer coating and contain a nut. Bayberry wax is used to make scented candles and soap.

Pacific bayberry *(Myrica californica)* is a shrub or tree with multiple trunks, growing up to 25 feet tall. Its glossy, bright green leaves are 2 to 4 inches long, and its berries are dark purple in color. The berries are consumed by many birds but are especially important to band-tailed pigeons. The Pacific bayberry grows along the Pacific coast from Washington to southern California.

Southern bayberry, or **wax myrtle,** *(Myrica cerifera)* is a shrub or tree growing as tall as 40 feet. Its foliage is yellowish green above and pale on the lower surface, with dots of resin on both the upper and lower surfaces. The pale blue berries appear in the autumn and serve as a minor food source for various birds. Southern bayberry is found in wet, sandy soil in the coastal plain of the southeastern United States.

Beech *(Fagus)*

Beeches are noble deciduous trees related to chestnuts and oaks. They grow 50 to 100 feet tall, with dense, rounded crowns and smooth pewter-colored bark. The unusual bark has tempted generations of romantics to carve initials and messages on it. Spring flowers are followed by small, triangular nuts enclosed in prickly, burrlike husks. As ornamentals, beeches are spectacular shade and specimen trees that do best in full sun and moist, well-drained acid soil.

The **American beech** *(Fagus grandifolia)* grows 50 to 70 feet or taller, with a short trunk, wide-spreading crown, and conspicuous surface roots. Young trees often sprout directly from the spreading roots of mature trees. The leaves are sharply toothed and grow 2 to 6 inches long. The male flowers are clustered into fuzzy green balls on a hanging stalk, while the female flowers grow singly or in pairs on short, thick stalks. In autumn the foliage turns golden-copper as the nuts mature and drop to the ground. American beech is widespread from southern Ontario across the eastern half of the United States. In the wild, American beech almost always grows in close association with Canadian hemlock, since both trees thrive in similar conditions. The seeds of the American beech, called beechnuts, are readily consumed by game birds and by mammals such as squirrels, raccoons, chipmunks, and bears. An American beech tree may live to be 300 to 400 years old.

Birch *(Betula)*

The birch is a deciduous tree that grows 40 to 100 feet tall, with an open crown. It has slender branches and double-toothed leaves that turn yellow in the fall. The thin bark peels away from the trunk in some species; it varies in color from white, silver, and yellowish or reddish brown to near black, and is distinguished by its characteristic, large, lens-shaped pores. Minute flowers in catkins are characteristic of birch and depend on the wind for pollination. Typically, these trees blossom in early spring before the leaves emerge; this allows complete exposure of their flowers to air currents that carry pollen. The tiny windblown seeds provide food for small animals. The trees themselves help to sustain some of the larger mammals through the cold, barren months of winter: moose and deer browse on the twigs in winter, while beavers feed on the inner bark. These fast-growing trees quickly become established after fire or logging has cleared an area. Most birches begin flowering at about 10 to 15 years of age; their normal life span is less than 150 years. Birches may be planted for shade or naturalizing and thrive in full sun and moist, cool soil. Yellow, sweet, and paper birches provide hardwood lumber for furniture, wood veneers, and plywood.

Paper birch *(Betula papyrifera)*, also known as canoe or white birch, grows to a height of 50 feet and may have single or multiple trunks. The striking white bark peels off in sheets. The leaves are 2 to 5 inches long, triangular to egg-shaped, with irregularly toothed margins. Paper birch was used by the Chippewas and other North

Southern bayberry *(Myrica cerifera)*

American beech *(Fagus grandifolia)*

Paper birch *(Betula papyrifera)*

American Indians to make their famous traditional birchbark canoes. A finished canoe light enough to be carried by one person could transport more than 1000 pounds.

Yellow birch *(Betula alleghaniensis)* grows 30 to 70 feet tall, with a straight trunk. The bark of young trees is yellowish or bronze and peels off in shreds; on older trees it is reddish brown and peels in sheets. Its leaves are 3 to 6 inches long, dull, dark green on the upper surfaces and pale yellow-green underneath. Conelike fruits are held upright on the branches and mature in autumn, when the foliage turns yellow. This species is unusually slow growing and long-lived for a birch: flowering begins after 35 to 40 years, and the trees may live 200 years. Yellow birch wood is especially valued for interior flooring, furniture, and cabinets. It is dark to reddish brown, close-grained, hard, and strong.

Box Elder see Maple

Buckeye and Horse Chestnut
(Aesculus)

The buckeye is a deciduous flowering tree that grows 20 to 50 feet tall. Its leaves are composed of five to seven leaflets radiating from the main stalk like the spokes of a wheel. The fruit consists of one or two glossy brown nuts enclosed in a leathery greenish husk that splits open when the seeds are ripe. Buckeye and horse chestnut seeds are poisonous and can cause serious reactions ranging from nausea to paralysis if eaten.

Ohio buckeye *(Aesculus glabra)* may reach 40 feet tall and has a low-branching crown. Small yellow-green flowers appear in spring and emerge along erect 6-inch stalks. The three-piece fruit husks are covered with blunt spines. The twigs, leaves, and blossoms all produce an unpleasant odor when crushed. The wood is white, close-grained, and lightweight and resists splitting. Although sometimes known as the fetid, or stinking, buckeye because of its odor, this otherwise attractive tree has been proudly chosen as the state tree of Ohio. The Ohio buckeye grows in fertile bottomlands and on stream banks from Ohio south to Alabama and west to Kansas and Oklahoma. West of the Allegheny Mountains, Ohio buckeye is one of the first trees to leaf out in spring. Ohio buckeye is a valuable timber tree, although its use has been restricted because it is relatively rare.

The **horse chestnut** tree *(Aesculus hippocastanum)*, a European species introduced to North America in colonial times, grows to 40 feet tall. It has white flowers marked with red or yellow, borne along upright foot-long stalks in midspring. Chestnut leaves are made up of five to seven leaflets that are widest above the middle. The fruit husks are spiny, and seeds ripen in early fall. The horse chestnut requires full sun, deep, moist soil, and ample growing space. It makes a fine shade tree.

Buckthorn *(Rhamnus)*

Buckthorns are shrubs or small trees, often with spiny branches. Their leaves are egg-shaped and many are deciduous. Buckthorn fruits resemble small berries.

The **Carolina buckthorn** *(Rhamnus caroliniana)* is a woodland tree of the southern United States that grows up to 40 feet tall. Its trunk branches close to the ground, and the deciduous leaves are 2 to 5 inches long and 1 to 2 inches wide. Tiny greenish-yellow flowers in small clusters emerge on short stalks in late spring. The small, black 1/2-inch berries are edible and ripen in the autumn.

Cascara buckthorn, bearberry, or **bitterbark** *(Rhamnus purshiana)* grows as a shrub or tree up to 40 feet tall. It is remarkable for being the only species of deciduous tree in the Northwest with winter buds that do not have bud scales; they are protected instead by dense rusty-brown hairs. The small black fruits mature in late summer and are sought after by such birds as the band-tailed pigeon, catbird, mockingbird, and thrush, which deposit large numbers of the seeds along fence rows. Cascara buckthorn is most common in the Puget Sound region of British Columbia and Washington. This species was discovered by the Lewis and Clark Expedition in Montana in 1805–06. Since the 1870's it has been well known for the laxative properties of its bark; in western Oregon, Washington, southern British Columbia, and northern California, bark has been stripped extensively from trees as part of a small extractive industry.

Butternut see Walnut

Buttonwood see Sycamore

Horse chestnut
(Aesculus hippocastanum)

Carolina buckthorn
(Rhamnus caroliniana)

Catalpa, or Indian Cigar Tree
(Catalpa)

Catalpas grow 30 to 90 feet high. They have pairs of heart-shaped leaves that look somewhat tropical. Many showy white flowers are produced in pyramid-shaped clusters. Their fruits are long, dry, beanlike capsules called Indian cigars that persist on the trees through winter and then split open to release papery-winged seeds in spring. Catalpa is a Cherokee Indian name.

Southern catalpa (*Catalpa bignonioides*) is 30 to 40 feet tall. A rapid grower, southern catalpa may begin to flower when it is only 6 to 8 years old. The leaves on the stout, brittle branches are 4 to 10 inches long and emerge in late spring, turning black before falling. In midsummer, white flowers spotted with yellow and purple are found at the tips of the twigs. The foot-long seed pods stay on the branches through fall and winter, releasing flattened seeds with tufts of hairs at each end in spring. Native from western Florida to Louisiana, southern catalpa is now cultivated from southern New England through Texas. It is a tough tree, adapting to poor soil, and has become a popular ornamental. Southern catalpa does best in full sun and thrives in hot, dry summers. It is recommended for open settings because of the messy flower, fruit, and leaf litter, and because its brittle branches are easily damaged in storms.

Cedar (*Cedrus, Thuja,* and others)

Cedar is a vernacular name given to a variety of unrelated conifers with fragrant wood, including several junipers (*Juniperus*) and arborvitae (*Thuja*). True cedars (*Cedrus*) are not native to North America. These trees are majestic evergreens with needles in brush-like clusters at the tips of stubby shoots, and woody, barrel-shaped cones with very tightly wrapped scales. They grow 40 to 60 feet or taller and have wide-spreading branches.

The **blue Atlas cedar** (*Cedrus atlantica*) is shaped like a pyramid in youth and becomes flat-topped with age. It may grow to some 90 feet tall. It has graceful, upward-sweeping branches and silvery-blue foliage. In landscapes it is used as an accent plant.

Cedar of Lebanon (*Cedrus libani*) is rare in North America but makes an impressive specimen tree. The long, massive branches extend horizontally for a magnificent effect. It has a round to flattened crown and grows to 100 feet or taller. Cedar of Lebanon is the hardiest of the true cedars and likes dry soil with full sun.

Some of the other trees called cedars and some species known as arborvitae are members of the genus *Thuja*. They are evergreens with reddish-brown trunks that flare at the base, and bark that peels in narrow, vertical strips. Leaves are scalelike and cling to the flattened branches in pairs.

Northern white cedar (*Thuja occidentalis*) has a compact, pyramidal shape and grows 40 to 50 feet tall. The scalelike leaves are leathery and dull yellowish green, with tiny gland dots. Northern white cedar is a tree of central and eastern Canada and the northern midwestern and northeastern United States. Taken to France in 1536, the northern white cedar was one of the first trees brought from North America to Europe.

Stands of **western red cedar** (*Thuja plicata*) were decimated in the early 20th century when the tree was practically the only source of wood for telegraph poles and railway sleepers. For a discussion of other native American cedars, see Juniper.

Cherry and Plum (*Prunus*)

This is a large genus of deciduous flowering trees yielding fruits that include plum, cherry, peach, apricot, and almond. All of these fruits are fleshy and their seeds are enclosed by a hard shell and called a stone or pit. Cherry trees grow from 15 to 40 feet tall and have attractive white or pink blossoms. Their leaves are leathery, with minute teeth along the edges, and are dark green above and paler beneath. All of the North American species are deciduous. Most cherries will flourish in full sun or partial shade, although cultivated varieties with purple leaves require full sun to bring out their colors.

Allegheny plum, or **purple sloe,** (*Prunus alleghaniensis*) is a thicket-forming shrub or small tree up to 20 feet tall. It flowers abundantly in spring, with the blossoms starting out white and fading to pink. The fruits ripen in late summer; they are reddish purple, about 1/2 inch across, with tart yellow flesh. Allegheny plum is found from Connecticut

Southern catalpa
(*Catalpa bignonioides*)

Blue Atlas cedar
(*Cedrus atlantica*)

Northern white cedar (*Thuja occidentalis*)

to Pennsylvania and through the mountains to Tennessee. It is a valuable food source for wildlife such as white-tailed deer, bears, foxes, and songbirds.

American plum, or **wild red plum,** *(Prunus americana)* is a shrub or small tree 6 to 15 feet tall with widespread, sometimes drooping branches that form a broad crown. Clusters of two to five white flowers appear before the leaves emerge. The sour red fruits are about 1 inch across and are palatable only when made into sugary preserves. American plum is widely distributed through eastern and midwestern North America. About 300 different varieties have been derived from this single species.

Bitter cherry *(Prunus emarginata)* grows to about 25 feet and has an oval crown. The leaves are widest from near the middle to near the tip. The white or greenish-white flowers grow in sprays of 5 to 12 blossoms, and its 1/2-inch fruits are ruby-red, turning black when ripe in summer. Bitter cherry is a western species that grows from British Columbia to southern California, Arizona, and New Mexico.

Black cherry *(Prunus serotina)* grows 50 to 60 feet tall and has an oval crown. Leaves are dark green in summer and turn yellow to red in fall. Edible fruits ripen to black in August. Black cherry grows throughout the entire eastern half of the United States, as far west as the Dakotas, and south to Texas. The tree provides a beautiful, lustrous wood of a reddish-brown hue that deepens with age. The wood is close-grained, hard, and resilient, and prized for cabinetry and furniture.

Chickasaw plum *(Prunus angustifolia)* reaches 25 feet tall, often with stubby, spurlike side branchlets along the twigs. It has bright green, narrow leaves 1 to 2 inches long, with two red glands near the base of each leaf. Tiny white flowers bloom in clusters of two to four blossoms and emerge before the leaves. The edible chickasaw plum fruits are yellow or red, about 1/2 inch across, and tart. The tree has a broad range throughout the southeastern and midsouthern United States.

Common choke cherry *(Prunus virginiana)* can grow either as a shrub or as a 20- to 30-foot tree with a straight trunk and small branches. The white flowers do not appear until late spring, when they emerge along upright or branching central spikes 3 to 6 inches long. The fruits, which ripen in summer, have a puckery, unpleasant flavor. The common choke cherry is very broadly distributed across the entire central portion of North America. The cultivated tree is suitable as a shade or border tree in a yard and requires sandy, well-drained soil.

Chestnut *(Castanea)*

Chestnuts grow either as nut-producing shrubs or as trees 40 to 100 feet tall; the shrubby species are often called chinkapin. Leaves are long, narrow, and coarsely toothed. Their long flower clusters, or catkins, emerge in summer after the leaves. Shiny, brown, rounded nuts are enclosed in spiny, burr-like husks that split open when the nuts ripen in autumn.

Allegheny chinkapin *(Castanea pumila)* is a shrub or tree that may grow as tall as 50 feet. Leaves are 3 to 5 inches long and about 1 1/2 inches wide. Each husk contains a single nut.

The **American chestnut** *(Castanea dentata)* at one time grew almost 100 feet tall, with a broad, rounded crown. This "spreading chestnut tree" of American poetry has now been driven to the verge of extinction by chestnut blight, a fungal disease that affects the bark. Today the American chestnuts can be found only as stump sprouts or small trees that reach about 20 feet tall and may not have a chance to reproduce before they are attacked by disease. Leaves are glossy and yellowish green, 6 to 11 inches long, with hook-shaped teeth. Fragrant, tiny male and female flowers are clustered along semi-erect stalks in summer. As the leaves turn yellow, one to three brown chestnuts mature in each spiny, velvet-lined husk in late autumn.

This tree ranged from Maine south to the foothills of the southern Appalachians and as far west as Mississippi. Of the 12 species of chestnut worldwide, the American chestnut had a reputation for yielding the most useful timber and the tastiest nuts. The reddish-brown wood was coarse-grained and light but relatively weak; it was valued for non-structural uses, such as interior trim, fence posts, furniture, and crates. Tannic acid, used for

Chickasaw plum
(Prunus angustifolia)

Commmon choke cherry
(Prunus virginiana)

Allegheny chinkapin
(Castanea pumila)

American chestnut
(Castanea dentata)

tanning leather, was also extracted from the wood. Were it not for the chestnut blight, the American chestnut would still rank among the eastern states' most important commercial and horticultural trees.

Chinaberry
(Melia azedarach)

Chinaberry is a shade tree growing to 50 feet tall, with a dense, low, rounded crown. Each broad leaf is made up of a number of leaflets and may be a foot or more in length. In spring masses of small, pale purple flowers emerge. In autumn the tree is covered with yellow berries about ½ inch long that contain a stone. Although eaten by catbirds, robins, and mockingbirds, the berries are poisonous to humans and may cause illness. Chinaberry is native to the Himalayas and eastern Asia. It was widely planted in the southern United States and is now found naturalized in the Southeast. Although it is a member of the mahogany family, chinaberry yields poor-quality wood of negligible commercial value. The inner stones of the berries, however, have been used for making beads.

Chinkapin see Chestnut and Oak

Cottonwood see Poplar

Crabapple see Apple

Crape Myrtle
(Lagerstroemia)

The crape myrtle belongs to a group of decorative trees 10 to 60 feet tall, with showy flowers. They usually develop multiple trunks and broad spreading crowns. The deciduous leaves grow in pairs along the branches.

Crape myrtle *(Lagerstroemia indica)* is a small tree with multiple trunks and a feathery spreading crown. Its two most distinctive features are its flowers and its bark. The flowers range from white through a broad spectrum of pinks and purples. They are produced in large clusters and have crinkled edges that look like crepe paper. The bark is smooth and gray, and flakes off in patches, revealing the lighter underbark.

Crape myrtle flowers best in full sun and does well in most types of soil. It has been widely planted in the South since the mid 18th century, especially

along city streets, and can be found growing wild in some parts of the Southeast.

Cypress
(Cupressus)

The cypress tree is a long-lived evergreen growing 40 to 90 feet tall, with fragrant, scalelike leaves. Woody seed cones are small and round, with only 6 to 10 thickened scales per cone. Cypress wood is yellowish brown and lightweight but tough and weather resistant. It is used for utility poles and fencing, as well as for some furniture.

Arizona cypress *(Cupressus arizonica)* has rough red bark that peels in thin strips, and small blue-green leaves that smell foul when crushed. Its cones are about 1 inch across. Arizona cypress can be found from southern New Mexico and Arizona to northern Mexico and northern Baja California. It is one of the hardier cypresses, suitable for mild, dry climates and requiring full sun and well-drained soil. It resists drought and is often planted to control erosion. Young trees are shaped like pyramids, making them popular Christmas trees in the southwestern United States.

Dogwood
(Cornus)

Dogwoods grow from 15 to 40 feet tall, with crowns that are generally broader than their height. As ornamentals, they provide year-round interest, with flowers in spring, bright berries and claret-colored foliage in autumn, and a delicate silhouette in winter.

Flowering dogwood *(Cornus florida)* is a graceful tree reaching 15 to 40 feet. The bark is blocky and coarse with deep fissures, almost resembling alligator hide. The deciduous leaves usually grow in pairs. The leaf veins are prominent and curve upward toward the leaf tip; when the dogwood leaf is gently broken, silky threads pull out from the veins. The structure we think of as the dogwood blossom is actually a group of tiny yellow true flowers surrounded by white or pink showy bracts that imitate petals. Clustered red fruits appear in late fall and are important in the diet of many birds and small mammals, although they are poisonous to humans.

Flowering dogwood is native from Massachusetts south to Florida and west to Texas. The bitter bark of the trunk and root was once used by North

Chinaberry *(Melia azedarach)*

Crape myrtle *(Lagerstroemia indica)*

Arizona cypress
(Cupressus arizonica)

Flowering dogwood *(Cornus florida)*

American Indians as a remedy for malaria and other fevers. Early pioneers soaked the bark in whiskey to relieve attacks of malaria before quinine from South America became available. Dogwood bark came back into use in the South during the Civil War when the blockade of Confederate ports reduced the availability of quinine.

Flowering dogwood makes a good lawn accent and landscape tree for a naturalizing effect. It requires partial shade and cool, acid, well-drained soil.

Douglas Fir *(Pseudotsuga)*
Douglas fir is an intriguing evergreen conifer that resembles spruces, firs, hemlocks, and yews.

Douglas fir *(Pseudotsuga menziesii)* is initially slow growing but grows more quickly as it matures. Although it may first reproduce at age 10, reproduction peaks only when the tree is 200 to 300 years old. Individual trees may live 800 to 1,000 years, reaching a height of 100 to 325 feet. Douglas fir is pyramidal in shape; its upper branches arch upward, while its lower branches droop. Its dark yellowish-green needles are 1 to 1½ inches long, flat, and blunt. Seed cones are egg-shaped, 2 to 4 inches long, and purplish, turning yellow-brown at maturity; a three-pointed bract extends from between the cone scales. The cones of the Douglas fir hang down from the branches in contrast to those of the true fir.

One of the most important trees of western North America, Douglas fir grows from British Columbia south to Mexico. The tree is extremely valuable to wildlife: the cones are taken for their seeds by Douglas squirrels and Townsend chipmunks, while fallen seeds are dispersed over wide distances and eaten by mice and seed-eating birds.

Douglas fir ranks among the principal economic woods of North America; in the United States it provides more timber by volume than any other tree. The yellowish to pale red wood is light and strong—it has the greatest strength by weight of any American timber. The tree's great height permits the extraction of standard-length boards free of knots and other defects. It is used for structural beams and trusses in building, dock, and bridge construction. Douglas fir is also known worldwide as an ornamental. In gardens it usually grows 40 to 60 feet tall. It is attractive as a specimen or massed as a windbreak. It needs full sun, humidity, and acid to neutral soil.

Elder *(Sambucus)*
Elders are shrubs or small trees with pairs of leaves divided into leaflets. Tiny flowers bloom in dense, spreading clusters and produce small berrylike fruits.

American elder *(Sambucus canadensis)* is a fast-growing but short-lived shrub that may reach tree size—about 20 feet—in the southern United States. It has a short trunk and round crown. New shoots often sprout from the root system. The lustrous dark green leaves consist of five to seven leaflets with toothed edges. American elder has tiny white flowers in sprays up to 7 inches across. The deep purple elderberries are about ¼ inch across and contain three to four seeds. The American elder grows across the eastern half of the United States, from Maine south to Florida and west as far as Minnesota and Texas. Its fruit provides food for more than 45 species of birds, including quail, pheasant, and grouse. An excellent red wine can also be made from the fruit. Cultivated varieties with large flower heads have been developed from the American elder. They are vigorous, sun-loving shrubs that do well in a variety of soil types.

Elm *(Ulmus)*
Elms are generally deciduous trees that grow 40 to 90 feet tall, with broad, open crowns. The thick trunks are covered with furrowed gray bark. Elm leaves are saw-toothed and lopsided at the base. The seeds are thin and flat and covered with hairs; they are an important part of the diet of small mammals and birds. Elms require full sun and moist, deep, well-drained soil. They are commonly used for lining avenues and in formal plantings.

The largest and most important of the six native North American elm species is the **American elm** *(Ulmus americana),* which grows from 60 to 120 feet tall, with a broad, spreading crown. Its inconspicuous light green flowers open in very early spring, and the tiny, greenish, papery fruits mature as the leaves unfurl. The leaves are 3 to 6 inches long, glossy dark green in summer, turning yellow in fall. This handsome species has an extensive range, from southern Newfoundland south to Florida and west to Saskatchewan and Texas.

Douglas fir
(Pseudotsuga menziesii)

American elder *(Sambucus canadensis)*

American elms have traditionally played a public role as centers for civic meetings, beginning with their role as council trees in the tribal lives of Native Americans. Under these trees, treaties and agreements with European settlers were made. The American elm was often planted in the town green and other public spaces in the colonies. The Washington Elm, under which George Washington assumed command of the Continental Army in 1775, remained standing for many years in Cambridge, Massachusetts. Nearly every town in the colonies, both before and during the Revolution, had an American elm designated as the town's Liberty Tree. A great elm in Boston, upon which unpopular British ministers were hanged in effigy in the furor that followed the Stamp Act, was the town's Liberty Tree until it was cut down by British soldiers during the occupation.

Many American elms have fallen victim to Dutch elm disease, a fungal infection spread by a bark beetle. First reported in 1930, Dutch elm disease has since ravaged the population of the American elms, which are especially susceptible. Botanists are attempting to promote disease-resistant strains of the magnificent trees.

Slippery elm (*Ulmus rubra*) grows 60 to 80 feet tall. The leaves are 5 to 7 inches long, with a sandpapery upper surface. Slippery elm is found from Maine and the lower St. Lawrence Valley south to Florida and west to South Dakota and Texas, most frequently along stream banks and wooded slopes. The inner bark of the slippery elm twig produces a slimy, aromatic substance used medicinally by early American settlers to reduce inflammation of wounds. It was also favored by spitball pitchers in the early years of professional baseball. The extract could be powdered and was sold in apothecary shops; the powder was mixed with water and drunk to relieve a sore throat.

Winged elm (*Ulmus alata*), sometimes also called wahoo, grows only 40 to 50 feet tall, with a narrow crown and small leaves 1½ to 3 inches long. The bark of the twigs extends in two flattened, corky wings about ½ inch thick. The fruits are reddish and covered with fuzzy hairs. It is native to the southeastern United States.

Eucalyptus, or Gum Tree
(*Eucalyptus*)

Eucalyptus is a large group of over 500 tropical and subtropical evergreen trees ranging from 20 to 100 feet tall. They are unusual in that the leaves have juvenile, intermediate, and adult phases, changing shape, color, and even position on the branches at each phase. The bark on some species flakes away, giving the trunks a mottled, shaggy appearance. Flowers may be produced singly or in clusters, and their color depends on the species. The fruits develop in the form of hard, woody capsules, which split along seams to release the seeds.

Blue gum (*Eucalyptus globulus*) is a large, fast-growing tree with a narrow, round crown. It sheds its bark in long strips, leaving a mottled green and tan trunk. Its aromatic leaves are round and bluish in the juvenile phase; they are often dried and used in floral arrangements.

Blue gum is the most common species of eucalyptus to have been brought from Australia. It grows well in a variety of soils and has been widely planted along the California coast; its fast-growing habit makes it popular as a windbreak. Fresh eucalyptus leaves produce an aromatic oil; the dried leaves are used in cough and cold remedies. The hard wood has been used for farm tools, tool handles, and even shipbuilding.

False Acacia see Locust

Fir (*Abies*)

Firs are a group of conical evergreen trees that grow 30 to 150 feet tall, depending upon the species. Their flat needles are fragrant, and in most species two whitish lines run along the underside of each needle. Fir cones are upright and cylindrical, and are found mostly near the top of the tree. Firs are not valued for their lumber, although several species provide sources of paper pulp. Balsam and Fraser fir are favorite choices as Christmas trees, since they hold their needles well and are beautifully aromatic. All firs thrive in moist, sandy, acidic soil and require full sun. As ornamentals, they are planted either as specimen trees or to provide screening or accents in a large yard.

The **balsam fir** (*Abies balsamea*) reaches 45 to 75 feet in height and 20 to 25 feet in

American elm (*Ulmus americana*)

Eucalyptus (*Eucalyptus globulus*)

Balsam fir (*Abies balsamea*)

diameter, and has lustrous, fragrant needles. The dark purple cones are 2 to 4 inches long. Balsam fir grows in eastern Canada as far west as Alberta and in the northeastern United States, where it is common in the central and northern Appalachian Mountains. In winter balsam fir helps sustain deer and moose, which feed on its foliage. A large plantation of balsam firs, for use as Christmas trees, was established on the Roosevelt estate at Hyde Park.

Fraser fir (*Abies fraseri*) generally reaches 30 to 40 feet tall and 20 to 25 feet in diameter. Modified leaves called bracts protrude conspicuously between the scales of the purplish cylindrical cones. Fraser fir is the only fir native to the southeastern United States; it is found at high elevations from Pennsylvania to North Carolina.

Subalpine fir (*Abies lasiocarpa*) is only 1 to 2 feet in diameter, although the tree grows 40 to 100 feet tall; this gives the tree its characteristic spire shape. The species grows at the snow line in the Rocky Mountains, from southeastern Alaska south to Arizona and New Mexico.

White fir (*Abies concolor*) grows 30 to 50 feet tall and 15 to 30 feet in diameter, and has bluish-or grayish-green needles 2 inches long. Its barrel-shaped cones are 3 to 6 inches long. White fir is found at higher elevations in the eastern Rocky Mountains, from Idaho to New Mexico and Arizona, and farther west, from southern Oregon to southern California.

Ginkgo, or Maidenhair Tree
(*Ginkgo biloba*)

The ginkgo is a deciduous tree that grows 30 to 80 feet tall with an irregular crown. Its exotic, fan-shaped leaves are striped with veins radiating from the stem and are often deeply notched at the top. Many of the leaves are borne on short branchlets. The leaves are pale green and turn bright yellow in autumn. Flower cones are either male or female and are produced on separate trees on the branchlets. The fruits resemble waxy orange-yellow cherries.

The ginkgo is one of the world's most fascinating trees. Often called a living fossil, it is the sole surviving member of a primeval order of plants that

thrived alongside the dinosaurs hundreds of millions of years ago. Ginkgo is believed to have been saved from extinction through cultivation in monasteries in eastern China, where the tree is sacred to the Buddhist religion. In the 1700's scientists discovered ginkgos growing in the Far East; the tree was introduced to North America in 1784. Whether or not ginkgos have survived naturally in the wild remains a mystery.

Ginkgo has a number of extraordinary features. The fleshy fruit and broad, deciduous, fan-shaped leaves suggest that ginkgo is a broadleaf species; however, it is thought to be more closely related to conifers because its pollen and ovules, or eggs, are found on rudimentary structures more like cone scales than flowers. On the other hand, it is not quite like any of the conifers. Like primitive plant groups, such as ferns, the male ginkgo produces swimming sperm cells.

Female trees are undesirable in lawn or garden settings because their fruits produce messy litter, smell like rancid butter, and may even cause a rash similar to poison ivy in some people. However, the nuts inside the fruit are considered a delicacy by

Asian Americans—roasted, they are a popular side dish with bird's nest soup. Ginkgo withstands the effects of pollution and tolerates poor, hard-packed soil. Thus the world's most archaic tree thrives in the most modern urban and industrial environments.

Gum Tree see Eucalyptus

Hackberry (*Celtis*)

Hackberries are deciduous trees 70 to 80 feet tall, with rounded crowns. Their long, tapering leaves are asymmetrical at the base and coarsely toothed. The flowers are inconspicuous and may be either bisexual or male, with both flower types found on the same tree. Hackberry fruits are fleshy berries that range in color from orange-red to blue-black. The fruits are important to many birds, including cedar waxwings, quail, pheasants, and woodpeckers. Soft, yellow hackberry wood is weak and of minor commercial importance; it is used mostly for sporting goods, furniture, and plywood.

Common hackberry (*Celtis occidentalis*) is a small to medium-size tree with an oval, somewhat ragged crown. Its gray bark may appear either warty or ridged. The leaves are 2½ to

White fir (*Abies concolor*)

Ginkgo (*Ginkgo biloba*)

Common hackberry
(*Celtis occidentalis*)

3¹/₂ inches long and sharply toothed along the margin. The foliage turns yellow in autumn, when fruits ripen from deep orange to a dark purple. The common hackberry is a forest tree, commonly growing in river valleys from New England south to Georgia and west to North Dakota and Oklahoma. The common hackberry is a popular street tree in the Midwest. It tolerates urban pollution and heavy, sandy, and rocky soils, but does best in limestone soil.

Hawthorn (*Crataegus*)

Hawthorns grow as shrubs or as broad-crowned deciduous trees up to 30 feet tall. Their spreading branches have prickly spines. Flowers open late in spring or early summer and produce small, fleshy fruits that remain on the tree in winter. Their toothed leaves are shallowly to deeply lobed. Hawthorns prefer a sunny exposure and well-drained loamy soil but adapt well to adverse conditions. As cultivated plants they make a fine hedge or screen. Numerous subtle differences, on which even botanists do not agree, make it difficult to distinguish among hawthorn species. Hawthorn thickets provide important nesting sites and cover for birds and small animals. Birds and rodents eat the fruits, while deer prefer to browse on the twigs and leaves.

Thorn plum, or **cockspur hawthorn,** *(Crataegus crusgalli)* grows up to 25 feet tall, with scaly dark brown bark and twigs scattered with 3- to 4-inch spines. The leathery leaves are usually unlobed. The foliage has a reddish flush when it first emerges in spring and turns vibrant orange or red in the fall. In midspring the thorn plum produces abundant clusters of flowers ranging from white to red. These in turn produce drooping, greenish or reddish fruits less than ¹/₂ inch across that resemble tiny apples. Native to the eastern and southeastern United States, the cockspur hawthorn is the most popular hawthorn in American gardens; it has been planted as an ornamental and trimmed into hedges since colonial times.

Hemlock (*Tsuga*)

Hemlocks are elegant evergreen conifers 30 to 70 feet tall, with arching branches and dense foliage. Most species have small, flat needles that lie along the branches in a flattened plane. Hemlock trees, unrelated to the herb poison hemlock, are so named because crushed foliage of the eastern hemlock smells like the toxic herb; their needles were once brewed to make a tea. Hemlocks are among the most popular evergreens for planting as hedges, screens, or accents. They prefer partial shade and a cool, damp climate.

Canada hemlock, or **eastern hemlock,** *(Tsuga canadensis)* is a broadly pyramidal tree with a forked trunk. It grows 40 to 80 feet tall, and occasionally even taller. The flat needles are about ¹/₂ inch long and dark yellowish green on the upper surfaces, with white bands on the undersides. In fall the egg-shaped seed cones, ¹/₂ to 1 inch long, mature and hang down from short stalks. Canada hemlock grows in the northeastern United States. It grows relatively slowly and does not mature until it is 250 to 300 years old; some trees may live 600 years. The bark of Canada hemlock was used for extracting tannin and was once of greater value than the wood—stripped logs were often left to decay in the forest. It is still in demand today; lumbering is done in spring and summer when the bark can be removed most easily.

The largest hemlock, **western hemlock** *(Tsuga heterophylla)*, grows 130 to 215 feet tall, with a narrow, steeple-shaped crown that droops at the very top. Its flat needles are about ¹/₂ inch long and are grooved on the upper surface, having two broad white bands underneath. Inch-long seed cones hang directly from the branches. This tree is found along the West Coast from southeastern Alaska to northern California and is one of the commonest trees in the Pacific Northwest. Individual trees may live for 500 years or longer. Indians of southeastern Alaska have used the inner bark to make a bread. Today the tree is important as a source of alpha cellulose, used in making cellophane, rayon, and plastics.

Hickory and Pecan (*Carya*)

Members of the walnut family, hickory and pecan are deciduous trees 60 to 100 feet tall. Flower clusters in the form of catkins emerge in spring and depend on the wind for pollination. The large leaves are aromatic and made up of a number of smaller leaflets. Hickories and pecans have hard, smooth-shelled nuts

Thorn plum (*Crataegus crusgalli*)

Canada hemlock
(*Tsuga canadensis*)

Western hemlock
(*Tsuga heterophylla*)

that ripen inside husks and fall from the trees in autumn. The taste of both types of nut, either sweet or bitter, depends on the species. Hickory and pecan nuts were an important staple in the diet of many North American Indians. In fact, the name hickory comes from *pocohicora*, an Indian word for a milky drink prepared from the crushed nuts. Pecan and hickory trees make beautiful specimen trees in a large yard; they need full sun and fertile, deep soil.

Pecan *(Carya illinoinensis)* grows 70 to 100 feet tall with an open crown 40 to 75 feet wide. The leaves are composed of 9 to 17 sickle-shaped leaflets. Thin, four-ribbed husks enclose smooth, thin-shelled, oval nuts with a lobed and furrowed edible meat. A tree of the Mississippi Valley, pecan is the state tree of Texas and the most valuable native North American nut tree. Once harvested in the wild by felling entire trees, pecans today are grown in orchards. Individual trees may produce an average of 500 pounds of nuts a year and may produce nuts continuously for some 200 years. Pecans are long-lived; in fact, the oldest trees at Mount Vernon are

pecans that began their lives as saplings at Monticello and were given by Thomas Jefferson to George Washington.

Shagbark hickory *(Carya ovata)* grows to 150 feet, with an oblong crown. It has gray, shaggy bark that peels off in long, curling strips. Each leaf is composed of five and sometimes seven leaflets; the leaflets are 3 to 7 inches long, with the terminal leaflet generally being the largest. They are edged with numerous fine teeth and tiny hairs. The yellow-green foliage turns golden yellow in autumn. A thick husk surrounds each nut. The nuts themselves are oblong, flat, and four-sided, and contain the sweet meat. Shagbark hickory is widespread in the eastern United States, growing as far west as Minnesota and Texas. Hickory is the world's foremost wood for making tool handles and, until the mid-20th century, was the most popular material for skis. The wood is also well known for its superior fuel value—a cord of seasoned hickory is almost equal to a ton of anthracite coal in number of thermal units produced. The

green, or unseasoned, wood is used to smoke hams and bacon.

Holly *(Ilex)*

Hollies come in both deciduous and evergreen forms. They grow 10 to 50 feet tall in a pyramidal shape. The leathery leaves are edged with spines in some species. Tiny flowers are white to greenish white, emerging in spring. Male and female flowers are borne on separate trees. When trees of both sexes are planted near each other, the female trees bear red or yellow berries in fall.

Hollies have been used for centuries in Europe and North America as decorations in houses and churches at Christmastime and were once called holy trees; the word holly may be derived from this usage. To this day the foliage and fruit of red-berried native species and cultivars are used for holiday arrangements. Hollies are also popular as hedges, borders, and accent plants. They need moist, well-drained soil and protection from winter sun and winds.

American holly *(Ilex opaca)* is a slow-growing tree that reaches 40 to 50 feet in height. Young trees are pyramidal, but their shape becomes irregular

with age as the trees develop short, crooked branches. The lustrous evergreen leaves have coarse, spine-tipped teeth along the margins and form a striking contrast to the red berries in autumn and winter. American holly is found in the southeastern and south-central United States. The berries are a valuable source of food for more than 20 species of songbirds and game birds, including thrushes, robins, grouse, quail, and turkeys. More than 300 cultivated ornamental varieties are derived from the American holly.

Common winterberry *(Ilex verticillata)* is a shrub or tree up to 25 feet tall, with a short trunk and rounded crown. The purplish leaves are deciduous, with minute teeth along the edges and dense hairs on the undersurface. The bright red berries mature in late fall and persist on the bare branches through winter. Winterberry thrives in swamps, bogs, and other soggy environments in the eastern United States. In late winter and early spring, birds, including the brown thrasher and bluebird, feed on its berries. The white, almost grainless wood is used in fine woodworking for highlights and inlays.

Pecan *(Carya illinoinensis)*

Shagbark hickory *(Carya ovata)*

American holly *(Ilex opaca)*

Common winterberry
(Ilex verticillata)

Cultivated in North America since colonial times, **English holly** (*Ilex aquifolium*) grows up to 20 feet tall and has leaves with spiny, wavy edges.

Possum haw (*Ilex decidua*) is a low-branching shrub or tree growing to 35 feet, with an open crown. Its deciduous leaves are edged with minute, rounded teeth. The orange to red berries persist on the bare branches throughout the winter. Possum haw is found in lowland sites in the central to southeastern United States. The berries are an important source of food for turkeys, quail, and many songbirds.

Yaupon (*Ilex vomitoria*) is a low-branching shrub or tree that may reach 25 feet tall. Its leaves are evergreen, with small, rounded teeth along the edges. The ruby-red berries ripen in late fall. Yaupon occurs in the southeastern coastal plain of the United States, roughly from Virginia to Texas. The berries provide food for many birds, while white-tailed deer browse on the leaves and young twigs. The Yaupon was a war symbol of North American Indian tribes; a Black Drink ceremony centered around a decoction of its leaves, intended to induce nausea.

Hoptree, or Wafer Ash
(*Ptelea*)
Hoptrees have leaves consisting of three and sometimes five leaflets. The hoptree fruit is a disc-shaped, winged, papery sac enclosing the seed.

Hoptree, or **wafer ash,** (*Ptelea trifoliata*) is a deciduous tree some 20 feet tall, with a slender straight trunk, short branches, and a rounded crown. Its twigs and gray, warty bark produce an unpleasant, citrus-like odor when bruised. Flowers are greenish white and form in groups at the tips of the branches. The numerous, brown disk-shaped fruits mature in the summer. They hang in dense clusters from the tree through winter and are released in spring.

The hoptree is widely scattered throughout North America but is found primarily in the southeastern and parts of the midwestern United States. It is slow growing and short-lived and of limited significance in providing shelter to wildlife. As the common name suggests, the fruit of the hoptree was once used as a substitute for hops in flavoring beer. Pioneers used the bitter hoptree root as a remedy for malaria and relief of indigestion.

Hornbeam (*Carpinus*)
The hornbeam is a deciduous, slow-growing tree ranging from 20 to 60 feet tall. Its leaves are toothed and prominently veined. Hornbeam flowers are pollinated by the wind; separate male and female flowers, appearing in mid-spring, are borne along different stalks on the same tree. Tiny nutlets in leafy bracts ripen in autumn. Hornbeams make fine shade trees or street trees. They grow in sun or shade and in any moist, well-drained soil.

American hornbeam (*Carpinus caroliniana*), also called blue beech, ironwood, or musclewood, is a small tree, usually only about 20 feet tall, with an irregular branching habit. The trunk is short, irregularly fluted, and gnarled, with bluish-gray bark. In autumn the foliage turns red-orange, and the bracts containing the fruit turn brown. Each fruit is a small, ribbed nutlet surrounded by a three-lobed, leafy bract; many fruits are clustered together on a hanging stalk. American hornbeam is widespread as an understory tree in mixed deciduous forests in the eastern United States, from Maine west to Minnesota and south to Florida and Texas. Its seeds are of minor importance as

food for small rodents. Fine-grained hornbeam wood is very hard and heavy, with light brown heartwood. Its resistance to splitting made the wood popular with pioneers for making bowls and dishes, as well as tool handles; it is used today in the manufacture of the striking hammers in pianos. Its small size limits the hornbeam's commercial use.

Indian Cigar Tree see Catalpa

Joshua Tree
(*Yucca brevifolia*)
The **Joshua tree** (*Yucca brevifolia*) belongs to the agave family, whose members prefer arid and sandy or rocky environments. The trunk begins branching only after the tree has flowered for the first time, which means that branches usually start about 10 feet above the ground. The Joshua tree is slow growing, but it may live as long as 1,000 years. It has tough, sword-shaped leaves. The greenish-yellow leathery flowers are abundant in early spring, appearing on upright, branching clusters about 10 inches long. The flowers open at night, when they are visited by

Hoptree (*Ptelea trifoliata*)

American hornbeam (*Carpinus caroliniana*)

Joshua tree (*Yucca brevifolia*)

yucca moths, with which these trees have developed a close symbiotic relationship. The female moths pollinate the tree as they fly from blossom to blossom to lay their eggs in the flowers. After hatching, moth larvae are nourished by Joshua tree pollen as they develop. The fruit of this tree matures by early summer; it is a three-sided, somewhat egg-shaped capsule, pale red to yellowish brown.

The Joshua tree is characteristic of the Mojave Desert and is found from Utah west to California and south to Arizona. The tree is important as shelter for several species of birds, including the cactus woodpecker, red-shafted flicker, and various owls and wrens. North American Indians used Joshua tree leaf fiber to make rope, sandals, mats, and baskets. Flowers and buds were eaten raw or boiled. The fleshy fruits were dried for winter use or fermented as a drink.

The tree has many other uses as well. Fibers of the Joshua tree have been used for making newsprint, and a soap can be made from the roots and stems.

The Joshua tree was named by the Mormons, who are said to have discovered it, recalling Moses' successor in completing the Israelites' sojourn in the desert. Joshua Tree National Monument is a "forest" of these trees near San Bernardino, California.

Juniper (*Juniperus*)

Junipers are pyramid-shaped, resinous, coniferous evergreens that grow 20 to 65 feet tall. The foliage of young trees looks like needles, while that of mature trees looks more like scales. Male trees produce cylindrical cones; female trees bear round bluish-gray or reddish semi-fleshy "juniper berries." Junipers are the most commonly planted evergreens in home gardens because of their variety of sizes, shapes, and colors. Rocky Mountain juniper and eastern red cedar are attractive as screening, background, or specimen plants. Junipers grow in full sun to partial shade. Generally, they are easy to grow and adapt to a broad range of conditions.

Common juniper (*Juniperus communis*) is usually a spreading shrub but may also grow as a small tree. Its needlelike leaves are sharp and curve inward. They are about 1/2 inch long and grow in whorls of three. The blue-gray berries take 3 years to mature and may persist on the plant for 3 or 4 years. The berries are eaten by cedar waxwings, quails, chipmunks, and raccoons. Common juniper is found in poor rocky soils from Alaska, across Canada, and south to the mountains of northern Arizona.

The **eastern red cedar** (*Juniperus virginiana*) grows to 40 feet or taller, with a dense crown that is conical to oval in shape. The young leaves are awl-shaped and prickly when young, and become scalelike and blunt when mature. This tree is the most widespread and drought-resistant conifer in eastern North America; it is found throughout the eastern United States as far west as the Dakotas. It is the only juniper of commercial importance in the United States. Its fragrant reddish wood is used in cedar closets and chests because the odor repels moths. The red color of both the wood and bark of this tree led French Canadians to call it *baton rouge;* when the same tree was encountered in Louisiana, its name was given to the state capital.

Rocky Mountain juniper, or **Colorado red cedar,** (*Juniperus scopulorum*) grows 30 to 40 feet tall and 3 to 15 feet wide, often with multiple main stems. This tree grows slowly and may live 200 to 300 years. The scalelike foliage has a silvery-blue cast; on younger stems the new leaves are sharp and prickly. The cones look like dark blue berries and ripen in two years. Turkeys, Bohemian waxwings, and evening grosbeaks consume the sweet berries, while antelope, mule deer, and bighorn sheep graze on the foliage. Rocky Mountain juniper ranges from central British Columbia south to Arizona and New Mexico.

Kentucky Coffee Tree (*Gymnocladus*)

Kentucky coffee tree (*Gymnocladus dioica*) usually grows 60 to 75 feet tall but can reach 110 feet. Its scientific name *Gymnocladus,* meaning "naked branch," refers to the fact that the leaves do not appear until late spring and are shed early in the autumn; the branches are bare 6 months of the year. The leaves are 3 feet long and 2 feet wide, with many leaflets per leaf. Kentucky coffee tree has separate male and female flowers that are borne on different trees. Both kinds of flowers are greenish white, tiny, and inconspicuous;

Eastern red cedar
(*Juniperus virginiana*)

Rocky Mountain juniper
(*Juniperus scopulorum*)

Kentucky coffee tree
(*Gymnocladus dioica*)

they appear in June and last for about a week. Members of the bean family, these trees produce thick, woody purplish-brown pods enclosing seeds in a sticky pulp. The pods appear in fall on the female trees and persist into winter, when they dry out and rattle in the wind. Kentucky coffee trees grow only in China and North America today, although fossils reveal that they once grew across Europe as well. In North America the tree is found in the midwestern and eastern United States. Its bitter seeds were once used by early settlers in an attempt to brew a drink resembling coffee. Neither the bitter seeds nor the sweet pulp surrounding them in the pod appears to be sought after by wildlife. The pale red to reddish-brown wood is coarse-grained and fairly hard, and takes a good polish. Because it maintains its strength in contact with the soil, it is used for railroad ties, fence posts, and other outdoor construction. It is too uncommon to be of much economic significance, however.

The male trees are preferred as ornamentals to avoid the litter from the pods. Because of its size, Kentucky coffee tree is suitable only in a large garden or park, or along a wide roadway. It grows in full sun or partial shade and tolerates dry soil and urban pollution.

Larch (Larix)

The larch is a conifer of mountainous regions that grows 40 to 90 feet tall. Its delicate branches arch gracefully and have peeling reddish-brown bark. The needles are arranged in spiral tufts on short shoots. Although larches are conifers, their needles turn yellow and drop off in autumn, and the trees remain bare through the winter. As a landscape plant, the larch provides a natural effect in a large yard that has full sun and acid soil.

The most common larch in North America is actually the **European larch** (*Larix decidua*), which grows 70 to 75 feet tall, with branches spreading 25 to 30 feet. It is distinguished by its 1- to 1½-inch scaly cones, which are cinnamon-brown and covered with soft brown hairs.

Generally smaller than the European larch is the native **tamarack** (*Larix larcinia*), a widespread, pyramid-shaped species 50 to sometimes 80 feet tall. Its needles are soft, about 1 inch long, and bluish green in summer. The tamarack begins to reproduce when it is 50 to 75 years old, with good seed production every 3 to 6 years. The cones are little more than ½ inch long, with fewer scales than those of the European larch.

The tamarack is a northern tree, found from Alaska to Newfoundland, where it is important to the forest ecology. Porcupines strip the outer bark to feed on the inner bark, often killing the tree in the process; red squirrels break off the cones and devour the seeds, or collect and bury the cones for later; other rodents, such as chipmunks, consume the seeds as well; in early fall, red crossbills break the cones apart to get at the seeds. Indians used the tough tamarack roots to stitch together sheets of bark, which they used in constructing their canoes.

Lilac (Syringa vulgaris)

The lilac is a shrub or tree growing little more than 20 feet tall. Native to southeastern Europe, it is quite popular in North American gardens. Its deciduous leaves are heart-shaped and grow in pairs. Lilac flowers, which are known for their fragrance, have four petals each and range in color from white to pale purple to mauve. The blossoms cluster in dense pyramids. The lilac fruit is a leathery capsule with two winged seeds in each chamber. Lilacs thrive in full sun and moist, loamy soil.

Linden, or Basswood (Tilia)

The linden is a deciduous tree that grows 50 to 100 feet tall, with a straight trunk and narrow crown. Its leaves are heart-shaped with toothed edges and long stems. The flowers are pale yellow or greenish and occur in small groups. This tree has two common names, depending on how it is used. In the lumber trade is it known as basswood and in the horticulture trade as linden. The English refer to it as lime tree, although it is not related to citrus trees. Lindens make elegant shade and street trees. They need full sun and moist, well-drained soil.

The valuable basswood lumber is soft and light, and has a straight grain. Linden flowers are known for attracting bees and have a reputation as a source of excellent honey. North American

European larch (*Larix decidua*)

Lilac (*Syringa vulgaris*)

American basswood
(*Tilia americana*)

Indians used the tough inner linden bark for cordage. After bark was peeled from the tree in spring, the fibers were soaked in water for about a month or pounded to remove the softer tissue. The remaining long, tough fibers were then twisted into rope or thread. Linden thread, being soft and silky, was used by Native Americans for suturing wounds as well as for weaving. The fallen leaves of this tree are especially high in calcium, magnesium, nitrogen, phosphorous, and potassium, and therefore play an important role in building soil fertility in the ecosystem.

American basswood *or Bee Tree (Tilia americana)* is a stately shade tree whose flowers produce excellent honey. The wood is most often used for the bases of the white keys on pianos.

Florida basswood *(Tilia floridana)* is a fast-growing tree 30 to 65 feet tall. Its leaves are 3 to 5 inches long and almost equally broad, and asymmetrical at the base. Its flowers appear in late spring, and hard, velvety gray fruits resembling peas mature in fall. The Florida basswood can be found in the southeastern United States from Virginia to Texas.

Liquidambar Tree
see Sweet Gum

Locust, or False Acacia
(Robinia)
Locusts are shrubs or trees that grow 25 to 80 feet tall. Leaflets combine to form leaves that fold inward at nightfall and open during the day. Locust stems are armed with a pair of spines at the base of each leaf. Long, hanging clusters of pea-shaped flowers are followed by dry pods.

Black locust *(Robinia pseudoacacia)* is a fast-growing tree 50 to 75 feet tall, with upright branches and an open, irregular crown. The leaves consist of seven to nine rounded leaflets about 2 inches long. Black locust trees may begin to flower at 6 to 12 years of age. Fragrant, white, wisterialike flowers appear through late spring and draw bees, which make honey from the nectar. The smooth, dark brown pods are 3 to 4 inches long. Native to North America, black locust became hugely popular in Europe in the late 1700's, and it is now found naturalized over much of central Europe. In North America its native range is the central Appalachian and Ozark mountains. As an ornamental, black

locust is recommended as a street tree or for use in land reclamation but is considered to be too messy for residential use. It needs full sun and does well in poor soil.

Black locust wood is brown, of medium to heavy weight, and very hard. It also resists rot—locust fences and beams can last a century or more. Locust wood is considered the strongest temperate American hardwood, but the live tree is subject to extensive damage from the locust borer beetle. This limits its availability as commercial lumber.

Madrone, Madroño, or Strawberry Tree
(Arbutus)
The madrones are evergreen, broad-leaved trees that grow 20 to 100 feet tall. Their bell-shaped flowers are white or pale pink; the round, berrylike fruits have a warty surface. Madrone wood is brown with a reddish blush, heavy, and hard, with a close grain. It is burned to make a high-quality charcoal that was once used in the manufacture of gunpowder. Madrones are stunning and unusual ornamentals, suitable as specimen or accent

plants. They need a sunny exposure and shielding from wind, and prefer dry, sandy, acidic soil.

Pacific madrone *(Arbutus menziesii)* is a slow-growing tree that may live for more than 200 years but reaches only 30 to 40 feet in height. It has a contorted and irregularly shaped or sprawling trunk, and papery, cinnamon-colored bark that peels off to reveal smooth, yellowish new bark. The glossy, evergreen leaves persist for 2 years and then are shed and replaced in either spring or late summer. The flowers are white to pink, about 1/4 inch long, and emerge in spring along hairy branched stalks 5 to 6 inches long. The blossoms attract honeybees. Pacific madrone berries are 1/2 inch across and bright orange-red with a finely bumpy skin; they are edible but lack flavor. They are quite popular among banded pigeons, chats, thrushes, and small mammals. Pacific madrone grows along the Pacific coast from southern British Columbia through California.

Magnolia *(Magnolia)*
Magnolias are deciduous or evergreen shrubs and trees, 20 to 80

Black locust *(Robinia pseudoacacia)*

Pacific madrone *(Arbutus menzi*

feet tall. They are well known for their large, showy, usually fragrant blossoms and leathery, dark green leaves. The fruit is a woody, conelike structure with individual compartments that open to release a vermilion seed dangling from a thin thread. Magnolias are spectacular ornamentals when they have ample space, as in a large yard or park. Unfortunately, they produce large amounts of leaf and fruit litter. They grow in full sun or partial shade and require deep, moist, slightly acid, well-drained soil and protection from wind. The fleshy, bowl-shaped magnolia flowers are pollinated by beetles and other insects.

Cucumber tree, or **cucumber magnolia,** *(Magnolia acuminata)* grows 50 to 80 feet tall and nearly as wide. It has massive, spreading branches and is pyramidal in youth, becoming broadly rounded with age. The deciduous leaves are 5 to 9 inches long with an abrupt point at the tip; they are dark green and glossy on the upper surface and pale green with tiny hairs below. The odorless flowers are 3 inches long, loosely cup-shaped, and pale green to yellowish. The conelike fruit is 1 to 2½ inches long. The cucumber

tree is found from western New York to Louisiana.

Southern magnolia, or **bull bay,** *(Magnolia grandiflora)* grows 60 to 80 feet tall, with low branches that spread broadly in a pyramidal crown. The tree blossoms at 10 to 20 years of age. The richly fragrant flowers are nearly one foot across, with fleshy white petals that are rounded at the tips. Evergreen leaves are 4 to 10 inches long; they are thick, glossy, and dark green on the upper surface, with velvety, rust-colored hairs on the lower surface. The conelike fruit is barrel-shaped and 2 to 3 inches long. The southern magnolia is native to the southeastern United States, from North Carolina to eastern Texas.

Maidenhair Tree see Gingko

Maple *(Acer)*

Maples range from 15 to 50 feet in height and have dense, round crowns and symmetrical branches. In most species, unremarkable small flowers appear in early spring before the leaves unfurl. The distinctive leaves grow in pairs and resemble a hand with the fingers spread. Maple trees produce paired, winged seeds called samaras, or keys, which

mature in either spring or fall. Among the most familiar woodland trees in North America, maples are popular for the vibrant displays of color the leaves provide in autumn. While the nearly 150 species are mostly Asiatic, 13 are native to North America, and the maple is the national tree of Canada. With the exception of Japanese maple, which needs partial shade, all maples need full sun and moist, well-drained soil.

Box elder, or **ash-leaf maple,** *(Acer negundo)* usually grows 40 to 50 feet tall but may reach 75 feet, with a trunk up to 4 feet in diameter. These trees grow about 1 inch in girth each year for the first 15 to 20 years and live a total of 60 to 100 years. The leaves, unlike those of most other maples, may consist of three, five, or seven coarsely toothed leaflets. Each leaf may be 6 to 15 inches long. The foliage turns yellow in fall. Box elder grows in the eastern United States, from New England to Florida; westward, it is found through much of the United States and north through Manitoba to Alberta.

Norway maple *(Acer platanoides)* usually grows to about 50 feet, with a short trunk. Greenish-yellow flower clusters

appear in spring. Its leaves have five or seven lobes, each lobe ending in a pointed tooth. The leaves are leathery and broader than they are long. An unusual feature of the leaf stems is that they exude a milky juice when broken. The foliage turns bright yellow in fall. The wings on the Norway maple seeds are shaped like mustaches.

Native to Europe, this species is widely planted and well known in North America. Norway maple takes city stress better than most other maples and is popular as a street, lawn, or park tree; however, grass grows poorly under Norway maple because of the tree's shallow surface roots.

Red maple *(Acer rubrum)* grows 40 to 50 feet tall and usually lives only about 150 years. Red maple is one of the first trees to flower in spring, with tiny, bright red blossoms. Its leaves usually have three to five lobes and double teeth around the edges. The stem of each leaf is often tinged with red; the foliage itself turns red and orange in fall. The winged seeds are pink when they emerge and are already mature by summer. Red maple grows in eastern North America, from southern

Southern magnolia *(Magnolia grandiflora)*

Norway maple *(Acer platanoides)*

Red maple *(Acer rubrum)*

Canada down to Texas and northern Florida.

Sugar maple *(Acer saccharum)* is a 50- to 70-foot-tall tree having a relatively short trunk when growing out in the open, and a large crown spreading some 35 to 45 feet. Its leaves have three to five lobes and are as broad as they are long. The leaves of the sugar maple turn brilliant combinations of yellow, orange, and red in autumn. Male and female flowers are produced in separate clusters on the same tree in the spring, and the winged seeds are produced in summer.

Sugar maple is widespread in eastern North America and occurs in the extreme south of Canada and throughout the eastern United States. American Indians who lived near the Great Lakes and the St. Lawrence River produced maple sugar and syrup long before Europeans arrived in North America. During the 1700's and 1800's maple sugar ranked as an important food item. The Canadian province of Quebec produces more maple sugar than all the United States, and while many people associate maple sugar with Vermont, New York outproduces all other states.

Most of the so-called hard maple used in the lumber trade is actually sugar maple. Its reddish-brown heartwood has the finest luster of all the maple species, and the hard, close-grained, strong wood is highly regarded for making furniture, flooring, veneer, and other goods. Bird's-eye maple, curly maple, and fiddleback maple are forms of sugar maple wood with decoratively distorted grain. They are valued highly for veneers used in cabinetmaking. While a fine ornamental, sugar maple is a poor choice as an urban tree because of its intolerance to road salt.

Mescal Bean see Sophora

Mesquite *(Prosopis)*
Mesquite is a small tree or shrub with a loose and straggling crown. The branches have a pair of spines at each point along the twig where a leaf attaches. The leaves of most types of mesquite are usually V-shaped and made up of 5 to 21 pairs of narrow leaflets. Minute individual flowers are grouped into long, dense, fluffy clusters, which attract bees. The fruits look like long, narrow bean pods. Mesquite is characteristic of the dry prairie and desert of Mexico and the southwestern

United States. There, the seeds and leaves are indispensable to deer, peccaries, rabbits, and smaller mammals, as well as roadrunners, quail, and some livestock. At one time the seeds were ground into a flour and eaten by Native Americans.

Glandular mesquite *(Prosopis glandulosa)* has 7 to 18 pairs of leaflets on each of the two leaf axes. Its flowers are grouped in fuzzy yellow clusters about 2 inches long. The fruit pods are 4 to 10 inches long, narrow, and slightly indented between the seeds. Glandular mesquite grows in southern California and Nevada, and from southern Kansas south through Mexico.

In **screwbean mesquite** *(Prosopis pubescens)*, each of the two or four leaf axes has five to eight pairs of leaflets. The flower clusters are greenish white, and the 1- to 2-inch fruits are in tight spirals, similar to the threads of a screw. Screwbean mesquite is found in southern Nevada and California, south to Mexico.

Mimosa, or Silk Tree
(Albizia)
The flowering mimosa tree grows 20 to 120 feet tall or more. It is flat-topped, with a

wide crown and low branches. Its flowers are clustered in fluffy heads resembling powder puffs. The leaves fold inward when touched; each comprises a central stalk bearing many lateral stalks with numerous pairs of tiny leaflets. In autumn, long, flat brown seed pods are produced.

The **mimosa tree,** or **silk tree,** *(Albizia julibrissin)* is a fast-growing tree that may begin to flower at only 3 or 4 years of age and eventually grows to about 40 feet. It has feathery leaves 9 to 12 inches long and fluffy, rosy-pink flowers. The mimosa tree is a shade tree that does well even in dry, hot climates and exposed to pollution; it likes full sun.

Mimosa trees are originally from Asia but now grow naturally in many parts of the world, including much of the southern United States. Thomas Jefferson obtained mimosa tree seeds from botanical explorers in 1785 and speeded its introduction in North America. Trees from the original seeds were able to survive only in the shorter winters in the area south of Washington, D.C. More than a century later Ernest Wilson, a botanical explorer, obtained seeds from a mimosa tree growing beyond the

Sugar maple *(Acer saccharum)*

Glandular mesquite *(Prosopis glandulosa)*

Mimosa *(Albizia julibrissin)*

northern part of its natural range in Korea. The seeds were brought to the United States and proved to be hardy in the region between Philadelphia and Boston.

Mountain Ash, or Rowan Tree *(Sorbus)*

Mountain ash is a deciduous tree, usually 20 to 50 feet tall. It has foamy sprays of flowers in spring and showy clusters of bright orange berries in late summer. Two species that were introduced from Korea and Europe are well-known lawn ornamentals that thrive in full sun and well-drained soil.

American mountain ash *(Sorbus americana)* is a shrub or round-topped tree up to 30 feet tall. The dark green leaves resemble feathers, with 9 to 17 long, narrow leaflets. White flowers form in dense, flat-topped clusters. In late summer the trees are laden with clusters of vivid orange-red fruits about 1/4 inch wide. The American mountain ash is occasionally planted as an ornamental but is much more important as a source of food for wildlife. Moose browse the twigs and leaves, while grouse, squirrels, and songbirds consume the berries. American mountain ash

is an understory tree in eastern North America and grows from Newfoundland south through the Appalachian Mountains and west to Manitoba and Illinois.

Mulberry *(Morus)*

Mulberries are deciduous shrubs or trees that grow 30 to 80 feet tall. Sweet, edible fruits resembling elongated raspberries are produced in early summer. White and black mulberries are two Asian species that have become naturalized in North America. Mulberries are planted to attract songbirds in the garden as well as for their fruit and foliage. The trees grow in full sun to partial shade and adapt to any good soil. Mulberries are fine trees for open areas; fruit litter and stains make them undesirable in small yards or near walkways.

The native **red mulberry** *(Morus rubra)* grows up to 65 feet tall with a spreading, rounded crown and a trunk that branches low to the ground. Its leaves are 3 to 4 inches long and irregularly toothed along the edges; the leaf is rounded to heart-shaped at the base, and the ends are either undivided or have one, three, or five lobes. The undersides are covered with whitish hairs. Male and female

flowers are produced separately on either the same tree or different trees, and the tiny greenish flowers form in tight 1-to 2-inch-long clusters that dangle from the stems. The fruits are red, turning almost black when ripe. Red mulberry is found scattered throughout the eastern United States and Canada, from Massachusetts west across southern Ontario to Minnesota, and south to Florida and Texas.

Nutmeg Tree see Torreya

Oak *(Quercus)*

Oaks are a large and diverse group of trees found mainly in the Northern Hemisphere; some 60 species grow in North America. Most oaks are trees, ranging from 35 to 100 feet tall, with leaf shapes varying from unlobed to deeply lobed, incised, or toothed. Depending on the species, oak leaves may be deciduous, evergreen, or semi-evergreen—remaining on the tree through winter but falling off and being replaced in spring. Oak flowers are pollinated by the wind; male and female flowers emerge in separate, dangling clusters on the same tree in spring, before or at the same time as the leaves appear. The

fruit of the oak is the acorn, a nut that is surrounded at the base by a scaly cup.

There are two major subgroups of oaks: the white oaks and the red and black oaks. All species that fall into the white oak group have leaves of varying shapes, with smooth tips; their acorns require only one season to ripen, and the inside of the acorn shell is smooth, with no hairs. All the leaves of the red and black oaks have bristlelike tips; the acorns require two seasons to mature, and the inside of the acorn shell is lined with hairs. Oaks provide the finest commercial hardwoods, notable for their strength and durability, the white oak species being distinctively harder and more resilient. The wood is blond to reddish brown and heavy, takes a hard polish, and can be cut to reveal a decorative grain. Oak wood is popular for furniture, flooring, paneling, and construction.

Acorns are a staple in the diet of several mammal species, including squirrels, white-tailed and black-tailed deer, bears, peccaries, and raccoons; they are also consumed by birds such as the wild turkey, wood duck, woodpeckers, and jays. Some oaks are grown as ornamentals to provide

American mountain ash *(Sorbus americana)*

Red mulberry *(Morus rubra)*

Black oak *(Quercus velutina)*

shade and natural beauty; some serve as street trees. Most oaks need full sun and acidic, well-drained, moist, deep soil.

The oak family provides a good example of how much basic research still needs to be done on even our most familiar North American plants. Recent studies revealed that the tree commonly known as Texas oak did not have a valid scientific name. Two botany students at the University of Texas fulfilled the requirements to name this "new species" officially. Thus in the 1980's one of the most common trees in Texas was at last given a scientific name, *Quercus buckleyi*, or Buckley's oak, in honor of the Texas explorer Samuel Bosworth Buckley.

Black oak *(Quercus velutina)* averages 60 to 80 feet in height. Its leaves are some 5 to 6 inches long and 3 to 4 inches wide, with deep U-shaped indentations between the five to seven main lobes. The lobes and marginal teeth are both tipped with bristles. The leaves are tough, glossy, and dark green above, and paler and velvety to smooth on the undersurface. The acorns, which develop in two seasons, ripen in late fall; they are 1/2 to 3/4 inch long, with a deep cup enveloping about half of the nut. Black oak is one of the commonest trees of the eastern and midwestern United States. The yellow to orange inner bark of black oak is dried to a powder to produce a yellow dye.

Blackjack oak *(Quercus marilandica)* grows 20 to 30 feet tall, although it occasionally grows as high as 50 feet. The name blackjack probably refers to the somewhat club-shaped leaves, which usually have a broad apex divided into three lobes. The leaves range between 3 and 7 inches long and between 2 and 5 inches wide. They are tough, dark green, smooth, and glossy above and have dense brown hairs below. The egg-shaped acorns mature in 2 years and are up to 1 inch long; they are enclosed about halfway by a deep cup. Blackjack oak is usually found in dry areas, primarily in the southern United States, most abundantly in Arkansas and eastern Texas.

Bur oak, or **mossy cup oak,** *(Quercus macrocarpa)* grows 70 to 130 feet tall. Its leaves are 6 to 12 inches long, widest above the middle, and often have a pair of deep U-shaped indentations just below the middle and five to nine rounded lobes. The acorn is up to 2 inches long and may be enclosed over half its length by the cup. The bur oak grows primarily in the midwestern United States.

California white oak *(Quercus lobata),* also called valley oak or weeping oak, grows 40 to 100 feet tall, with an enormous spreading crown. Its leathery leaves are up to 4 inches long and 2 inches wide, with 7 to 11 rounded lobes. The upper and lower surfaces are finely hairy. The distinctive acorns are almost bullet-shaped, 1 to 2 inches long, with a shallow cup enclosing only the base. The California white oak is found only in the valleys and foothills of California.

Chinkapin oak, or **yellow chestnut oak,** *(Quercus muehlenbergii)* is 65 to 100 feet in height, with a rounded crown. Its oblong leaves, tapering toward the tip and with wavy teeth along the margins, resemble those of the chinkapin or chestnut. The acorn nuts are usually less than 3/4 inch long and are covered half their length or less by the cup. Chinkapin oak is found scattered on upland sites in the midwestern and eastern United States.

Pin oak *(Quercus palustris)* grows 60 to 90 feet tall. The bottom branches sweep low, and the upper branches stand upright to form a pyramid shape. The name pin oak refers to the numerous short, pinlike lateral twigs along the branches. The leaves are 3 to 6 inches long and have five to seven bristle-tipped lobes with deep, rounded coves between the lobes. The globe-shaped acorns are 1/2 inch across and enclosed only at the base by a shallow cup. Pin oak is a tree of the midcentral to eastern United States.

Post oak *(Quercus stellata)* is 30 to 65 feet tall with a dense, round crown. The leathery dark green leaves are 4 to 6 inches long, 3 to 4 inches wide, and shaped vaguely like a Maltese cross. The acorn is about 3/4 inch long, with a cup that encloses less than half the nut. Post oak grows throughout the southeastern and southcentral United States.

Southern live oak *(Quercus virginiana)* is a semi-evergreen tree that grows 40 to 80 feet tall, with a massive spreading crown and contorted branches. Its leaves are 1 1/4 to 3 inches long and 3/8 to 1 inch wide and have margins that roll inward

Bur oak *(Quercus macrocarpa)*

California white oak *(Quercus lobata)*

Southern live oak *(Quercus virginiana)*

slightly. They are dark green and leathery on the upper surfaces, gray-green and woolly underneath. The egg-shaped acorns are about 1 inch long, and a shallow cup encloses about one-quarter of the nut. Southern live oak is a striking tree of the Gulf and Atlantic coastal plains from Virginia through Texas.

White oak (*Quercus alba*) grows to 75 feet or more. Its leaves have 7 to 10 rounded lobes. The foliage is bright green in summer, turning to burgundy and crimson in fall. Acorns are $1/2$ to $3/4$ inch long, with a shallow cup that envelopes just the base of the nut. White oak is a common tree of the southcentral and southeastern United States. Wood ducks and blue jays feed extensively on the acorns.

Palms

(Family *Arecaceae* or *Palmae*) Palms are evergreen trees mainly of tropical regions and are easily recognized by their characteristic form. Palm trees almost always have a columnar trunk, often ringed where the older leaves have peeled off, with a tuft of leaves at the apex. The leaves are very large and either long and divided into leaflets or rounded; the leaf blade is pleated like a fan and split into numerous lobes radiating out like the spokes of a wheel. Palm flowers are usually white and fragrant, and have a leathery or fleshy texture. The flowers are found along stalks emerging from within or directly below the crown. Although they may vary greatly in size and color, palm fruits have either a fleshy or fibrous outer layer that encloses a hard-shelled seed.

The **date palm** (*Phoenix dactylifera*) has a rough, fibrous trunk with a cross-hatched pattern created by its old leaf bases. At maturity, the trunk may be 50 feet tall and as much as 3 feet across. Its leaves are stiff, dark grayish green, and up to 20 feet long. Tiny white flowers, followed by the sticky and sugary date fruits, are produced in huge quantities in large, hanging clusters. The date palm is cultivated in California and Arizona and, to a lesser extent, in Texas and Florida. It lines the avenues of Phoenix, Arizona, a city whose name is derived from the Latin name of this tree. Date palms need full sun and fertile soil to thrive. Dry summers are best for producing fruit. The date palm was probably cultivated by humans before any other tree. Sun-baked bricks, made in Mesopotamia more than 5,000 years ago, contain instructions for growing the tree.

The **sabal palm**, or **cabbage palmetto**, (*Sabal palmetto*) grows up to 80 feet in height. The stout trunk is covered with dried leaf sheaths that form a cross-hatched pattern. The fan-shaped leaves split into ribbon-like segments as they develop. White or pale yellow flowers appear in spring. The fruits are round, $1/2$ inch across, and black when they mature in fall. The cabbage palmetto occurs along the southeastern coastal plain from North Carolina to the Florida Keys and is the state tree of Florida. Cabbage palm is often used as an accent plant, either in clusters or in groves. It grows in full sun or partial shade and in sandy soil, especially in seaside areas.

The palm known variously as the **California washingtonia, desert fan palm, petticoat palm,** or **washingtonia** (*Washingtonia filifera*) grows 50 to 70 feet tall. A thick skirt of withered leaves clings to the trunk below the crown. The light green leaves are shaped and pleated like a fan, 3 to 5 feet across. They tear between the folds into narrow segments on a spiny leafstalk, with fibrous threads fraying between the sections. In summer, clusters of fragrant flowers bloom along 9-foot branches. The black, berrylike fruit is $1/4$ inch in diameter and ripens in autumn. California washingtonia is native to a small area at the junction of southern California, southwestern Arizona, and Baja California. It needs full sun and moist soil.

Paloverde (*Cercidium*)

Paloverdes are small shrubs and trees of the desert Southwest. As their name suggests, they have green stems and branches. Their leaves are composed of multiple leaflets with a pair of spines at the base of each leaf. The fruit looks like a flattened bean pod.

Blue paloverde (*Cercidium floridum*) is a deciduous tree up to 33 feet tall, with bluish-green branches and leaves, and a crooked trunk. The leaves have a V-shaped axis with one to nine pairs of leaflets, each about $1/4$ inch long. The five-petaled yellow flowers grow in small clusters and appear in early spring. The pods are somewhat flat and

Date palm (*Phoenix dactylifera*)

California washingtonia (*Washingtonia filifera*)

Blue paloverde (*Cercidium floridum*)

contain one to four seeds. Blue paloverde is found in dry scrub and grassland from Texas to southeastern California and Mexico. The blue-green twigs and leaves are eaten by sheep and burro deer, while the seeds are consumed by smaller mammals. The Pima and Papago Indians of Arizona cook the young pods and seeds or grind the mature seeds to prepare a thick soup.

Pawpaw (*Asimina*)

The pawpaw is a North American group of shrubs, with one species of tree. It is unusual in being a temperate member of a largely tropical family of plants, the custard-apple family.

Pawpaw (*Asimina triloba*) is a tree or large shrub, 15 to 35 feet tall, with delicate, spreading branches. The leaves are light green and turn pale yellow in the fall before drooping and withering on the stem. In spring exotic flowers emerge from the older stems. The cup-shaped blossoms are 2 inches across, with a cushionlike mass in the center and six fleshy round petals that turn from green to deep burgundy. Pawpaw fruits are lumpy and irregular to somewhat cylindrical in shape and about 2 to 4 inches long. When ripe in late fall, the skin is black and wrinkled, but the sweet, custardy flesh inside is yellow to orange.

Pawpaws were cultivated by the Creeks, Cheraws, and Catawbas, who preferred the more flavorful, orange-fleshed fruit. Pawpaws are understory trees found in forests mainly of the southeastern United States. The fruit is a favorite of raccoons, opossums, bears, and turkeys.

Pecan see Hickory

Pear (*Pyrus*)

Pears are some 20 to 60 feet tall and may be deciduous or semievergreen. They have ornamental white flowers and distinctive, edible fruits that are wider at the base than near the stem and have gritty flesh. Pear trees make fine accent and shade trees, as well as street trees. They prefer full sun, but are easy to grow, adaptable, and tolerant of pollution, drought, and wind.

The **common pear** (*Pyrus communis*) is widely cultivated but is also found in the wild. It is a deciduous tree that may grow some 65 feet tall, with a straight trunk and dark brown to gray bark. The leaves are 1 to 3 inches long; they are hairy when young, turning smooth, glossy, and dark green above and paler beneath at maturity. The fruit, about 4 inches long, is soft and juicy when ripe; there are gritty stone cells in the flesh, especially near the core.

Persea (*Persea*)

Perseas are handsome tropical trees and shrubs that grow 30 to 60 feet tall. They have evergreen leaves and small, inconspicuous flowers. Depending on the species, the trees may bear anything from small berries to large, fleshy fruits.

The **avocado** (*Persea americana*) often grows up to 65 feet tall. Its leathery leaves are 4 to 12 inches long. The pear-shaped fruits are 3 to 8 inches long. The avocado, native to Central America, was introduced in Florida by the Spanish and is now naturalized in that region. The fruit has become an important food crop in Florida and California.

The tree known by the names **red bay, sweet bay, laurel tree, tisswood,** and **Florida mahogany** (*Persea borbonia*) grows 30 to 40 feet tall. Its aromatic leaves are 2 to 8 inches long, glossy green in color, and fuzzy to smooth on the undersides. The dark blue to blackish fruit, about 1/2 inch across, is borne on a red stalk. Red bay is found in moist lowland areas of the Atlantic and Gulf coastal plains from Virginia to Texas. This species provides the fragrant bay leaves that are used in flavoring soups and stews. In the cultivated landscape red bay makes an unusual lawn accent. It needs full sun and moist soil.

Persimmon (*Diospyros*)

Persimmons are deciduous fruiting shrubs or trees reaching 35 to 70 feet or more, with rounded crowns. Their leaves are glossy and dark green, turning yellow, orange, or purplish red in fall. Small flowers bloom in spring and are followed in fall by juicy, edible fruit. The tangerine-size persimmons called kaki, occasionally found in supermarkets, are the fruit of an introduced Asian species now cultivated in California. They are ripe for eating when the flesh is soft and the skin becomes wrinkled.

A member of the ebony family of plants, persimmon has very dark brown to almost black, hard, very heavy wood. It yields a

Pawpaw (*Asimina triloba*)

Common pear (*Pyrus communis*)

Red bay (*Persea borbonia*)

Common persimmon
(*Diospyros virginiana*)

poor quality lumber, however, that is not of significant commercial value. Persimmons can serve as small shade trees; they need full sun and moist, well-drained soil to thrive.

The **common persimmon** (*Diospyros virginiana*) is a small to medium-size tree with a broad crown. Its dark green, leathery leaves are 3- to 5-inch-long ovals. The common persimmon bears fragrant, bell-shaped, whitish flowers in early summer. The orange to purple fruit is 1 to 2½ inches long and has four leathery green lobes at the stem; it ripens only after the first frost.

Persimmons are usually found in disturbed sites and woodlands in the southeastern United States. The fruits are eaten by deer, raccoons, foxes, skunks, and a variety of birds. At one time Native Americans made a bread by mixing mashed persimmon pulp, which tastes sweet and fruity, with crushed corn.

Pine (*Pinus*)

Of all needle-leaved evergreens, pines have the widest range of characteristics, habits, and distribution. They are evergreen conifers that grow 10 to more than 100 feet tall. They generally have pyramid-shaped profiles in youth and become more rounded with age. The long, narrow leaves, or needles, are clustered in bundles of two to five along the outer branches. There are distinct male and female cones, but both are found on the same tree. Wind carries the male pollen cell, which has two balloonlike wings, to the female cones. Although the pollen is transferred to the female cones in the spring, fertilization does not happen until one or two years later. The mature pine cones are brown, with woody or sometimes leathery scales, each of which contains two seeds. Pines need full sun and moist, well-drained soil.

Eastern white pine (*Pinus strobus*) is the largest conifer in the Northeast, growing 75 to 100 feet tall, with an open, airy crown and tiers of whorled branches. Its blue-green needles are 3 to 5 inches long. This tree is the only pine east of the Rocky Mountains that has five needles in each cluster. The curved, cylindrical cones are 4 to 8 inches long. This species of pine spans a wide range over eastern North America.

Eastern white pine was the most important timber tree in North America in the 18th and 19th centuries. Early lumberers recorded trunks 250 feet long and 6 feet in diameter. Pine is still one of the principal commercial woods; it is straight-grained, has white sapwood and orangish heartwood, and takes a good polish, but is soft and not exceptionally strong.

Loblolly pine (*Pinus taeda*) has needles 6 to 7 inches long in clusters of three. The seed cone is 4 to 5 inches long, and there are sharp spreading spines on the scales. Loblolly pine is native to the southeastern United States. The name loblolly, originally a word for a thick gruel, refers to the swampy or poorly drained areas in which the tree often occurs. This fast-growing tree is cultivated for pulpwood and its pale, coarse-grained lumber. Loblolly pine plantations are remarkably productive; one acre can yield 300 to 1,000 board feet of timber annually.

Longleaf pine, or **southern pine,** (*Pinus palustris*) grows slowly to a height of 75 to 120 feet. Needles are in clusters of three, usually concentrated toward the ends of the branches, and are 8 to 18 inches long. Seed cones are 6 to 10 inches long and have a prickle at the top of each scale. This tree is native to the southeastern United States. Southern pine is cultivated as the raw material for products like turpentine and resin. It is also logged for lumber, since the reddish to yellowish wood is hard and strong.

Colorado pinyon (*Pinus edulis*) is one of four species of pinyon pine. It is a small tree with edible seeds that grows 20 to 60 feet tall with a rounded crown. Needles are 1 to 1½ inches long in clusters of two. The seed cones are round and about 2 inches long. Colorado pinyon is frequently encountered in the Southwest, particularly in Utah, Arizona, New Mexico, and Colorado.

Ponderosa pine, or **western yellow pine,** (*Pinus ponderosa*) has a cone-shaped crown of upswept branches and may grow to 150 to 180 feet tall and live 350 to 500 years. Its pinkish-gray to pinkish-brown bark grows in long plates that shed in pieces. The cones are 4 to 5 inches long. When young the cones stand upright; as they mature, they turn upside down to spill the winged seeds.

Eastern white pine *(Pinus strobus)*

Loblolly pine *(Pinus taeda)*

Colorado pinyon *(Pinus edulis)*

Ponderosa pine is a dominant tree of the mountains of western North America, where it often grows in almost pure stands. The name ponderosa, conferred on the tree by one of its earliest collectors, David Douglas, refers to the tree's ponderous mass. Its wood is pale red, fine-grained, and strong, and is often used for general construction.

Red pine (*Pinus resinosa*), sometimes called Norway pine although it is native to North America, grows 50 to 80 feet and has an oval crown. The glossy, dark green needles are 5 to 6 inches long and found in clusters of two; they are somewhat brittle and will snap in two when bent sharply. The oval seed cones are 1 to 2½ inches long. Red pine is common in New England; it grows in Newfoundland west to Manitoba and south through the Great Lakes region.

The world's tallest and longest-coned pine is the **sugar pine,** or **Douglas pine,** (*Pinus lambertiana*). This species has been reported to reach 300 feet tall, although few are known to be over 220 feet. The gently twisting needles form in groups of five. Seed cones 15 to 20 inches long hang from the branch tips. The seeds are about the size of a corn kernel and are sought after as food by many birds and mammals. The sugar pine is found in the mountains from southern Oregon to southern California.

Planetree see Sycamore

Plum see Cherry

Poplar *(Populus)*

The trees known as cottonwood, aspen, quaking aspen, and poplar are among the 13 North American species belonging to the genus *Populus*. All are fast-growing, deciduous trees that reach 40 to 100 feet tall. The catkins emerge before the leaves, and the fruits mature quickly before the leaves are fully expanded. The fruits are usually tiny capsules that separate into two or four pieces. This releases cottony seeds that are carried in the wind by their long silky hairs. In general, cottonwoods and poplars have sticky buds, dark bark with deep fissures, and thick-walled fruits. In contrast, aspens have buds that are not sticky, light-colored bark, and thin-walled fruits. All of these trees are suitable shade trees in a large area.

Although poplars were planted frequently in the past because of their hardiness and rapid growth, they are currently out of favor as landscape plants because their invasive roots damage sidewalks, pipes, and sewer drains. Seed and leaf litter can also be a nuisance. They do best in difficult growing situations where few other plants will grow.

Quaking aspen is impressive planted as a mass or grove, or for naturalizing. Poplar, cottonwood, and aspen are adaptable to difficult conditions, including drought and pollution, but they grow best in full sun and deep, moist, well-drained soil. Poplars are most significant as part of the natural landscape, where they are vitally important in the winter and early-spring diet of many woodland animals. The twigs and leaves are eaten by moose, white-tailed deer, and mule deer, and beaver and hares consume the bark, leaves, and buds. Game birds eat the buds and young flower stalks. Poplar wood is light, soft, and weak, and is used for paper pulp and crates.

Balsam poplar (*Populus balsamifera*) reaches 100 feet with branches high on the trunk to form an irregular, open crown. Its teardrop leaves are 3 to 5 inches long and have small blunt teeth along the margins. The small brown seeds ripen quickly and are released in spring. Balsam poplar grows from Alaska through most of Canada, northern New England, and the Great Lakes area, and at higher elevations in the Rocky Mountains. Honeybees often use the resin of balsam poplar to waterproof their hives.

Eastern cottonwood (*Populus deltoides*) is a lowland tree usually 70 to 100 feet tall—although occasionally much taller—with an irregular crown and a massive trunk. Its bright green leaves are triangular, with rounded corners and wavy teeth along the edges. Eastern cottonwood is a tree of the eastern United States, ranging as far west as Minnesota and Texas.

Quaking aspen (*Populus tremuloides*) grows 40 to 50 feet tall; the crown becomes broader and rounder as it matures, spreading to as much as 20 to 30 feet. Catching the slightest breeze causes the long, flat leaf stalks to flutter and rustle. The leaves are 1½ to 3 inches long and equally wide. They are dark green in summer and turn brilliant gold in the fall. The bark is smooth and whitish green on

Ponderosa pine *(Pinus ponderosa)*

Quaking aspen *(Populus tremuloides)*

young trees, becoming fissured and dark on mature trunks. Quaking aspen has the widest distribution of any tree in North America. It is found from Alaska southeast through almost all of Canada and the northeastern United States, and southwest into Mexico.

Possum Haw see Holly

Quaking Aspen see Poplar

Redbud *(Cercis)*

The redbud is a graceful tree, growing 20 to 40 feet tall. Tiny flowers in clusters of four to eight are produced along the branches in spring before the appearance of heart-shaped or kidney-shaped leaves. A member of the bean family, redbud has flat, papery seed pods.

Eastern redbud *(Cercis canadensis)* grows 20 to 30 feet tall. With its 30-foot spread and heart-shaped foliage, the eastern redbud is striking in early spring, when the small, magenta-pink flowers cover the branches and stand out in the green woodland. The flowers can be eaten in salads. Redbuds are some of our most beautiful native ornamental trees, effective as lawn accents or specimen trees.

George Washington was so fond of the sight of redbud in early spring that he often transplanted trees from the woods to his garden at Mount Vernon. They thrive in any well-drained soil and in full sun or partial shade.

Redwood *(Sequoia and Sequoiadendron)*

Redwoods are massive, narrow-crowned evergreen conifers reaching 360 feet in height. Their trunks are 35 feet or more in diameter.

Redwood, or **coastal redwood,** *(Sequoia sempervirens)* is the tallest tree in the world, towering to 360 feet. It has a reddish-brown trunk that flares out at the base to support its massive bulk and a slender, irregular crown. Its flat needles are less than 1 inch long; the seed cones are 1 inch long with some 12 to 20 scales. The tree has amazing powers of regeneration; new sprouts often emerge from stumps, roots, or even felled trunks. Coastal redwood grows in the fog belt along the Pacific coast from southern Oregon to central California—which represents only a portion of its original range.

The name sequoia commemorates the Cherokee Indian

Sequoyah (1770–1843), who developed the Cherokee alphabet. This tree yields a valuable, naturally rot-resistant timber that was once widely used for shingles, fences, and general construction, including bridges. Overexploitation of the redwood has endangered its survival, although beautiful stands are now protected in the Redwood National Forest.

The **giant sequoia,** or **sierra redwood,** *(Sequoiadendron giganteum)* is an enormous tree, 200 to 300 feet tall or more, with a buttressed trunk that grows 20 to 50 or more feet in diameter. The bark may be up to 2 feet thick. The giant sequoia has a tremendous life span of 2,000 to 3,000 years or more; none have ever been known to die of old age, disease, or insect attack. Its tiny, scalelike leaves lie flat along the stem, overlapping each other. Seed cones are 1½ to 2½ inches long and have some 25 to 40 scales.

Giant sequoias are native to the western slopes of the southern Sierra Nevada of California.

In the mid to late 1800's vast numbers of giant sequoias were plundered for timber; many felled trees were left to waste because machines were not available to remove the enormous logs from steep slopes. Large stands are now protected by the creation of Yosemite and General Grant national parks and the expansion of Sequoia National Park in 1890. The largest living organism on earth is the giant sequoia tree named General Sherman. At 295 feet tall and 110 feet in diameter, it is estimated that this single tree would yield more than 600,000 board feet of lumber.

Rhododendron *(Rhododendron)*

The rhododendron is a large and diverse, mostly Asian group of about 800 species of plants, many of which are well known as attractive ornamentals. Technically the genus *Rhododendron* includes the woody shrubs with papery deciduous leaves, known by gardeners as azaleas, as well as the leathery-leaved, usually evergreen plants we all recognize as rhododendrons. Many of the ornamental rhododendrons and azaleas used as foundation plantings are hybrids.

Eastern redbud *(Cercis canadensis)*

Redwood *(Sequoia sempervirens)*

Giant sequoia
(Sequoiadendron giganteum)

Rosebay rhododendron
(Rhododendron maximum)

Rosebay rhododendron (*Rhododendron maximum*) is a sprawling shrub or small tree with sinuous stems. Its narrow evergreen leaves are 4 to 12 inches long. Flowers appear in dense showy clusters of 12 to 30 at the tips of branches in late spring or early summer. The blossoms range from white to reddish pink, with flecks of green on the uppermost petals. Its fruits are sticky capsules about 1/2 inch long.

The rosebay rhododendron attracts many bees, but the honey produced from its flowers is toxic to humans. From time to time, wood of this tree is used to make handles for small tools, but rosebay rhododendron is most often utilized as a hardy evergreen ornamental. This species is native to an area extending from Maine to northern Georgia; it grows mostly along streams in upland areas.

Rowan Tree see Mountain Ash

Saguaro *(Cereus)*

Saguaros and organ-pipes are cacti that reach tree size. They have leafless, succulent, columnar stems, with clusters of spines running along lengthwise ridges. The showy, exotic flowers may be as large as 10 inches across, depending upon the species, and have vast numbers of yellow stamens and delicate petals. The cacti have spiny, bulb-shaped edible fruits.

Symbol of the desert Southwest, the **giant saguaro** (*Cereus giganteus*) reaches 50 feet in height. It grows as a single, straight trunk, or column, for many years and eventually develops one to five upward-bending side branches. The column has vertical ribs with spine clusters along the ridges and a green, leathery surface. The white flower, about 2 inches across, is the state flower of Arizona. The egg-shaped, fleshy fruit is green with a reddish blush and grows to 2 or 3 inches long; it splits open along three seams to expose a red pulp and a mass of tiny black seeds. The fruit is edible and can be made into jelly and preserves.

The saguaro grows in the high deserts of Arizona and in the Mexican state of Sonora. Although its water content varies throughout the year, the average saguaro is 98 percent water by weight. Wide-spreading, shallow roots are efficient in taking advantage of the seasonal July rains, sudden flash floods, and night dews; the long ribs allow the stem to expand and contract like a bellows to accommodate fluctuations in water content.

Sassafras Tree *(Sassafras)*

The **sassafras** (*Sassafras albidum*) is a deciduous tree 30 to 60 feet tall. It develops an irregular, open shape with a short trunk and horizontal, twisted branches. Its extraordinary leaves appear in late spring and may be mitten-shaped, trident-shaped, or unlobed; all forms may appear on the same tree at the same time. Sassafras foliage is yellow-green on the upper surface and whitish below, and turns orange and scarlet in the fall. The inconspicuous flowers are yellowish green; male and female flowers are produced by separate trees. The olive-shaped blue fruits are about 1/2 inch long and are borne in red cups on red stalks in autumn.

Sassafras is native to the eastern United States, from New England south to Florida and west to Michigan and Texas. Like other members of the laurel family—cinnamon, bay leaf, and camphor tree—sassafras is noted for its aromatic bark, roots, branches, leaves, flowers, and fruit. The bark of the sassafras root is brewed to make sassafras tea, which is often available in supermarkets.

In past centuries, sassafras enjoyed a fantastic reputation as a cure-all. A large demand for sassafras was created in Europe in the late 1500's following publication of an overblown description of the tree's curative powers against malaria, liver and stomach ailments, and chest colds, among other ills. The price of sassafras root bark soared to 336 pounds sterling per ton. Shipments of sassafras were demanded from Virginia as a condition of the charter of Jamestown Colony, although it was soon after this that the tree's reputation began to wane. Sassafras was one ingredient in the medicinal spring tonic that was given to pioneer children and was used in other medicines, if not for its curative properties, then to help disguise their medicinal taste. Until banned for human consumption, sassafras was important in the manufacture of soaps and perfumes and in flavoring root beer.

As an ornamental, sassafras makes a fine shade tree for naturalizing. It grows in full sun or partial shade and does best in loamy, acid, well-drained soil.

Sequoia see Redwood

Giant saguaro *(Cereus giganteus)*

Sassafras *(Sassafras albidum)*

Silk Tree see Mimosa Tree

Silverbell, or Snowdrop Tree
(Halesia)
Silverbells, or snowdrop trees, grow from 20 to 50 feet tall, with drooping, white to pink, showy, bell-shaped flowers that form on the previous year's stems. The fruit is a capsule with either two or four wings.

Carolina silverbell *(Halesia carolina)* is a stunning tree, 20 to 30 feet tall, with a wide-spreading, rounded crown. The white, inch-long, snowdrop flowers appear in midspring. The bright green leaves have minute teeth. Yellow fall foliage provides a striking backdrop to the red, winged fruits, which persist on the tree through winter. As an ornamental, silverbell is used as a patio accent or woodland border. It does well in full sun or partial shade and in acid soil.

Snowdrop Tree see Silverbell

Soapberry *(Sapindus)*
Soapberries are persistent-leaved and deciduous shrubs and trees that grow 30 to 60 feet tall. The berrylike fruit contains a single seed and has a leathery skin that produces a soapy lather.

Western soapberry *(Sapindus drummondii)* is a deciduous tree or large shrub that grows 25 to 50 feet tall. Its leaves are composed of three to nine pairs of sickle-shaped leaflets and a single terminal leaflet. The bark is scaly and reddish brown. Tiny yellow-white flowers in showy 6- to 10-inch sprays appear in spring. The fruit is 1/2 inch in diameter, turning from yellow-orange to black and often persisting through winter. The foamy lather from the fruits was used for washing by Native Americans. Soapberry wood has mostly been used for firewood or basketry. Soapberry is planted as a shade or urban tree in dry locations; it thrives in full sun or light shade and in sandy or rocky soil.

Sophora, Mescal Bean, or Texas Mountain Laurel
(Sophora)
Sophoras are deciduous and evergreen trees with compound leaves, showy flowers, and bean-pod fruits. A genus of about 50 species worldwide, *Sophora* contains several ornamentals, including the Japanese pagoda tree, a popular shade, street, or specimen tree. Texas mountain laurel is popular as a native ornamental

planting in the Southwest. Sophoras need full sun and, once established, they can withstand heat, drought, and air pollution.

Texas mountain laurel *(Sophora secundiflora),* also called mescal bean or frijolito, grows up to 35 feet tall. It keeps its leaves throughout the year. The lavender flowers emit a fragrance like grape-flavored chewing gum when they appear in abundant clusters in early spring. The woody pods are up to 8 inches long and contain ruby-red seeds.

Texas mountain laurel is found in limestone areas of central and southwestern Texas, New Mexico, and Mexico. Although they smell delectable, the purple flowers are highly toxic, as are the red seeds, which contain hallucinogenic alkaloids. Before the use of peyote, Texas mountain laurel seeds were the principal hallucinogen in the Southwest. The ground seeds were mixed in small doses in a beverage to induce an intoxicated state as part of ceremonial rituals of Native Americans. The seeds are deadly in higher doses.

Sorrel Tree see Sourwood

Sourwood, or Sorrel Tree
(Oxydendrum arboreum)
Sourwood is a deciduous tree 25 to 30 feet tall with multiple stems and sinuous, gracefully drooping branches. Glossy, leathery leaves with fine teeth unfurl in spring, followed by ivory, bell-shaped flowers on clusters about 1 foot in length. The flowers are visited by bees, which cling to the petals and buzz their wings to release the powdery pollen. Scarlet foliage and yellow to brown persistent fruit are handsome in fall.

Sourwood grows from Pennsylvania south through northern Florida. The tree flowers best in full sun and very acid soil. Sourwood needs shelter from wind and does not tolerate air pollution.

Spruce *(Picea)*
Spruces are evergreen conifers that grow 20 to 100 feet tall in a pyramid or spire shape. Their stiff, sharp needles are 1/2 to 1 inch long and arranged in spirals around the twigs. Seed cones hang down from the branches and are either woody or leathery in texture.

Carolina silverbell *(Halesia carolina)*

Western soapberry
(Sapindus drummondii)

Texas mountain laurel
(Sophora secundiflora)

Sourwood *(Oxydendrum arboreum)*

Black spruce, or bog spruce, *(Picea mariana)* grows between 15 and 60 feet tall with a slender crown. Its needles are square in cross section and have a bluish cast. The small, egg-shaped cones are about 1 inch long and may persist on the branches for 4 or 5 years; only fire stimulates them to release the seeds. The black spruce has a broad range from Alaska across Canada to Newfoundland, but not further south than the Great Lakes region and New England. Squirrels, which consume the seeds, are apparently the only animals that value the tree for food. The small size of black spruce limits its commercial use, although spruce gum and spruce beer are made from this species.

Blue spruce *(Picea pungens)* is 80 to 100 feet tall with silvery blue, bristly needles that curve toward the branches. The cones are 2 to 4 inches long and have toothed scales. Native to the central Rocky Mountains, blue spruce is cultivated widely as an ornamental in eastern North America and in Europe. Some blue spruce trees may live 600 to 800 years.

White spruce *(Picea glauca)* is 80 to 140 feet in height; branches begin about halfway up the long trunk. Its green to bluish-green needles are square in cross section. The slender, hanging seed cones are leathery and have flexible, round-edged scales. This tree has a broad range—from Alaska to the northeastern United States. The white spruce is an important commercial timber tree in Canada, where it is used mainly for pulpwood. The lumber is soft, straight-grained, and resilient. White spruce is used in landscaping as a lawn highlight, windbreak, or screen, often in combination with other conifers. It is extremely hardy, capable of tolerating winters of −70°F and summers of 110°F. Like most trees in this family, white spruce needs full sun and sandy, acid soil.

Strawberry Tree see Madrone

Sumac *(Rhus and Toxicodendron)*
Sumacs are fast-growing, thicket-forming trees, shrubs, or vines with foliage of either single leaves or multiple leaflets. They may be either evergreen or deciduous. Flowers are small; fruits are small berries with a seed enclosed in a hard stone. The crushed fruits of staghorn and lemonade sumacs are used to make a drink like lemonade.

Lemonade sumac *(Rhus-integrifolia)* is a small tree or shrub with simple, leathery, evergreen leaves. White or pink flowers appear from early through midspring in dense clusters 1 to 3 inches long. The fruit, which matures in late summer, is deep scarlet, fuzzy, and sticky. Lemonade sumac is native to sandy soils of the southern California coast and Channel Islands.

Poison sumac *(Toxicodendron vernix)* is closely related to poison ivy and poison oak but is the only one of these species that regularly reaches tree size. The oil of poison sumac can cause a skin condition similar to that often caused by poison ivy. Poison sumac is a shrub or small tree up to 25 feet tall, with drooping branches forming an oval crown. The deciduous leaves are 7 to 13 inches long and composed of 7 to 13 leaflets. Small, yellowish flowers are produced in early spring in clusters emerging from the junction of the leaves and stem. Male and female flowers are found on separate trees. Fruits are white waxy berries about 1/2 inch across. Poison sumac ranges from southern Quebec south to Florida and west to Texas.

Staghorn sumac *(Rhus typhina)* is a shrub or straggling tree growing as tall as 35 feet. The stout twigs contain a milky sap; when young, they are covered with long, velvety brown hairs and resemble the fuzzy surface of new deer antlers. Leaves are deciduous and 1 to 2 feet long, with 11 to 31 leaflets. The flowers are densely packed in cone-shaped clusters found upright at the tips of the branches and are followed by the bright red, fuzzy fruits. Staghorn sumac is native from New Brunswick to the southern Appalachians and west to Iowa.

Sweet Gum, or Liquidambar Tree *(Liquidambar styraciflua)*
Sweet gum is a deciduous tree that grows 25 to 80 feet tall. It is easily distinguished by its five-to seven-lobed, star-shaped leaves with saw-toothed edges. The lustrous, light green foliage remains on the tree until late in the season and turns rich shades of yellow, burgundy, and scarlet. The round, woody fruits, called sweet gum balls, are actually composed of many individual capsules with pincerlike spines, massed together in a ball. The tree produces a sticky, golden,

Blue spruce *(Picea pungens)*

Staghorn sumac *(Rhus typhina)*

Sweet gum *(Liquidambar styraciflua)*

sweet-smelling resin known sometimes as liquid amber or gum. This resin, obtained by peeling the bark from the trunks and scraping off the thick droplets, was used in pioneer days to treat lesions and skin problems and, although bitter tasting, for chewing as well. The resin was used again during both world wars as the base of medicines, soaps, adhesives, and ointments when imported ingredients became scarce.

Sweet gum is an important commercial timber, second in popularity only to oak among the hardwoods in terms of production. It is widely used in the manufacture of furniture wood, used for cabinetry, veneer, plywood, and pulpwood. The sweet gum is native from southern Connecticut west to Illinois and south to Florida and Texas. As a shade, border, boulevard, or street tree, sweet gum does well in full sun to partial shade and needs acid soil.

Sycamore, Buttonwood, or Plane Tree *(Platanus)*

Sycamores are massive shade trees that grow to 75 to 100 feet tall, with broad, open crowns and stout trunks and branches. Sycamores are recommended as lawn highlights or shade trees in areas with ample growing space, such as large yards or parks. They are adaptable and can grow almost anywhere, but they do best in full sun and moist, well-drained soil.

The tree known as **American plane tree, American buttonwood, eastern sycamore,** and **buttonball** *(Plantanus occidentalis)* has large, broad leaves 4 to 9 inches wide, with three to five triangular lobes. The leaves are bright green on the upper surface, paler and downy beneath. The fruits are round "buttonballs" of tightly compressed old flowers and numerous individual nutlets buried in fuzzy hairs. The buttonballs hang singly from long stalks and often remain on the tree through winter. The bark of the tree is grayish brown and peels off in thin, irregular flakes to reveal a cream-colored inner bark, creating a mottled appearance.

The American plane tree grows from Maine west to Nebraska and south to Texas and Florida. In the wild it is a lowland tree of stream banks, floodplains, and bottomlands. The wood is light brown, hard, and heavy but coarse-grained and relatively weak. It was once popular for the manufacture of Pullman cars and stereoscopes but is used today for making crates, furniture, and butcher-block countertops.

Tamarack see Larch

Texas Mountain Laurel see Sophora

Torreya, or Nutmeg Tree *(Torreya)*

Torreyas are evergreen conifers with flat, needlelike leaves but no seed cones. Instead, as the seeds ripen, a fleshy outer covering called an aril grows out and envelops the seed completely. Two years are required for the seeds to mature. Although not related, the ripe fruits resemble those of the spice-yielding nutmeg tree. Torreya needles are aromatic, with a sagelike odor.

California torreya, or **California nutmeg,** *(Torreya californica)* is a pyramid-shaped tree 15 to 65 feet tall. Flat, dark green needles lie flush along the branches and are 1 to 3 inches long. The fruit is about 1 inch long and resembles a purple-streaked olive. California torreya is a rare tree of the central California Sierra Nevada. The strong wood was once used by American Indians for making bows.

Florida torreya, or **stinking cedar,** *(Torreya taxifolia)* is similar to the California species but has shorter, sharply pointed leaves, 1 to 1½ inches long, with a putrid odor. It is a very rare species of northwestern Florida—particularly in Torreya State Park—and southeastern Georgia.

Tree-of-heaven *(Ailanthus altissima)*

Tree-of-heaven is a fast-growing deciduous tree that reaches 60 feet or more, with loose, spreading branches. It has dark green leaves that produce an unpleasant odor like burned popcorn when crushed. The leaves are 1 to 3 feet long, with some 11 to 41 oval-shaped leaflets along a central stalk. Male and female flowers are usually produced by separate trees; the male flowers emit a vile odor. The fruits are narrow, flat, winged seeds that hang in large, dense clusters. The seeds are yellowish green to orange-red in late summer, turning brown and persisting on the tree through winter.

American plane tree *(Plantanus occidentalis)*

Florida torreya *(Torreya taxifolia)*

Tree-of-heaven *(Ailanthus altissima)*

Originally from China, tree-of-heaven is now among the most familiar trees in the North American landscape, where it is naturalized in many areas. It was first imported as an urban ornamental, for which it is still widely used. Tree-of-heaven is probably the most tolerant of all trees to stressful conditions, from seaside to urban environments. It is the best choice for growing under circumstances that no other tree can tolerate and can grow as much as 10 feet a year. If possible, the female tree should be chosen for planting to avoid the odor of the male flowers. While tree-of-heaven thrives along city streets, in vacant lots, and on woodland margins, it can also take over an area and become difficult to get rid of.

Tulip Tree (*Liriodendron*)

Tulip tree is a massive deciduous tree that may eventually grow more than 100 feet tall. The branches start high on the trunk, spreading to form a crown up to 50 feet wide.

The tree known variously as **tulip tree, yellow poplar, tulip magnolia, tulip poplar,** and **whitewood** (*Liriodendron tulipifera*) grows 60 to 100 feet tall and changes from a conical to an oval shape as it ages. Its leaves are 5 to 6 inches across, blunt along the top, with four or six pointed lobes. They turn buttery yellow in fall. In spring the tree produces bowl-shaped, leathery blossoms that are pale green with a splash of orange at the base of the petals. Tulip tree fruits are narrow cones composed of numerous flat, winged seeds that flutter to the ground in autumn, while the base of the cone persists into winter.

Tulip tree is native from extreme southern Ontario south to northern Florida. Early pioneers hollowed out the long, straight trunks to make thin-walled, lightweight canoes—it was into such a canoe, 60 feet long, that Daniel Boone packed his family and belongings and left Kentucky for the Spanish territory.

Tulip tree has long been appreciated for its pale, soft and lightweight wood, known in the lumber trade as yellow poplar. This tree is spectacular when planted in a large lawn or park with sufficient space for adequate development of its massive roots and branches. It grows in full sun and needs moist, well-drained, slightly acid soil.

Tupelo (*Nyssa*)

The tupelo is a deciduous tree that grows 25 to 75 feet tall or more. It has splendid autumn coloration, its leaves first becoming mottled yellow, orange, and red, and finally bright scarlet. Tupelo is an American Indian name for the tree; the scientific name *Nyssa*, from a water nymph of Greek mythology, was given in reference to the preference of the tree for swampy soils.

Tupelo wood is yellow to light brown. Its growth rings and twisted grain make it tough and difficult to work with; despite this toughness, tupelo is susceptible to rot and must be treated with creosote or some other preservative before it can be used outdoors. Thin sheets of the lumber are used for crates, boxes, and baskets. Tupelos make handsome specimen, shade, and street trees. They require a moist location with deep, acid soil.

The **black tupelo** (*Nyssa sylvatica*), also known as sour gum or black gum, grows 30 to 90 feet tall. The branches stretch out horizontally to give the tree a spreading form in youth, drooping and becoming somewhat irregular with age. The leaves are glossy and dark green in summer. The flowers are small and greenish; male flowers form in dense clusters while the female blossoms are in sparse groups. The blue-black fruit is fleshy but bitter tasting and is eaten by many birds and mammals. Black tupelo is native from southern Ontario, Maine, and Michigan to Texas and Florida.

Water tupelo (*Nyssa aquatica*) has a longer and more tapered leaf than other members of this species, some having a few vague teeth. The fruits are shaped like teardrops. The base of the trunk is naturally thickened or buttressed to support it in the swampy, seasonally flooded environment in which it thrives. It is native to the southeastern United States from Virginia to Texas; the greatest stands are found in the Louisiana delta region.

Wafer Ash see Hoptree

Wahoo (*Euonymus*)

The wahoo is a deciduous shrub or tree up to 25 feet tall, with gray scaly bark and four-sided branches. The leaves occur in pairs, with sharply toothed edges.

Tulip tree
(*Liriodendron tulipifera*)

Black tupelo (*Nyssa sylvatica*)

Eastern wahoo
(*Euonymus atropurpurea*)

Wahoo is a name that also applies to other trees with winged stems, such as the cascara buckthorn and winged elm.

Eastern wahoo (*Euonymus atropurpurea*) has dark purple flowers in groups of 7 to 15. Each blossom is about ¹/₂ inch across, with four petals. The reddish-purple fruit capsules have four lobes and contain red seeds.

Walnut and Butternut
(Juglans)

Walnuts and butternuts are deciduous trees known for their edible nuts and fine hardwood. They usually grow 30 to 130 feet tall, with coarse leaves that are aromatic when crushed. Walnut and butternut trees are an excellent choice for shade in a large space; however, they are not recommended for a small garden because they produce a substance called juglone that hinders the growth of neighboring plants. They do best in areas ranging from full sun to partial shade and moist, well-drained soil that is deep enough to support their massive root systems.

Black walnut (*Juglans nigra*) grows 100 to 130 feet tall. The leaves have 7 to 11 leaflets along the central axis and may or may not have a terminal leaflet.

Nuts grow individually or in pairs on the branch. They form inside a thick, yellowish-green husk that turns brown when the nuts are ripe in late fall.

Black walnut is widely scattered in mixed forests in the eastern United States. Black walnut wood is a fine-grained hardwood with a beautiful figure and a rich, dark color that polishes well. It is esteemed for cabinet and furniture veneer as well as for gun stocks. Black walnut burl and crotch wood are highly figured, and the wood is so valuable that a single large tree may be worth tens of thousands of dollars in the lumber trade.

The **butternut**, or **white walnut**, (*Juglans cinerea*) grows up to 100 feet tall and has a broad, open crown. The leaves are composed of five to eight pairs of lateral leaflets and one terminal leaflet. The butternuts occur in clusters of two to five; each nut is 1 to 2¹/₂ inches across, has four obvious ribs on the shell, and is enclosed by a sticky husk.

Butternut ranges in bottomlands and floodplains from New Brunswick west to Minnesota and south to northern Georgia, Missouri, and Arkansas. Butternuts must be harvested as soon as

they ripen because the nut meat quickly becomes rancid. A yellowish pigment can be extracted from the bark and husks of butternut. This dye, used by early settlers, came back into use during the Civil War when yellow dyes from other sources were difficult to obtain. Backwoods Confederate troops, sometimes dresssed in homespun cloth colored with dye from these trees, were called "Butternuts."

Whitewood see Tulip Tree

Willow (Salix)

Willows are deciduous, rapidly growing trees that reach 15 to 75 feet tall or more. The leaves are long and narrow, with short stems. Male and female flowers are produced on separate trees; the flowers are minute, borne in long catkins that may be drooping or upright. Individual willow species are separated by subtle differences and are often difficult to distinguish. The smallest member of this group is a tiny, 1-inch-tall shrub that grows in the Arctic and above the timberline; the largest may grow to 120 feet tall or more. Some 100 species of willow are native to North America; although most are shrubs, 35 or so are large

enough to be considered trees. In landscaping, willows are favored as lawn highlights or screens; they are especially effective along a waterside, where they may be planted to prevent erosion. They thrive in full sun or partial shade and need wet soil.

Black willow (*Salix nigra*) is a tree growing 30 to 40 feet tall, with very dark brown or black, deeply cracked bark. Narrow, lance-shaped leaves are 3 to 6 inches long, bright green and shiny on the upper surface and paler below. The flowers appear at the same time as the leaves. Black willow grows from Minnesota east to southern New Brunswick and Maine and south to Texas, particularly in wet lowland sites. Young shoots are eaten by deer and rodents. The light, flexible wood is often used in basketry.

Goodding willow (*Salix gooddingii*) is a medium-size tree that branches close to the ground, giving it a loosely spreading shape. This species is very similar to the black willow but is distinguished by its yellowish twigs that snap off the

Black walnut (*Juglans nigra*)

Black willow (*Salix nigra*)

Pussy willow (*Salix discolor*)

main branch when pulled. Its leaves are a dull green in color. The American Indians of the Southwest remove the bark of the flexible branches; from the bark they weave baskets that are tight enough to carry water. Goodding willow is native from California southeast to Texas and Mexico and is especially common along the floodplain of the Colorado River.

Pacific willow (*Salix lasiandra*) also resembles black willow, but its leaves are gray-green on the undersurface with glands where the leaf blade meets its stem. Pacific willow is native from central Alaska south to southern New Mexico and California and east to Saskatchewan.

Pussy willow (*Salix discolor*) is a shrub or small tree with upright, dark reddish-purple branches. Leaves are bright green on the upper surface and blue-green below. They are 2 to 5 inches long and have sparsely toothed margins. The soft, silky gray "pussyfeet" appearing on leafless branches in the early spring are the catkins of male flowers; they fluff open when mature and are sprinkled with yellow pollen that is sought by bees later in the spring.

Pussy willow ranges from Newfoundland south to the Smoky Mountains and west to British Columbia. Flowering pussy willow branches are often sold by florists for use in flower arrangements.

Weeping willow (*Salix babylonica*) grows 30 to 40 feet tall and has a short, stout trunk and a dome-shaped crown of sweeping branches. The sickle-shaped leaves of the weeping willow emerge pale green in spring, turning dull green in summer and yellow in autumn. Weeping willow is native to China. It was introduced to North America in 1730 and remains popular as an ornamental.

Winterberry see Holly

Witch Hazel (*Hamamelis*)
Witch hazel is a shrub or small tree with an open crown of spreading branches. Its unusual yellow flowers have four ribbon-shaped petals; they may appear either in spring or in autumn and winter, depending on the species. The fruit forms as a hard, two-piece capsule and requires a year to mature.

Witch hazel (*Hamamelis virginiana*) is a slow-growing tree that reaches 25 feet in

height and has a trunk that branches close to the base. The leaves are 3 to 6 inches long and lopsided at the base, and have wavy teeth toward the tips. Witch hazel flowers from October through December. When the small, woody capsule is mature, its walls dry and contract, abruptly squeezing out the shiny black seeds with a loud pop; the seeds may be propelled a distance of 30 feet.

Witch hazel is common in woodlands from southeastern Canada south to Florida. The leaves, twigs, and bark of witch hazel are the source of the mildly astringent toilet water of the same name, which is frequently used in lotions. A forked witch hazel branch is the preferred divining rod used in the mystical practice of locating underground water, hence the reference to witches in its name.

Yaupon see Holly

Yellow Poplar see Tulip Tree

Yew (*Taxus*)
The yews are evergreen coniferous shrubs and trees that grow 10 to 60 feet tall. Their flat, needlelike leaves can be up to 1 inch long. The greenish seed is

surrounded by a bright red gelatinous cup called an aril. Yew lumber is very dense and strong and takes a good polish. North American species are popular for making small, decorative items. The Canadian yew is extensively used as an ornamental shrub and is often used as a hedge or foundation plant. Yews thrive in full sun or partial shade and require moist, well-drained soil.

The Pacific yew (*Taxus brevifolia*) reaches 30 to 60 feet tall and has a conical crown. Its bark is reddish purple and peels in thin, irregular flakes. This bark is the source of taxol, a promising new anticancer drug. Stripping the bark kills the tree, however, and with 100,000 potential users of the drug annually—each requiring the taxol of six trees—efforts are underway to develop synthetic substitutes. The Pacific yew is a scattered understory tree that grows in forests along the Pacific coast from southeastern Alaska to California.

Weeping willow (*Salix babylonica*)

Witch hazel (*Hamamelis virginiana*)

Pacific yew (*Taxus brevifolia*)

CREDITS

Cover: Misty morning in Chequamegon National Forest, northern Wisconsin, by Richard Hamilton Smith.

Foreword: 6 Sycamore tree, Livermore Valley, California, Carr Clifton; 7 Nitinat Lake, British Columbia, Canada, Gary Braasch/Woodfin Camp, Inc.; 9 Tree planting, Maryland, Greg Pease/Folio.

Chapter One:
The Presence of Trees
10 (top left) Buds of Ohio buckeye, Mike Blair; 10 (bottom) Dan McCoy/Rainbow; 11 Baron Wolman; 12-13 Whit Bronaugh; 13 (right) Jeff Matthewson; 14 (left) William E. Ferguson; 14-15 Gary Braasch; 15 (right) William E. Ferguson; 16 (left) William E. Ferguson; 16 (middle) Stephen P. Parker/Photo Researchers, Inc.; 16 (right) Art Wolfe/Allstock; 17 Nurisdany et Perennou/Photo Researchers, Inc.; 18 (left) Tom McHugh/Photo Researchers, Inc.; 18 (right) Gary Bistram/The Image Bank; 19 Bridgeman/Art Resource, New York; 20 (top) Jerry Jacka; 20 (bottom left) Alon Reininger/Woodfin Camp, Inc.; 20 (bottom right) Smithsonian Institution photo no. T13,301; 21 Smithsonian Institution photo no. 1713; 22 courtesy, Winterthur Museum; 23 (top) Richard Hamilton Smith; 23 (bottom) Grant Haist; 24 Benjamin Mendlowitz; 25 Richard Hamilton Smith/Allstock; 26 David Stoecklein/Allstock; 27 Priscilla Connell/Photo Nats; 28 29 Darius Kinsey Collection/Whatcom Museum of History and Art, Bellingham, WA; 29 (right) Landslides/Alex S. MacLean; 30-31 I.N. Phelps Stokes Collection, Miriam and Ira D. Wallach Division of Art, Prints and Photographs, The New York Public Library, Astor,

Lenox and Tilden Foundations; 32-33 (top) Ric Ergenbright; 33 (bottom) National Park Service; 34 Michael Goodman/Photo-Nats; 35 George Wuerthner; 36-37 Michael S. Quinton.

Chapter Two:
What Is a Tree?
38 (top left) Red oak acorns, Al Bussewitz/Photo-Nats; 38 (right) Carr Clifton; 39 Richard Hamilton Smith/Allstock; 40-41 David Muench; 42 Carr Clifton; 43 (top left) Gary Braasch/Woodfin Camp, Inc.; 43 (top right) Mark E. Gibson; 43 (bottom left) Mark E. Gibson; 43 (bottom right) Gary Braasch; 44 (left) David Muench/Allstock; 44 (inset) Dan McCoy/Rainbow; 45 Andrew Syred/Science Photo Library/Photo Researchers, Inc.; 45 (inset) Al Bussewitz/Photo-Nats; 46 (top) Dan McCoy/Rainbow; 46 (bottom) Dan McCoy/Rainbow; 47 Laboratory of Tree-Ring Research, University of Arizona, photograph by Jeff Matthewson; 48 (top) Grant Haist; 48 (bottom) Stacy Pick/Folio; 48-49 Harald Sund/The Image Bank; 50 Carr Clifton; 51 Richard Hamilton Smith; 52-53 illustration by Les Devenirs Visuels; 54 (middle) Cheryl Kemp/Photo-Nats; 54 (others) Valorie Hodgson/Photo-Nats; 55 Jeff Gnass; 56 Richard Hamilton Smith; 57 Dewitt Jones/Woodfin Camp, Inc.; 58 (top left) Grant Haist; 58-59 Dan Suzio; 59 (top right) Michael Dirr; 60 (top) Jim Brandenburg/Allstock; 60-61 illustration by Les Devenirs Visuels; 62 (left) Pat Lynch/Photo Researchers, Inc.; 62 (right) Jeff Gnass; 63 Connie Toops; 64 Steve Kaufman; 65 Gary Braasch.

Chapter Three:
An Intimate Partnership
66 (top left) Hopi kachina doll, John Running; 66 (bottom) Library of Congress; 67 Al

Bussewitz/Photo-Nats; 68 (top left) Al Bussewitz/Photo-Nats; 68 (bottom left) Robert Llewellyn; 68-69 Robert Walch; 69 (top right) John A. Lynch/Photo-Nats; 70 Smithsonian Institution photo number 86-4132; 71 (left) Jeff Gnass; 71 (right) Al Bussewitz/Photo-Nats; 72-73 illustration by Les Devenirs Visuels; 74-75 Paul Kane, "Indian Encampment on Lake Huron," Art Gallery of Ontario, Toronto; 75 (right) Al Bussewitz/Photo-Nats; 76 (both) The Mariners' Museum, Newport News, VA; 76-77 Bruce Matheson/Photo-Nats; 77 (right) Museum of the American Indian/Smithsonian Institution; 78 (top) Steve Kaufman; 78 (bottom) Gregory K. Scott; 79 Frances Anna Hopkins, "Voyageurs Manning a Canoe," National Archives of Canada, Ottawa; 80 (left) Steve Kaufman; 80 (middle) Susanne Page; 80 (right) Gary Braasch; 81 Elliott Varner Smith; 82 (top left) Debby Crowell/Photo-Nats; 82 (bottom right) Minnesota Historical Society; 83 copyright British Museum; 84 Jerry Jacka; 85 (top left) John Running; 85 (top right) Elliott Varner Smith; 85 (bottom) Kim Todd/Photo-Nats; 86 Gary Braasch; 87 Landslides/Alex S. MacLean; 88 (top) David Barnes/Allstock; 88 (middle) Smithsonian Institution photo no. 56759; 88-89 courtesy of the Thomas Burke Memorial Washington State Museum, catalog no. 1- 3004, photograph by Eduardo Calderon; 89 (top) courtesy of the Thomas Burke Memorial Washington State Museum, catalog no. 96,97, photograph by Eduardo Calderon; 90-91 Library of Congress; 91 Jerry Jacka; 92 Alon Reininger/Woodfin Camp, Inc.; 93 (top) British Columbia Archives and Records Service, catalog no. HP 33613; 93 (bottom) Scott Landis.

Chapter Four:
An Exploitable Resource
94 (top left) Massachusetts pine tree shilling, circa 1670, courtesy, Winterthur Museum; 94-95 Linton Park, "Flax Scutching Bee," gift of Edgar William and Bernice Chrysler Garbisch, copyright 1992, National Gallery of Art, Washington, DC; 95 (right) Dana Levy; 96 courtesy Hagley Museum and Library; 97 Steve Dunwell/The Image Bank; 98 (top) Hal Gieseking; 98 (bottom) U.S. Forest Service, courtesy Forest History Society; 99 David Muench/Allstock; 100 (all) Old Sturbridge Village, nos. B26161, B26151, B26157, photographer, Henry E. Peach; 101 (top) Robert Villani; 101 (bottom) East Machias Public Library, East Machias, ME, from *THE OLD WEST: The Loggers*, photograph by Ellis Herwig, copyright 1976, Time-Life Books Inc.; 102 (left) Joe Sohm/Chromosohm/Allstock; 102 (right) Mark E. Gibson; 103 John F. Waggaman; 104 (left) Scott Landis; 104-105 Landslides/Alex S. MacLean; 105 (right) Benjamin Mendlowitz; 106 (top) Landslides/Alex S. MacLean; 106-107 Larry Gilpin/Allstock; 108 (left) courtesy, Winterthur Museum; 108-109 RSI/Allstock; 109 (right) courtesy, Winterthur Museum; 110 (top and bottom left) Shelburne Museum, Shelburne, VT, photograph by Ken Burris; 110 (top right) courtesy, CIGNA Museum and Art Collection; 110 (bottom right) courtesy, Western Reserve Historical Society; 111 (top left) Matt Bradley; 111 (top middle) Scott Landis; 111 (top right) Scott Landis; 111 (bottom left) Matt Bradley; 111 (bottom middle) Baron Wolman; 111 (bottom right) courtesy, Peter Joseph Gallery; 112 Michael Baytoff; 113 (all) Scott Landis; 114-115 illustration by Les Devenirs Visuels; 116-117 James G. Evans, "Celebration of

Washington's Birthday at Malta on board USS Constitution," courtesy, United States Naval Academy Museum; 117 (right) Steve Kaufman; 118-119 Robert Llewellyn; 120 American Philosophical Society; 121 (both) courtesy of the National Agricultural Library, Special Collections; 122 (top) Independence National Historical Park Collection; 122 (bottom) American Philosophical Society; 123 David Muench/Allstock.

Chapter Five:
Mining the Forest
124 (top left) Logging in Minnesota, Richard Hamilton Smith; 124 (bottom) From *Here's Audacity! American Legendary Heroes* by Frank Shery, Eben Giben, illustrator; 125 Darius Kinsey Collection, Whatcom Museum of History and Art, Bellingham, WA; 126 From *A View of the Cultivation of Fruit Trees in America* by William Coxe, courtesy of the National Agricultural Library, Special Collections; 127 copyright Roger R. Trahan, Sr., courtesy Assumption College; 128-129 Michigan Historical Collections, Bentley Historical Library, University of Michigan; 129 (right) Randy Wells/Allstock; 130-131 Library of Congress; 132 Library of Congress; 133 Minnesota Historical Society; 134 Buffalo and Erie County Historical Society; 135 Landslides/Alex S. MacLean; 136 (bottom) Minnesota Historical Society; 136-137 (top) Library of Congress; 137 (bottom) State Historical Society of Wisconsin; 138 Courtesy of the Atwater Kent Museum; 139 Warshaw Collection, Archives Center, NMAH, Smithsonian Institution, photograph by Jeff Matthewson; 140-141 illustration by Les Devenirs Visuels; 142 courtesy of the Weyerhaeuser Archives; 143 from the Collection of the Louisiana State Museum; 144 Darius Kinsey Collection,

Whatcom Museum of History and Art, Bellingham, WA; 145 (left) Darius Kinsey Collection, Whatcom Museum of History and Art, Bellingham, WA; 145 (right) courtesy of the Weyerhaeuser Archives; 146 (top) courtesy of the Weyerhaeuser Archives; 146 (bottom) courtesy of the National Agricultural Library, Special Collections; 147 David Barnes/Allstock.

Chapter Six:
Trees—Present and Future
148 (top left) Northern spotted owl, Willamette National Forest, OR, Greg Vaughn; 148 (right) Richard Hamilton Smith; 149 Ric Ergenbright; 150-151 Mark E. Gibson; 151 David Frazier/Folio; 152 illustration by Les Devenirs Visuels; 153 (left) Elvin McDonald; 153 (right) Gary Braasch; 154-155 Jeffrey E. Blackman; 155 (top) Jeffrey E. Blackman; 155 (bottom) Elvin McDonald; 156-157 Alon Reininger/Woodfin Camp, Inc.; 157 Michael S. Yamashita/Woodfin Camp, Inc.; 158 Michael Baytoff; 159 illustration by Les Devenirs Visuels; 160-161 Grant Haist; 162-163 illustration by Les Devenirs Visuels; 164 (top) Michael S. Quinton; 164 (bottom) Art Wolfe; 165 Gary Braasch; 166 (left) J. A. Lynch/Photo-Nats; 166 (right) Valorie Hodgson/Photo-Nats; 166-167 Steve Kaufman; 168-169 Gary Braasch; 170 Virginia Twinam-Smith/Photo-Nats; 171 Dr. Charles Steinmetz/Photo-Nats; 172 Momatiuk and Eastcott/Woodfin Camp, Inc.; 173 Mark E. Gibson; 174 Gary Braasch/Woodfin Camp, Inc.; 175 Carr Clifton; 176-177 Jodi Cobb/Woodfin Camp, Inc.

Tree Identification Guide
Photographs listed from left to right by page:
178 Don Johnston/Photo-Nats; Horticultural Photography, Corvallis, OR; 179 Elvin McDonald; Pamela Harper;

Pamela Harper; Pamela Harper; 180 Michael Dirr; Michael Dirr; Pamela Harper; 181 Michael Dirr; Michael Dirr; 182 Ann Reilly/Photo-Nats; Pamela Harper; Michael Dirr; 183 Michael Dirr; Pamela Harper; Pamela Harper; Thomas E. Eltzroth; 184 Pamela Harper; Thomas E. Eltzroth; Joanne Pavia; Michael Dirr; 185 Michael Dirr; Michael Dirr; 186 Michael Dirr; Thomas E. Eltzroth; Michael Dirr; 187 Robert E. Lyons/Color Advantage; Gay Bumgarner/Photo-Nats; Steven Still; 188 Elvin McDonald; Pamela Harper; Michael Dirr; 189 Elvin McDonald; Pamela Harper; Michael Dirr; Robert E. Lyons/Color Advantage; 190 Al Bussewitz/Photo-Nats; Steven Still; Pat Toops; 191 Pamela Harper; Michael Dirr; Michael Dirr; 192 Pamela Harper; Pamela Harper; Joanne Pavia; 193 Elvin McDonald; Jerry Pavia; 194 Michael Dirr; Michael Dirr; Pamela Harper; 195 Michael Dirr; Peter Margosian/Photo-Nats; Al Bussewitz/Photo-Nats; 196 Pamela Harper; Michael Dirr; Michael Dirr; 197 Michael Dirr; Jo-Ann Ordano/Photo-Nats; Pamela Harper; 198 Pamela Harper; Pamela Harper; Peter Margosian/Photo-Nats; 199 Michael Dirr; Thomas E. Eltzroth; Pamela Harper; Liz Ball/Photo-Nats; 200 Michael Dirr; Michael Dirr; Mary Nemeth/Photo-Nats; 201 Pamela Harper; Jeff March/Photo-Nats; 202 Pamela Harper; Michael Dirr; Pamela Harper; Robert E. Lyons/Color Advantage; 203 Don Johnston/Photo-Nats; Clyde Mitchell/Color Advantage; 204 Pamela Harper; Michael Dirr; Pamela Harper; Pamela Harper; 205 Michael Dirr; Pamela Harper; Pamela Harper; 206 Michael Dirr; Michael Dirr; Pamela Harper; 207 Michael Dirr; Pamela Harper; Michael Dirr; 208 Jerry Pavia; Michael Dirr; John J. Smith/Photo-Nats; 209 Pamela Harper; Michael Dirr; Greg Vaughn.

FOR FURTHER READING

America's Renewable Resources: Historical Trends and Current Challenges, edited by Kenneth D. Frederick and Roger A. Sedjo; Resources for the Future, Washington, D.C., 1991.

Americans and Their Forests: A Historical Geography, by Michael Williams; Press Syndicate of the University of Cambridge, Oakleigh, Victoria, Australia, 1989.

The Audubon Society Nature Guides: Eastern Forests, by Ann Sutton and Myron Sutton; Alfred A. Knopf, New York, 1986.

The Audubon Society Nature Guides: Western Forests, by Stephen Whitney; Alfred A. Knopf, New York, 1985.

A Natural History of Trees of Eastern and Central North America, A Natural History of Western Trees, by Donald Culross Peattie; Houghton Mifflin Co., Boston, 1953.

North American Wildlife, edited by Susan J. Wernert; Reader's Digest, Pleasantville, N.Y., 1982.

REDEFINITION

President
Edward Brash

Editor
Glen B. Ruh

Picture Editor
Rebecca Hirsh

Design Director
Edwina Smith

Production Coordinator
Glenn Smeds

Researchers
Susan Sonnesyn Brooks
Mary Yee

Copy Editors
Claudia S. Bedwell
Debra Greinke

Design
The Watermark Design Office
Alexandria, VA

Illustrations
Les Devenirs Visuels
Paris, France

Color Separation
Colourscan Overseas
Co. Pte. Ltd.,
Singapore

Gerald Jonas is a free-lance writer in the arts and sciences. He has written five other books, including *Dancing: The Pleasure, Power and Art of Movement,* a companion volume to the public television series. A staff writer for *The New Yorker* magazine, he has also been a regular reviewer for *The New York Times Book Review.* Living in New York City, he appreciates the importance of trees in the urban environment.

Ed Zahniser, Contributing Editor, has written books on U.S. National Parks and the natural wonders of North America. He is the editor of *Where Wilderness Preservation Began: Adirondack Writings of Howard Zahniser* and the author of a poetry collection, *The Way to Heron Mountain.*

For planting the original seed for this book and for his many contributions to its development, special thanks to Ed Zahniser. For her oversight of the Tree Identification Guide, thanks to Lisa Barnett.

For advice, consultation, and other contributions, thanks to the following individuals and organizations: Susan Arritt, Carlos Alexandre, Robert Barkin, Andy Bornstein, Richard Burrows, Linda Busetti, Irv Garfield, Mel Ingber, Laura Kreiss, Scott Landis, Michele Italiano-Perla, Louis Plummer, Elizabeth Simon, Edwin Taylor, Marilyn Wandrus. Stanwyn Shetler, National Museum of Natural History/Smithsonian Institution; Deborah Gangloff and Steve Stetson, American Forestry Association; John Forbes, National Agricultural Library; Susan Chapman, Eric Newman, and Wayne Olson, National Arboretum.